Scattered
Seeds

Scattered Seeds

In Search of Family and Identity
in the Sperm Donor Generation

Jacqueline Mroz

SEAL PRESS

ISBN 978-1-58005-616-8
ISBN 978-1-58005-617-5 (e-book)

Library of Congress Cataloging-in-Publication Data for this book is available.

Published by SEAL PRESS
An imprint of Perseus Books, LLC
A subsidiary of Hachette Book Group, Inc.
1700 Fourth Street
Berkeley, California

sealpress.com

Cover Design: Faceout Studio
Interior Design: Cynthia Young

Printed in the United States of America

Distributed by Hachette Book Group

LSC-C

10 9 8 7 6 5 4 3 2 1

To Simon, Lucas, Will, and Owen,
for all their love and support.

Contents

PART THREE

Introduction

It's a cold winter day, and my sister and I are sitting at her kitchen table, drinking tea against the cold. We hover over her laptop, checking out profiles of sperm donors on the California Cryobank website. It reminds me a little of the shopping trips we sometimes take together—except this time, instead of browsing the latest styles in dresses and shoes, we are shopping for the man who will father her child. Will it be the tallish anthropology student who likes to hang out with friends and resembles football player Drew Brees, or maybe the blond, blue-eyed athlete who enjoys traveling and spending time with his family, and who looks a bit like actor Paul Bettany?

Profiles of exceptional men parade before our eyes. We bookmark a few standouts and consider paying the extra $250 fee to view the donor's childhood photos, staff impressions of him, and a facial features report. It's a little surreal, like *The Handmaid's Tale* for men.

That's when my sister tells me something incredible. She'd been on a website for single mothers, reading through a forum for women trying to conceive, when she came across a message from a woman who had had a child through a sperm donor. This woman had just found out that her daughter—conceived with a sperm donor—had seventy-five half siblings!

The woman had used an open donor so that her daughter could get in touch with her biological father when she turned eighteen, but she now realized there was no way her sperm donor was going to be at all interested in any personal contact with her child.

My sister is understandably upset.

"This is freaking me out! I can't believe a child could have seventy-five siblings. I don't know what I'd do," she says.

The thought of my niece or nephew having that many half siblings *is* worrying. There were so many things to consider: would my sister ever get to know the other families? Would her child be able to contact the biological father? How could the donor possibly keep track of all his kids or maintain relationships with them?

Still, I'm fascinated. Could one sperm donor actually have fathered nearly a hundred children? What does it mean? I'm intrigued and find myself pulled into an investigative journey that will ultimately make me reconsider the very definition of family and the concept of identity.

I speak to my editor at the science section of the *New York Times*, and he, too, is curious. He wants me to start digging and confirm the story. As I begin my research, I learn that seventy-five kids is, in fact, a relatively small number. There are much larger groups out there—including one that is comprised of 150 children.

It's unfathomable. The most children I'd ever heard of one man having are a dozen or so (think Anthony Quinn). But 150! I quickly calculate: that means that in 800 years, one donor could have *millions* of descendants. To put this in context, Genghis Khan, during his global rampage, is thought to have sired the equivalent of 16 million descendants.

I'm curious to find out how we got to a place where a man could father so many children. As I begin looking into it, I'm surprised to discover that America's fertility industry is only loosely regulated. Compared with countries such as Britain, which strictly regulates its fertility industry, the U.S. is the Wild, Wild West of baby making.

Here, anything goes.

My *New York Times* story, "One Sperm Donor, 150 Offspring," generated an extraordinary amount of publicity. It was the *Times'* most emailed, most viewed, and most blogged story of the day, and it was picked up all over the world. *The Today Show* interviewed me for a segment it did on my piece. People were interested. People wanted to know more. Clearly, it had hit a nerve.

Through my story, I was able to meet several mothers of the 150 children I wrote about—all born with the help of Donor B155A. They were by any measure a secretive group, unwilling to talk to the press or be identified publicly. But some of the mothers were different. Susanna Wahl, for instance, wanted her kids to know who they were and where they came from. And she didn't keep secrets. She took her children on a remarkable cross-country trip to meet as many of their half brothers and sisters as they could. I'll share more of her story in Chapter 3.

Susanna's experience is just one example of the remarkable changes taking place in human society's central organizing element: the family. And these changes will have profound and widespread consequences on the future of how human beings connect with one another. Today's blended families, gay couples with kids, and children born out of wedlock are almost unrecognizable in makeup compared to the traditional nuclear families of the 1950s. Regardless of how the pieces of today's families may differ from those of a half century before, they all share the same bonding agent: love and kinship.

In the past few decades, the number of women who have decided to reproduce without a male partner has exploded, a development made possible through the growing sophistication and accessibility of assisted reproductive technology. The number of lesbian couples and single women using sperm donors to have children has transformed how families are created today, giving women new choices about how they'd like to structure their family. This change started slowly, but now hundreds of thousands of children are born through donor eggs or sperm in the United States every year and more than one million people born through donor gametes worldwide.

As for the sperm donors, in most cases, they were never told how many kids they would father, or the sperm bank lied to them and said it would only be a few. The concept of having any real relationship with dozens, perhaps hundreds, of offspring must be mind-boggling. One sperm donor who is in touch with his multiple offspring uses an

Excel spreadsheet to keep track of them all. He's not sure what he'll do if more of his children are born.

Meetings between sperm donors and their offspring are also becoming more common—especially as it's become easier for children to find their donors through genetic testing and online searches.

It's very difficult to quantify how many of these relationships are taking place—or even how many sperm donors or donor-conceived people are out there. That's because nobody is keeping track—not the federal government, not the sperm banks. No one. That's one of the biggest complaints that critics make of the fertility industry in this country. The most accurate numbers for donor-conceived children are probably on the Donor Sibling Registry (DSR), a website that serves donor offspring and sperm donors, and those are self-reported by the families. However, Wendy Kramer, the founder of the DSR, says that of the 2,800 sperm donors in her database, there have been 1,400 donor to offspring matches (as of March 2017). That means that more than a thousand sperm donors have become connected to their children. And that number is probably even higher now. It's a remarkable concept to consider—all these new and complicated families that are being formed at this very moment.

Of course, scores of offspring means dozens of half brothers and sisters. How do donor children make sense of their place in the world when they are one of so many? Not knowing the identity of one's parent can be devastating for some, leading them to relentlessly search for clues as to who they are.

Andrew Solomon, author of *Far from the Tree: Parents, Children, and the Search for Identity*, says that children and adults search for their identity to get a sense of who they are and how their experience of their life or their world differs from other people. But he notes that there are particular challenges associated with being a donor child, and that it can be even more difficult for children who have multiple siblings.

"I won't say that it's exactly the same as any other childhood, because it's not. There are complexities and nuances and layers to being a donor child. And I think some of those children do grow up with a real sense of yearning," says Solomon. He knows about this well because he and his partner used an egg donor and surrogate to have their son, George.

This search for identity is leading more and more donors, parents, and donor-conceived children to look for those who share their biological and genetic background. For many of these people, the genetic ties they share create powerful bonds between them.

Chase Kimball was a prolific sperm donor in his youth who was never able to have children of his own. He later started searching for his biological offspring. His story is told here, too.

Then there is Ryan Kramer, a child born through a sperm donor. When he was just ten, Ryan started searching for his donor, which inspired his mother to create the Donor Sibling Registry. It would eventually help thousands of families connect to their donors.

A profound need to answer this question of her children's identity is what led Susanna Wahl to take her kids on their cross-country odyssey to meet their half siblings and extended families. The journey expressed her unusual vision of "family," one that is different from most everyone else's; it bleeds the boundary between family and the rest of the world.

I'll examine these stories and more, and how they fit into the history of fertility in this country and elsewhere. I'll also look at how politics—and the lack of regulation of this country's fertility industry—affects those who use sperm banks.

There are troubling society-wide implications to sperm donation as well. For example, some donor children are inheriting rare and serious genetic illnesses from their sperm donors and spreading them throughout the population at a rapid rate, which I'll share more about in Chapter 8.

How did this all come to be?

It began in 1790, when a fearsome Scot named John Hunter helped a couple have a child by performing the world's first artificial insemination. But over time, the fertility industry began to exploit couples that were trying to conceive, along with the fertile young men and women who could help them.

Like a detective novel, this book will go back to the roots of the fertility industry, trace the steps that led to the case of Donor B155A, and examine the impact it had on the 150 children he fathered.

Note to the reader: Due to the sensitive nature of some of the material in this book, some of the names of the people that I interviewed have been changed. When only a first name is used, it means that person's name was changed. When the first and last name are used in the book, that is the person's real name.

Part One

1

Finding a Father

A Young Boy's Quest to Discover His Donor

When he was still very young, Ryan Kramer became deeply curious about the identity of his biological father. His mother had conceived him through an anonymous sperm donor when her husband discovered he was infertile, so Ryan had no idea who his biological father was. But within one year his mother and the only father he knew had divorced. His father had had issues with addiction, so Ryan's mother retained full custody. When Ryan was a small child, only around two years old, his mother, Wendy, told him he'd been born through a sperm donor. She believed that it was best to tell children at an early age where they came from.

When he was only a toddler, Ryan, a bright boy, started asking his mother questions about his real father. Who was he? Did he look like him? What did he do for a living?

"When I was two years old, I asked my mom in preschool, 'So did my real dad die or what?' I always knew that my father wasn't my real father. It was never an issue for me. It was just a part of who I was," says Ryan. "And I really appreciated her openness and honesty."

Academically, Ryan excelled in math and science. But no one on his mother's side shared those interests. Ryan wanted to know if his biological father worked in the sciences. Was that something he'd inherited from him? Perhaps this was something they had in common?

In fact, Ryan was so precocious as a child that when he was six years old, his mother had his IQ tested. It was 181. (Anything over 140 is considered genius.) The boy was a prodigy. Ryan went on to graduate from high school at age fourteen, and when he was eighteen, he'd finished one of the most difficult college science programs in the nation. He loved playing with numbers. Once, bored on an airplane, Ryan memorized Pi out to forty digits. His favorite formula is the definition of a derivative.

But his curiosity about his father persisted. Ryan thought about him all the time.

"When some children are told they were donor conceived, they feel desperately curious. They feel like a part of them is missing, and they can't be whole until they find the answers," says Ryan. "I always felt like a complete person, but it was still important for me to know where I came from. I felt like I could have been happier if I had an understanding of my genetic roots."

His mother, Wendy, understood her son's need to find some key to who his father was and what he was like. And she wanted to help him find any half siblings he might have. She would ultimately spend nearly a decade helping Ryan find them.

"It's about honoring that curiosity," says Wendy. "Some moms try to minimize the place of a donor in their child's life. But to kids, it's half their genetic identity. My son told me, 'I just want my donor to know that I exist.'"

There were times when Ryan was desperately curious about his father, and other times when it was in the background, says Wendy. But she wanted her son to have a sense of his ancestry, and she told him as much about her family as she knew. Still, it wasn't enough for Ryan. He had to know about his father's side of the family, too.

Wendy knew the sperm bank wouldn't help her (they generally don't give out this information to families who have used sperm donors), so she started a Yahoo group to help donor siblings connect. She thought, if her son was curious, maybe other kids were curious, too.

When they started getting media exposure for the concept, Wendy and Ryan created the Donor Sibling Registry website in 2000 when he was just ten years old. This website helps donor children and their families find their half siblings and donors.

Wendy firmly believes that people have the fundamental right to information about their biological origins and identities, and her website is a testament to this conviction. She has become an advocate for more openness in the fertility process and for more rights for the children who are the result of sperm and egg donation.

Since its founding, the DSR has forever changed the way donor children and their families interact with their half siblings. Before the website was started, there was virtually no way for families or donor children to find each other. Now, they can go on the site to see if anyone has posted their sperm donor's number to find any half siblings they might have—or even their sperm donor, if they have agreed to be identified. Each donor gets an identifying number; however, sometimes the sperm bank will tell the donor his number, and sometimes it does not.

In her search for answers about her son's donor, Wendy would call California Cryobank every few years to see if she could get information about any half siblings Ryan might have and to get help finding his donor. Ryan even wrote the sperm bank a handwritten letter himself when he was only seven years old, asking if they could give him information about this father. The bank knew Ryan's sperm donor's number—it was 1058. During one call that Wendy made, someone at the sperm bank inadvertently told her that Ryan had either three or nine half brothers and sisters out there. She knew that as soon as she told Ryan, he would want to meet them.

Then, Wendy and Ryan had a bit of luck. A posting on the DSR website for Donor 1058 showed up. It was from a thirteen-year-old girl who was looking for any half siblings she might have. Wendy was nervous about telling Ryan, who was sixteen, because she didn't want to get his hopes up if it didn't work out. He'd already found out about two other half siblings, but their parents hadn't wanted them to meet Ryan, and he was devastated when it fell through.

This time, Wendy immediately contacted the girl's parents to see if she had her parents' permission to contact Ryan, since she was under eighteen. Wendy received this message:

Dear Wendy,

My daughter, Anna, just responded to a posting by you regarding donor number 1058. This is the first time we have explored the registry and are very anxious to find out if your son is indeed a match. My husband and I allowed Anna to register herself last night, with our supervision. She is thirteen years old and was born on May 22, 1993. Our donor was a Mechanical Engineering student. He was born in 1967. He has one brother who is a pilot. Does any of this sound familiar to you? As you can imagine, we are looking forward to a response and hope to hear from you soon.

Regards, Eileen (Anna's Mom) and John (Anna's Dad)

Then Anna sent a message to Ryan:

On the posting page you and I are in a pale yellow box, both with donor number 1058. Does this mean that there is a match?

Not only were they a match, Ryan was surprised to find that he and Anna shared the same birthday—three years apart. That day, Wendy and Eileen spoke on the phone. Wendy remembers it vividly: "We were giddy. And in shock. I told her that even though we were essentially strangers, we shared something so precious. We quickly traded a few bits about each of our kids, and Anna asked to speak with me so that she could ask questions about the other half siblings."

Ryan and Anna connected on social media later that evening. Over the next few weeks, the two families spoke on the phone and planned a meeting. They all wanted to get together as soon as possible.

So six weeks after finding each other, the families flew to New York City, where they would meet and get to know one another over two days. Ryan was excited about the meeting and brought Anna a University of Colorado sweatshirt as a gift (Ryan had begun attending the university at age fourteen, studying aerospace engineering). At the same time, Wendy had been contacted by ABC Primetime about updating a story they'd done on the DSR for the television show. Both families agreed to be filmed, so a TV crew was there in Central Park to document the encounter.

The families bumped into each other on the way into the park, rather than at the appointed spot, and as soon as Ryan and Anna saw one another, they felt an instant connection.

"Meeting Anna was really cool. I was incredibly curious about this half of my DNA that came from my father, and I hadn't met anyone who shared it," remembers Ryan. "To see Anna for first time . . . seeing all those mysterious traits that were in myself, in someone else. It was really wild. She was incredibly sweet and delightful."

At the park, Ryan looked at Anna and noted the striking similarities in their physical characteristics—some of their facial features were the same: they had similar eyebrows, chins, and teeth. Even the tone of her laugh was very much like his own, he thought. Walking behind her on the sidewalk, he noticed that their strides were almost identical. Even their temperaments were the same—they were both outgoing and friendly. Even so, the encounter was a little awkward at first, recalls Ryan.

"You're meeting this person that you have so much in common with, genetically 50 percent. You're more than just strangers, but at same time you are strangers. I thought, 'what do I say to her? What is this person to me?' I tried to have as few expectations as possible for the meeting. These sibling meetings can go very differently: people can either have an immediate brother and sister connection, or meet and have nothing in common and not feel the need to see each other again. It's like meeting a cousin or some distant relative, someone who is part of your family but is still a stranger to you."

Still, within a few minutes, they were pretty comfortable with each other. When half siblings meet for the first time, there's often a feeling of familiarity and kinship that they experience right away.

The families asked each other questions about themselves, took pictures, and compared notes. Anna immediately put on her University of Colorado sweatshirt even though it was warm out. Over the next two days, the families spent time getting to know each other and were amazed by the similarities between Ryan and Anna. They already felt like family.

"It was tremendous. We all hugged," says Wendy. "The smiles on Anna and Ryan's faces were beatific. It was like they sensed 'home' in each other. There was an undeniable bond and recognition of the familiar. We parents scoured the faces of the kids, looking for resemblances. It was very emotional, to say the least. I was overwhelmed with gratitude for Anna's parents' honesty with their daughter and how they honored her curiosity and need to search and connect with Ryan.

"While Eileen and I had a more obvious bond, I was deeply moved by John's willingness to put aside any possible fears or concerns about Anna finding her biological family. In this matter, he made his daughter more important than anything else. That is the best dad anyone could want."

Wendy, John, and Eileen told the half siblings that they should define the terms of their relationship, and that there should be no pressure to make it more than they wanted it to be.

While the parents had been calling them "half brother" and "half sister," Ryan and Anna were already referring to each other as "brother" and "sister."

A few years later, Ryan was able to meet Christina and Natalie— full biological sisters who were also his half siblings. He spent the weekend in New York with Anna and their sisters so that they could all get to know each other. Ryan says he was astonished by how much Anna and Christina, especially, looked and acted alike, with very similar temperaments.

Since then, he's connected with three other half siblings, although he hasn't met them yet. Some live in Boston and New York, which makes it hard for them to get together, since Ryan lives in California. He likens it to having cousins who live on the other side of country;

they mainly keep in touch these days through social media, and they see each other occasionally.

"Meeting Anna, and seeing the traits that she and I shared, did a huge amount for my identity and sense of self. I felt like a whole person. I knew that those traits had to have come from our donor," says Ryan.

WHILE FINDING SOME of his half siblings helped Ryan find some peace, he was still left with a void when it came to knowing about his donor. He wanted to meet his biological father, to talk to him, to look into his eyes, and to be in his presence.

Tall and handsome, with thick, russet hair and warm, brown eyes, Ryan is remarkably self-assured for someone so young. And while some donor children are bitter about their experiences, about the emptiness they feel from the missing piece of their past, Ryan is not like that. He's upbeat and enthusiastic.

"It's an intrinsic basic human desire to want to know where you came from," says Ryan. "I've always had an interest in math and science and engineering. I've known I wanted to be an engineer since I was three years old. I didn't share that with anyone on my mom's side. So I wanted to know where this came from. Why was this interesting and important to me?"

So when Ryan was fifteen, he decided to do a little detective work and try and find his donor himself.

Until fairly recently, most sperm donors who donated through sperm banks did so anonymously. That is, their identity could never be disclosed, and they could not be contacted by their offspring. Sperm banks give these donors a number, and only that was used to identify them. Sometimes, additional information about a donor's background was shared with families, such as place of birth and college major. The sperm banks prided themselves on their ability to guarantee absolute anonymity to these men.

On the other hand, sperm donors who agreed to be open donors *could* be contacted by their offspring, usually once their biological children turned eighteen. California Cryobank, one of the largest sperm banks in the country, urges its open donors to commit to one contact with each of their offspring once the child reaches eighteen, should they request it—and even then, the sperm bank facilitates the contact. The communication may be through a letter, an email, a phone call, or even a meeting in person. Both the donor and the child must mutually decide on the type of contact.

Since Ryan's donor was anonymous, he knew there was no way he'd find him through his sperm bank, and he doubted he'd turn up on the Donor Sibling Registry (those were sperm donors who decided they wanted to find their offspring). Why would his donor reach out now when he signed up to be anonymous? At the time that Wendy had Ryan, she was not given a choice to use a known donor—the clinic that she and her husband used in Denver chose a donor for them. They didn't even know that they had used California Cryobank until Ryan was three years old. There were only anonymous sperm donors available in 1989. So in the summer of 2005, when he was fifteen, Ryan decided to do a little detective work on his own. By this time, technology had caught up with his objective.

While anonymous sperm donors may want to maintain their right to privacy, some, such as Wendy, believe that children conceived through donors have a basic right to know their genetic heritage. Those children didn't ask to be born through an unknown donor, they say, and their desire to know their biological father is more important than a donor's right to remain anonymous. The issue has sparked a debate over whose rights are more important—the donor's or the offspring's.

After contacting her clinic, Ryan's mother had been given his donor's date and place of birth and his college degree. When Ryan's donor had signed up with California Cryobank, he had given this information about himself, but no doubt he never thought this would be enough for any of his offspring to find him. But Ryan was about to change all that. He would soon become the first donor offspring to find his anonymous sperm donor through the Internet and a genetic test, forever changing the concept of guaranteed donor anonymity.

To be sure, they worried about invading their donor's privacy. But Wendy firmly believes that a child's right to know their ancestry, medical background, and biological relatives trumps any right a donor might have to anonymity. "If you don't want to be known, don't donate," she says. "Giving a donor a right to choose, like Ryan did, was Ryan's right. The donor had a choice, too. He could not respond. He could say, 'Thanks, but no thanks,' or he could accept Ryan's invite to get to know each other."

So Ryan began his search. First, he combed through public records for the names of all the people who had the same birthday as his sperm donor in the city where he knew he had been born. That brought up about 300 people.

Then Ryan went on the website for Family Tree DNA and ordered an online genealogical test that, for $289 (the price has since gone down to $89), would allow him to find any family members. The company's Family Finder is an autosomal DNA test that finds relatives within five generations. It compares your DNA to the DNA of others in its database. Of course, if Ryan's biological father didn't have his or her DNA in the database, it would make finding him trickier. But he had a plan.

First, Ryan had to take the test. To collect a DNA sample, he swabbed the inside of his cheek with a "buccal swab," which looks like a mini-toothbrush. He rubbed for about a minute, moving the scraper up and down, back and forth. He placed the scraper into a vial, waited four hours, then scraped another sample from his cheek, which the site suggested. Then he sent the samples to Family Tree DNA and waited for a response. The test was expected to take eight to ten weeks to complete. Family Tree's website touts its ability to help users "discover unknown family connections, confirm uncertain relationships, and connect with living relatives."

It was this last part that ended up helping Ryan. The DNA test turned up a match with two men who were Ryan's closest genetic relatives on the site. They both had the same unusual last name but with slightly different spellings. That seemed promising. He knew he was getting closer to finding the man whose genetic material had made his existence possible. Ryan had a feeling that these men would somehow lead him to his father.

The rare surname ultimately helped Ryan find his father. If his father's last name had been Smith or Johnson, it would undoubtedly have been much harder, says Bryan Sykes, a fellow at Wolfson College, Oxford University, who has studied human genetics and has been researching what DNA can tell us about the human past.

It was Sykes and his colleagues who first discovered the unexpectedly strong link between surnames and Y chromosomes, which has since become crucial to genetic genealogy. They were working on Y chromosomes, and trying to determine what kind of information they could discover about the history of the world, when it occurred to them that there might be a connection between surnames and chromosomes.

Surnames first came into use in England more than eight hundred years ago, after the Norman Conquest. Before that time, people lived in small villages and went by one name, either a personal name or a nickname. But as the population grew, there came a need to identify people further—so that the different "Johns" living in a town, for instance, could be distinguished. Thus, individuals were given surnames based on their occupation, such as Weaver or Smith (as in blacksmith), or place of residence, such as Lancaster or Bristol. This custom was based on the medieval practice of giving people bynames or nicknames in the same way. Later, the practice of giving surnames would grow to include using physical attributes, places of origin, and father's names. For instance, the name Reed comes from red, as in having red hair, and Boyce comes from the French word "bois" meaning wood, for someone who originally lived by or near the woods.

Surnames or family names aren't used in all parts of the world. In some countries, individuals still use only one name, and in some cultures, such as many Asian societies as well as in Hungary, a surname is used before a given name.

The issue of surnames is still controversial in some countries: the Japanese high court recently ruled that married couples must share the same surname, delivering a blow to women who fought to keep their maiden surname. The court upheld a law dating back more than a century. Whereas in Chile, women don't take their husband's name after marriage and are forever known by the same name. In Quebec, women have been forbidden since 1981 from taking their husband's surname after marriage. Greece has a similar law on the books. In Malaysia and Korea, it is the custom for women to keep their maiden names.

Since surnames came into use, Sykes estimates that about 10 percent of all given family names are a result of misattributed paternity, meaning that the putative father is not actually the biological father (because the mother had an affair, for instance, or the child was adopted). That can make genealogical research much more difficult, since actual blood relatives may not be who we think they are.

Sykes' discoveries about the link between surnames and genetics led the University of Oxford to create Oxford Ancestors, the first company in the world to pioneer the use of DNA to connect us to our ancestors and to our relatives. Sykes is the chairman of that company.

"It's far more difficult to find a relative with a common name," says Sykes. "Ryan would have had hundreds of men matching him. Indeed, people who share the same surname are often curious to know if they are related."

Coincidentally, a chance meeting with another Sykes was the catalyst to his research on surnames and genetics. While giving a talk at GlaxoSmithKline Pharmaceutical in England, he met the chief executive, a man named Sir Richard Sykes. People kept asking Bryan if they were related, and he wondered the same. So he obtained a sample of DNA from Richard Sykes and tested it along with his own. It turned out that they had exactly the same Y chromosome—they were, in fact, kin.

Curious, Bryan Sykes decided to pursue this connection between surnames and genetics. So he wrote to a couple of hundred men in Yorkshire with the same surname and asked to test their DNA. He found that 70 percent of them all had the same Y chromosome—they were all related.

That's how it all began, says Sykes. After he published a paper on that finding, DNA testing began to catch on. And that led Ryan to turn to Family Tree DNA to find his biological father. Although neither his biological father nor any of his close relatives had ever entered their own DNA online, Ryan was still able to find him through a fragment of shared genetic code from distant cousins.

Once Ryan had the names of two of his relatives, he cross-referenced those with the names of the 300 people he had found who had been born in the city where he knew his donor had been born, with the same birthday. He couldn't believe it. There was only one man with the same last name. He had to be a match.

But before contacting him, Ryan wanted to be sure. He knew that his biological father was an engineer, so he guessed where he went to college based on his major and his place of birth. He then wrote to the alumni association of that college and asked if they had had anyone graduate with an engineering degree on the date he speculated his donor had finished school and with the last name Ryan had provided. The alumni association wrote back: he had the right man.

From there, it wasn't difficult to find an email address for Lance, the man whom Ryan had been waiting for years to meet, the man he had fantasized about and speculated about. The man who was his biological father.

"It was bizarre to have his name in my hands. I'd spent half my life wondering who he was. I was excited but also very nervous," remembers Ryan. "I wanted him to know that I didn't want money, and I didn't need him to be my father. I wanted him to know that I existed, and that I was curious about him."

Within ten days of discovering this information, Ryan had found his father's email address and wrote to him, telling him who he was. It was June 2005. The subject line was: "interesting information."

The email read:

Lance, where to begin? My name is Ryan Kramer. I'm fifteen years old, and I live in Nederland, Colorado. Fifteen years ago, my mother was impregnated with a sperm donation from California Cryobank Donor 1058. You may want to sit down for this next part.

It was something out of a science fiction movie, says Ryan. Nobody emails you out of the blue to tell you they're your father. He told Lance a little about himself, and he asked him to get back to him, but only if he wanted to and on his own terms.

Then he waited.

Ryan and his mother, Wendy, were extremely nervous about what the donor's response would be—if he responded at all. Wendy just hoped that the donor wouldn't disappoint her son.

"As we waited the 48 hours for the donor to reply to Ryan's email, I just kept thinking, *Please be kind, please be kind, please be kind.* So in other words, even if he were to say, 'Thanks, but no thanks,' in regard to contact, I wanted him to be kind about it and not hurt Ryan in any way. Ryan and I talked a lot about it and he was very mature in his thinking. His thinking was that the donor signed up for anonymity, and if he wasn't up to meeting at that point, that would be okay. Ryan said that when he turned eighteen, he'd 'jump on a plane, go to California, and shake his hand,'" says Wendy.

A few days later, he heard back.

"He said he was thrilled to hear from me and excited to learn that he was my father. And he was happy to talk to me. It was cool—as good as I'd hoped for," says Ryan.

In a radio interview with Ryan and his father that later aired, Lance recalls the day he received that email: "Yeah, I mean, even remembering it now, my heart starts to pound a little bit."

At the time, Lance was thirty-eight and single, a tech worker in Silicon Valley. He spent his weekends playing Ultimate Frisbee and drinking Bud Light.

"It was quite an email. It had a link to a four-page human-interest story about Ryan in the *Denver Post*. I wasn't quite sure how to respond. I had never expected anyone his age to contact me. It was very exciting," says Lance.

It took him a few days to write back to Ryan. "I had no idea what to say. Imagine finding out a total stranger is a close relative."

Ryan and Lance emailed back and forth for about three months, with Ryan asking him an array of questions. He wanted to know what his father's taste in music was (electronic music; he sent Ryan a link to a music video for the song "Weapon of Choice" by Fatboy Slim), what he did for a living (he was an engineer in Silicon Valley), and what he liked to do for fun (Ultimate Frisbee, which, coincidentally, Ryan liked to play, too). And, most importantly, he sent Ryan a picture of himself.

"Imagine going your whole life not knowing what your father looked like? It was wild," he says.

When they had their first phone conversation, Ryan found more remarkable similarities. His father was talkative and high energy, as he was. He was also working as an engineer at the time, and Ryan would later receive the exact same degree as Lance in graduate school—engineering management. In many ways, their lives would end up following similar paths. Ryan eventually went to work for Apple, while Lance had worked for a Silicon Valley company for many years. People asked Ryan if he was trying to follow in his father's footsteps, but he assured them that it was just a coincidence.

Lance says he donated sperm in college because it was good money for a student, and he also thought it might be an opportunity to reproduce. He did it two to three times a week, on and off for about five years.

Did he ever think about the children that could result from his donations? "Other than wondering if they were out there, no. I didn't actually know what the sperm was used for, or if it was used," he says. However, he thought it was possible that one of his offspring might one day contact him.

In August of that same year (2005), Lance invited Ryan to come to California to meet him and his parents. Since his parents didn't have any grandchildren, Lance thought they'd like to meet Ryan, and he was keen to give them the opportunity. He'd never told them that he had donated sperm in college, so it all came as somewhat of a shock to them. But his mother was excited to meet her grandchild.

Ryan couldn't believe it was actually going to finally happen—he was overjoyed to meet his father. Lance was living in the Bay Area at the time, but his parents lived in Pasadena, so they decided to meet there.

Ryan and his mother immediately booked a flight to Southern California. When they arrived at the Hilton Pasadena, Lance's mother had left them a welcome basket in their room, with ideas for things to do in the area. Ryan was bouncing off the walls with excitement when they got there—he was jumping from bed to bed, doing flips, unable to control his enthusiasm. They had set up an initial meeting in the lobby of the Hilton Pasadena, where Ryan and his mother were staying. It was rather cloak and dagger at first, because Lance was worried that they might surprise him with a media presence, and that was the last thing he wanted. He needn't have worried. Although Wendy and Ryan had appeared on the *Oprah* TV show and other media outlets to talk about the Donor Sibling Registry, they had no intention of bringing anyone from the press along that day.

On the first day, Ryan and his mother visited the Norton Simon Museum in Pasadena and were told to wait for Lance's phone call for the meeting place. They had gone to a nearby Banana Republic store to kill time, when Ryan's cell phone rang. Wendy remembers their excitement when they saw Lance's name on the phone.

"It was like a comedy—we were pushing the phone back and forth, saying, 'You answer it!' 'No, you answer it!'" says Wendy. "Finally, I answered and got the instructions of where and when to meet, which was in our hotel lobby in 45 minutes."

They raced back to the hotel room to get cleaned up before the meeting. They wanted to make their entrance into the lobby seem casual, like they weren't there waiting for him, so they took the elevator down, hoping to walk out into the lobby and meet Lance. But he wasn't there. So they went back into the elevator and tried the same thing a few more times, casually exiting the elevator. Eventually, mother and son went into the bar area to wait, their eyes glued to the front door, staring at every man who entered the lobby to see if it was him. They were both tense with the anticipation of this meeting, one they had both waited for so long. Ryan was full of nervous energy. He remembers thinking, *Is that him?* every time a man walked in.

The minute Lance entered the lobby, it was immediately obvious that he was Ryan's father. They looked so much alike—they had the same eyebrows, the same chin. Ryan and Wendy nonchalantly came out from the bar area and headed toward him. Wendy recalls that the situation felt surreal.

"I remember walking toward him and seeing him smile. I said, 'Oh my God, he has Ryan's teeth!' He walked toward us, and we shook hands. I thought, 'this stranger is just as related to my son as I am.' It was a weird thought, since I'd been my son's only parent for all fifteen years of his life," says Wendy.

Ryan and Lance shook hands warmly. Ryan says there was a bit of awkwardness, and they took long pauses to look at each other. He noticed that his father was very handsome and clean cut, with a recent haircut. He was six foot one, a little taller than Ryan. He had dark hair, broad shoulders, and looked athletic—it was obvious to Ryan from the way Lance carried himself that he'd been a football player when he was younger (and he later found out that he was right). He also had the same eyebrows as Ryan.

"We had a moment where we looked at each other. Your brain is trying to take all this in—and this person looks a lot like you. It's pretty weird," recalls Ryan. "Meeting him was fascinating. For many years, I'd had conversations about myself—about my physical characteristics, my talents and my interests, and where they'd come from. And now, I'd found this person who shared my interest in science and engineering. Even the tiniest mannerisms caught my attention. I stretch a lot, and my father also stretches his arms when he talks. We even have a similar gait. And he's got a wild, goofy side, which I admit to as well."

As for Lance, he also remembers the first meeting as being slightly awkward, since they were strangers. "But I could tell by looking at Ryan that we were related. He had very similar eyes as mine," he says. "Ryan does look like me. He is a very interesting, likable guy."

Ryan remembers having a huge sense of relief and satisfaction when he finally met his father, as though an enormous weight had been lifted.

"It gave me closure. I look back and remember it was something I thought about a lot. Then, almost overnight, making contact with him absolved me of all that. It was thrilling," he says.

How did Lance feel about being discovered by one of his biological children? Here's what he said in the radio interview: "It is very difficult to imagine that anyone will be able to keep their DNA lineage anonymous. It's something they're gonna live with in the future, and we're living with today, apparently. He's my donor offspring, and he's a great kid. He's my younger-half clone."

So FAR, LANCE, who is now in his late forties, has met only one of his other biological children. He never married and has no kids of his own besides those he helped to conceive as a sperm donor.

Like Ryan, there are many other donor offspring searching for their biological parents and looking for some contact with their donor father or mother. But do people have the right to know who their biological parents are? Should sperm donors be able to maintain their anonymity? And will the debate over donor anonymity become irrelevant, as new technology makes it possible for children, such as Ryan, to find their relatives, making the concept of anonymous sperm and egg donation obsolete?

To be sure, Ryan's discovery has important implications for the many people conceived using donor sperm, as well as for all the sperm donors who thought they were donating anonymously. Now, any of those men could potentially be traced by their offspring, and the promises that the sperm banks made to maintain their anonymity might be significantly compromised.

"When those confidentiality contracts were agreed upon, they were based on the conditions at the time. Then you have this new technology come along . . . you have to reassess that," says Sykes, founder of Oxford Ancestors. "There might be a need to legislate. These kinds of ethical questions crop up in genetics all the time, and we debate them."

Ryan's mother, Wendy, says that she is now helping other donor offspring—and adoptees—find their biological fathers and mothers. The Donor Sibling Registry even has a guide to researching paternal genealogy on its site.

"Ryan's story isn't unusual anymore. When you make a place for people to find each other [on the DSR], they do. I know a lot of sperm donors and offspring who have become family," she says. "These kids aren't looking for a dad or money. What that curiosity is about is they want to know about their ancestry and their medical background. These children want to look in the face of the person with whom they share half their genetic background."

Wendy says that her son has sisters who don't even know they were donor conceived because their nonbiological fathers don't want them to know. "I see them on Facebook, and they look just like Ryan. But they don't know," she says.

There are, however, many who are open to meeting their half siblings and even their offspring. Of the 2,800 donors in the DSR's database, so far about half have been matched to their children, says Wendy. And while that's encouraging, she is critical of the sperm banks for failing to advise the men who donate sperm about the people they will help to create, and how to handle any potential contact in the future.

"They need to properly counsel the donors and the parents [who buy the sperm]. And they need to stop promising anonymity to the donors, because that's a myth. They aren't telling them about DNA searches. It's only a matter of time," she says.

There are some experts who agree with this prediction. Yaniv Erlich is an assistant professor of computer science at Columbia University and a member of the New York Genome Center. The center is a consortium of academic, medical, and industry leaders who focus on translating genomic research into clinical solutions for serious diseases. Erlich's team at the Genome Center has been investigating the intersection between social media and genetic information, among other things.

"Any sperm bank that promises that its sperm donors' identity will remain confidential for the rest of their life are very likely to be wrong," he says. "You cannot protect your genetic privacy if you give your genome [through your sperm] to someone. It's totally wrong to say that your privacy can be protected. There's a very high likelihood that someone will be able to breach that privacy."

And he points out that the databases with genetic information available online are only getting stronger, not weaker. So there is more data out there and better technology for finding someone. Microscopes, for instance, are so much more powerful that scientists can see almost every detail in a genome, and thus can acquire much more information.

In June 2016, the British medical journal *Human Reproduction* published an article, "The end of donor anonymity: how genetic testing is likely to drive anonymous gamete donation out of business." In an editor's note in the same issue, Hans Evers wrote, "All parties concerned must be aware that, in 2016, donor anonymity has ceased to exist."

With all this new information available, Erlich was interested in finding out if Ryan was just lucky in discovering his biological father so quickly, or if it was something that anyone could do. So his team analyzed nearly 1,000 Y chromosomes available online in the United States and found there was a 15 percent chance of recovering a surname just by running someone's Y chromosome through a database. They already knew the surnames attached to the Y chromosomes, but they created an algorithm and did the search blindly so that they could compare what they found to the real names.

If his team found a close relative to someone they were searching for—a fifth cousin or closer—they would guess that they had the same surname and were often right. Once they had a surname and additional information on an individual—such as the state and year of his birth—they found it relatively easy to use other tools, such as public databases and social media, to find the identity of this person.

What does this mean for all those sperm donors out there who thought they were donating anonymously? Sykes finds the situation disturbing.

"You have two conflicting desires here: you have the sperm donors who want to remain anonymous, set against the desire of the children to know who their father is. This has to be resolved through discussion and legislation, because both sides have a point of view," says Sykes.

"But at the end of the day, if you are a sperm donor and you're worried about keeping your identity anonymous, then don't be a sperm donor."

Of course, it's too late for Lance and others like him to change their minds now about sperm donation. However, Lance doesn't seem to regret his choice, even though he was an anonymous donor who was tracked down by one of his offspring.

ON THE DAY they first met in the hotel lobby, there was a certain amount of awkwardness between them. Ryan thought, *What do I say to this guy?* Lance was naturally quiet, so that didn't make things go smoother in the beginning.

The three of them decided to go out for a soda so that they could talk. They walked to a nearby California Pizza Kitchen, a restaurant chain. It was spring, and the weather was typical of Los Angeles, sunny and warm. Wendy let Ryan and Lance walk ahead of her, and she noticed that they had the same walk. She also realized that women were looking at Lance as they passed him. He was strikingly good looking. (Ryan would later ask her, "Do you think I'll have a jaw line like Lance when I grow up?" They actually do have similar jaw lines.)

Ryan says it was uncomfortable, but that his father seemed very nice and was open about himself. In some ways, it didn't seem weird at all that they were meeting for the first time as father and son.

As they sat down, Wendy remembers Ryan looking at her, then at Lance, and then back at her. He later told her that it was so weird to think he was sitting between his mother *and* his father for the first time! Almost right away, Ryan and Lance began to compare the size of their hands, and then their feet. Wendy says she has heard this from a lot of donor-conceived guys who have met their donor dads. It must be a guy-bonding thing, she says.

At the restaurant, Lance was great with Ryan, asking a lot of questions about his life and about school.

"It was an unusual lunch. I did find myself noticing that Ryan was obviously my offspring, and that was kind of shocking," he says. He thought that Wendy seemed like a great mom, and that she was very bright and cultured.

Ryan was very respectful during lunch, keeping his personal questions to a minimum, and waiting for Lance to divulge what he was comfortable with. There was a lot of staring going on, which became the norm whenever they got together. "I think that we all were so amazed at the resemblances; it was hard not to stare," says Wendy. Lance was very polite and probably just as nervous as they were. At that point, he may not have fully trusted Wendy and Ryan, so his guard was up.

After a few drinks, Lance surprised Ryan and his mom by inviting them to have dinner at his parents' house. When they got back to the hotel, Ryan turned to his mom with big eyes, clearly awestruck, and said, "I know who my donor is."

Later that day, as they drove toward the Pasadena hills to the home of Ryan's paternal grandparents, Ryan was nervous. What if they didn't like him? What if they had nothing in common and it was uncomfortable? But the evening turned out much better than Ryan could have imagined.

When they arrived, Lance's parents, Ronald and Doris, warmly greeted them, hugging them when they walked in. Everyone was nervously laughing, and Lance's father said, "Who wants some wine!" and Doris said, "I know we're all a little nervous here!"

As quiet as Lance was, his mother, Doris, was the opposite: bubbly, energetic, and talkative. She immediately made Ryan and Wendy feel at home. Ronald and Doris live in a quiet, well-kept neighborhood in one of the canyons near Los Angeles. It's an elegant ranch-style home with a pool and a deck in the back, overlooking the canyon, with well-manicured landscaping, and tastefully decorated with contemporary furnishings. They all sat out on the deck and enjoyed the view while they chatted. Ryan, who was already an aerospace engineering college sophomore at the time even though he was only fifteen, was a big topic of conversation.

Lance's parents ordered pizza, and when the pizza deliveryman rang the doorbell, Lance joked (sort of), "That better not be Oprah!" They all laughed—it was a good icebreaker.

"I was very happy that they could meet. That's what I was happiest about," remembers Lance, of the meeting between his son and his parents.

During the visit, Ryan immediately took to Doris.

"She's a character, kind of like Betty White [the actress]. She's adorable and super friendly," says Ryan.

Wendy noticed a faint resemblance between her son and his grandparents. Lance's father, Ronald, was more reserved than his mother. He was less trusting and rather unemotional, and he didn't really understand why Ryan was so curious about Lance, and what he wanted of him. Of course, he grew up in a very different generation, where sperm donation and donor children were not commonly talked about. Some things take longer for older generations to absorb and get used to. It took Ryan a while to convince Ronald that he didn't want anything from Lance—that he was just curious.

But Doris had no problem with Ryan's existence. In fact, she was thrilled to meet him and Wendy, and she immediately adopted Ryan as if he were her own grandchild. Until then she hadn't had any grandchildren, since Lance didn't have any kids—nor did his brother, his only other sibling. To Doris, Ryan was already family.

"I had such a feeling of contentment afterwards," recalls Ryan. "I finally had the answers to all my questions. I thought, even if I never see these people again, I'll have what I wanted."

While he was there, he looked at all the photos of his father in the house. Some had an astonishing resemblance to Ryan. There was one in particular where Lance was in his twenties, with a beard. He looked so much like Ryan that they all joked, "Now you don't need to grow a beard to see what you'd look like with one!"

They stayed for several hours and everyone seemed to be having a great time. As they were leaving, Ryan and Wendy hugged everyone goodbye, and they all made plans to meet up the next day at the house, then head to the Huntington Botanical Gardens. They ended up spending the weekend together.

"The most beautiful moment in that first weekend was that Sunday morning [when they went back to the house]. The smell of French toast cooking, the sun streaming through the windows, and Ryan sitting at the piano with his grandfather playing. Lance and I looked on as his mother came out of the kitchen, wearing an apron, holding a spatula and singing along. I was holding back tears," remembers Wendy.

Since his first meeting with Lance, Ryan has been redefining his relationship with his father. "He's like a friend or an uncle, not a dad," he says. Now that Ryan, who is twenty-seven, lives in the Bay Area near Lance, who is in his late forties, they see each other about once a month, meeting for happy hour or a holiday party, or getting together when Lance's parents are visiting.

"We've known each other for about a decade now. We have our expectations pretty well established. He's at a much different part of his life now than I am," says Ryan.

Wendy understands her son's now-casual attitude toward his biological father.

"People ask Ryan, 'what's it like?' Ryan has answered in many different ways. It's something completely different. It's your biological father that you didn't grow up knowing," says Wendy. "I know that Ryan's father cares very deeply for him. He's so protective of Ryan and proud of him. It was very touching for me to learn that he really cares about my son."

As for Lance, he says the two are friends. "We're a lot alike, just in different generations. It's nice to be in touch with Ryan. I see him or chat with him fairly often. We don't live far from each other." He says that knowing he has donor offspring may have made him less motivated to have his own children.

As for his new grandparents, Ryan's relationship with them built over time. That first year, he flew out by himself to see them for Christmas, and he and his mother fly out to see them occasionally for holidays. But they became much closer when Ryan decided to attend graduate school for engineering nearby, at the University of Southern California in Los Angeles, only a twenty-minute drive to Pasadena. He says he chose that school over Duke University in North Carolina because he thought it might give him a chance to get to know his grandparents better. And he was right.

Ryan would see them frequently, having dinner with them on Sunday nights. Over time, their relationship grew, and by the time Ryan finished grad school, they felt like his actual grandparents. He still keeps in touch with them and sees them a few times a year.

Wendy has also developed a strong rapport with Ryan's paternal grandparents.

"I adore Lance's parents. I have bonded with his mother and talk to her at least once a month. We have conversations that last an hour or two, talking about absolutely everything. I feel so lucky to have her in my life. When we hang up the phone, she always says first, 'love you.' It is very evident that Lance and his parents adore Ryan," she says. Of that first visit with Lance and his parents, she says, "I was watching my child's wish finally come true. It was a profound experience."

In his search for keys to his identity, Ryan learned something important about himself from his grandparents: engineering, something no one on his mother's side had any interest in, was in his blood. Not only was his father, Lance, an engineer, but so was his grandfather, and his father before him. In fact, engineering went back more than one hundred years in his father's family.

"I always felt it was weird that I was interested in math and science and engineering," says Ryan. "Learning where that came from, that it's been in their family for so many generations, I realized that it was totally normal to feel that way. It made me feel ok about it all."

2

Sperm Donor 007
One Man's Mission to Find His Children

As a young man, Chase Kimball always had a feeling he wouldn't have a family of his own. So when he was approached about donating sperm while a student at the University of Utah, it seemed like the right thing to do. He could contribute to the gene pool and potentially spread his genetic material far and wide, while also helping others.

The year was 1976, and sperm donation was still a relatively new concept in the United States. Since sperm banks were just starting to open, Chase, who was twenty-two, donated through the hospital at the University of Utah. Chase was young, tall (about six foot two), athletic, attractive, healthy, and highly educated (he was working on his second master's degree at the time). He had thick, light brown hair and a beard, and green eyes, and could frequently be seen riding his motorcycle around Salt Lake City. All those factors (besides the motorcycle) made him an ideal candidate to be a sperm donor.

Raised in a devout Mormon family, the notion of having children was important to Chase, as it is to many Mormons. And the fact that he could potentially help other families—including Mormons (he was in Utah, after all)—to have kids was an added bonus. He donated every Wednesday afternoon for more than three years, making $25 each time. The whole donor thing was still so new that his donor number was 007. The staff jokingly called him James Bond.

After college and graduate school, Chase stayed in Salt Lake City and became a lawyer, working as a civil litigator, handling divorces, personal injury cases, business disputes, and the like. He dated, but he had a hard time finding the right person. He became convinced that he would never get married and have kids, and that the only way he would reproduce would be through his sperm donation.

When he turned thirty-eight, he finally found a woman he really liked through mutual friends. Kimberly was smart and funny and shared his love for the outdoors. She was also game for taking long motorcycle trips with him. They married a year after they met, in 1993. They both wanted kids, so they began trying right away, but nothing happened. They tried fertility specialists, spending thousands of dollars on doctors and treatments, but they still couldn't get pregnant. Eventually, the marriage fell apart from the stress. After three years together, Chase's wife left him, and he was alone again.

Chase, now in his early sixties, is a big man, tall and broad with a salt-and-pepper beard and a deep, guttural voice. He walks with a slight stoop and shuffles a bit because of a back problem. Chase is kind, big-hearted, and self-deprecating, with a profound love for music and his family. He is chivalrous: he still holds car doors open for women and says his grandmother taught him the importance of good manners. But he also has a daredevil streak—he spent a good chunk of his spare time tearing up the West on his motorcycle. And while he's known formally as "Chase," his family and friends call him "Kim." When he was a small child, he says, his parents thought Chase was too "high-falutin'" a name for a small boy, so his father started calling him "Little Poop." When he was about two and a half years old, a family friend decided the boy might get a complex from such a moniker, so he gave Chase the nickname "Kim," saving him from a lifetime of embarrassment. His family has called him Kim ever since.

AFTER HIS MARRIAGE ended, Chase dated, but he had a difficult time finding anyone special. He'd always wanted kids, so the prospect of being childless saddened him enormously.

"I'm really, really unhappy about that. I'm very family-oriented. I'm not much of a Mormon anymore, but that doesn't mean I didn't learn things from the Mormons. The fact that I never reared any children was devastating to me," he says.

So he began to think about the children he might have fathered through his sperm donation. He would scan the faces of boys and girls in crowds, wondering if any could be his.

"I always wondered if I'd meet them. It was a matter of constant curiosity. When I saw groups of children, I'd look at them intently and see if any of them looked like me," he says.

The years went by, and Chase filled his spare time playing the piano, working, socializing with friends, riding his motorcycle, and occasionally dating. He thought he'd never find the woman of his dreams. And he thought longingly about any children he might have out in the world—he didn't know that finding them could be a mere click away on his computer.

In 2004, when he was fifty-two, Chase heard about the Donor Sibling Registry and discovered that the website allows sperm donors and their offspring (as well as half siblings) to find each other by using the donor's identifying number. Chase checked out the site. You had to pay to be a member, but you could look to see if there were any matches or messages for you without signing up. He checked again and again, every few months, looking to see if anyone wanted to get in touch with Donor 007 from the University of Utah Hospital. Nothing.

He did this for two years, checking back whenever he remembered, hoping for some kind of sign. Then on August 12, 2006, he decided to check the website again, something he hadn't done in months. He looked, and to his amazement, there was a message waiting for him from one of his donor children. He became so excited, he started shaking. He couldn't believe that he might have found a son or a daughter.

What he had dreamed about for years had come true: he would finally get to meet one of his offspring.

Having children of his own was something that had always been fundamental to Chase's life, in part, because as a Mormon, he'd been taught from an early age how important it was to have kids and a family. Mormons are fiercely devoted to their families, and they consider it a blessing to have children. They believe that God's commandment to Adam and Eve to multiply and replenish the earth is still relevant. They also think that family relationships continue beyond the grave, so that children will carry on as a source of joy and happiness in the afterlife, when they are all together again.

The tradition of having many children can be traced back to the creators of the Mormon Church, many of whom were polygamists. Among them was Chase's great, great, great grandfather, Heber Chase Kimball, whom he is named after. He had sixty-six children.

Heber Kimball was a member of the early Latter Day Saint movement and served as one of the original twelve apostles. He was later a leader in the church, second only to Joseph Smith, who founded the Mormon religion. Initially, Heber Kimball was reluctant to practice polygamy, but Joseph Smith eventually convinced him, and Heber later married a total of forty-five women and had sixty-six children by seventeen of his wives.

It turns out that Heber Kimball's great, great, great grandson was probably even more prolific than he was when it came to having children. Chase estimates that, based on the number of times he donated sperm over seven years, he now has between 100 and 200 donor children.

There's no way of knowing for sure how many kids Chase really has because no one keeps track of the numbers. Certainly not the sperm bank. Or if they did, they weren't telling anyone. Chase says the sperm bank at the University of Utah hospital purposely kept him from knowing how many kids he had. In the beginning of his sperm donation, the nurses would tell him if he'd fathered a child, but when they realized that he was keeping track, they stopped. Sometimes they would ask him to come in to donate for a particular person who wanted to have another child with his sperm. After a few years, they told him he'd fathered enough kids locally, so they were shipping his sperm out of state. Finally, when he was around twenty-five, they told him that he had to stop donating because of all the children he had.

Chase's parents were very devout Mormons, and sticklers for the conventions of the religion. Like many devoted followers, that meant no caffeine, tobacco, or alcohol. They had an occasional Pepsi. Church was every Sunday, and they were expected to attend for most of the day.

Chase was born in Winston-Salem, North Carolina, but his family moved to New York City when he was around a year old so that his father could enter a PhD program in Eastern European history at Columbia University. His father had gone on a Mormon mission to Czechoslovakia in 1947 and became fluent in Czech. He was a history buff, so he decided to teach Slavic history. Chase's father had always been a hard worker and very bright, so he finished his degree in four years while teaching nights at New York University. When he finished his degree, his father was offered a job teaching at Southern Illinois University, so the family moved to the St. Louis, Missouri, area, just across the river from the college.

Although Chase grew up in a strict Mormon family, he never really felt much of anything for the religion. "It was something I did out of habit. When I was fourteen, I'd had enough. I told my parents I didn't want to go to services anymore. That went very poorly. They made me go. It became a constant contest of wills from when I was age fourteen to eighteen, and it led to very disagreeable home life," he says.

He ended up going to college at the University of Utah because his parents told him that if he went to school in Utah, they'd pay for it. "They hoped I'd be surrounded by Mormons and meet a nice Mormon girl and see the error of my ways," he says. Chase tried a few different majors, including education (for which he received a master's degree) until he found something that appealed to him: a degree in musicology. But eventually, he realized that he'd be fighting for a teaching job, so he decided to enter law school.

ON THIS DAY in late summer, sitting at his computer, Chase was excited to communicate with just one of his kids. After reading the notification on the DSR website that he had a message, he ran upstairs to grab his wallet. He found his credit card and immediately opened an account so that he could read his note. It was from a young woman named Jane. She said that she thought he might be her biological father, and she was interested in speaking to him. Jane, who was nineteen at the time, also told him that she had a twenty-two-year-old sister, Nina, who was probably also his daughter, and that they both lived in Utah, not far from Salt Lake City. (Jane and Nina also had an older sister, but she was born through a different sperm donor.)

"I was just over the moon," says Chase. "I couldn't believe it."

He wrote back immediately:

Subject: biological father

Assuming you are correct about your donor's number being 007 at the University of Utah, I am your biological father. I have wondered about you and my other children for years. It is amusing that you are an English major. I am deeply interested in literature, and love poetry. My favorite poet is Gerard Manley Hopkins. I am not surprised that one of my children would be an English Major. Even more than literature, I am interested in music, particularly classical music. I come from a very old LDS family (you WILL recognize my last name), but am no longer active. I would love to know more about you and your sister.

When Jane read the message from Chase, she was overwhelmed.

"I opened my email, and thought, 'Wow!' It said, 'I'm your dad,'" says Jane. "I had this nervous excitement. I had to call my sister, who didn't know that I had contacted him. I told her, 'I don't know how to tell you this, but I found our dad.'"

Her sister, Nina, was stunned. She wasn't thrilled with the thought of Jane, who was nineteen, contacting a stranger. In fact, she thought the whole thing was a bad idea. And she wasn't so quick to believe that he really was their father. This man said he was a Kimball, which meant that he was of the distinctive Mormon lineage that goes back to Heber Chase Kimball (which, of course, meant that they were, too). He would know this was important to them if he had guessed that Jane and Nina were both raised as Mormon. And since 60 percent of all Utah residents are Mormon, it would have been a pretty good guess. Nina, who was six years older, thought everything seemed too perfect. This man didn't work in a fast-food restaurant, as Jane and her sister had feared—but a lawyer? And a Kimball? It was just too good to be true. She thought he was trying to swindle them somehow. She thought he was a liar.

"They thought I was just saying the things that Jane would want to hear," recalls Chase.

Regardless, Jane wrote back:

Subject: We're a match!

I had my mother bring me the receipts from your donation just to make sure, and yes, you are my biological father. My oldest sister was fathered by a different donor, and my mother accidentally told me his physical description, which is where the mix up came from. To be thorough, I checked the blood type of my sister and I, and they are consistent with yours and my mother's. Almost seems too good to be true, since we've been wondering about you for such a long time, but I guess there is no way to deny it now.

I was so shocked when I checked my email and found that you had written me, because I don't think I ever really believed the site would work. I've been curious about you ever since I found out that my dad is not my biological father. I don't look like my mother, which made me wonder if we had any similar features. I definitely got your height and your olive complexion. That was something that really struck me, because everyone in my family is fairer, shorter, and has lighter hair, and here I am with dark skin, hair, and eyes, towering over everyone else.

I was so excited to find that we share an interest in literature. I don't yet have a favorite author or poet, mostly because I feel that I haven't read nearly enough to make an educated decision.

I am also an avid lover of poetry and plan to look into Hopkins' work. My other passion in life is dance. I have danced since I was three years old. I was in a performing group for six years; competed in tap, jazz, and ballet; was captain of my high school dance team; and I began learning ballroom at BYU. I also love films and am constantly frustrated by the fact that so many classics are R-rated, making them off-limits. I try to get them edited when I'm at school, but I am a very serious student, so there isn't much time for that hobby.

You've probably already realized that I am also LDS (Church of the Latter Day Saints, or Mormon). I was thrilled to find that I come from an old LDS family. My father's parents and my mother are converts, so I always felt a little left out when people would talk about ancestors coming across the plains or being related to someone like Brigham Young or Joseph Smith. I guess it is also good that I am finding this out now, so I don't end up marrying a cousin or some other unknown relative.

I am not sure what is and isn't appropriate to ask about you, but I'm an extremely curious person and want to know as much as you are willing to tell me. I would love to exchange photos and even meet you when I come down to school. I also invite you to ask me any questions you might have, because I'm not sure exactly what you'd like to know.

I'm very excited to have found you.

Nina and Jane first learned that their dad was not their real father when they were very young—barely old enough to understand about sperm donors and how babies are born, says Nina. She was four years old, and Jane was about eighteen months old at the time.

"I was not at an appropriate age to understand this," says Nina. "But my family has a gossip problem, and I remember thinking that I already knew about this [because her relatives had talked about it]."

But having their mother tell them at an early age helped them get used to the idea that their biological father was a sperm donor. It made it seem normal to them. They soon learned that their eldest sister, Linda, was also born through a sperm donor, but a different one.

"My sister and I like to tell people that we cost our mother money to have us," says Nina, joking about their mother's use of a sperm donor.

Both sisters are very pretty, with very different personalities. Jane, who has long brown hair and brown eyes and a warm, open smile, is now in her late twenties, and is outgoing, vivacious, and deeply religious. She is a devout Mormon. She's a stay-at-home mother with two young children, and she likes to write and draw and is learning how to play the piano. She lives with her husband and children in Northern California.

Nina, who is now in her early thirties and is three years older than her sister, has long blond hair and blue eyes. She is more guarded than her sister and takes a little while to warm up to people. She is quieter, more bookish, and not as social as Jane. She likes to garden and read and spend time with her friends and her boyfriend. Nina and Jane are both very intelligent: each graduated magna cum laude, and Jane was valedictorian of her high school.

Nina's life has had its ups and downs: she is divorced, but now has a new boyfriend, and is a recovering alcoholic. She works in health care for the state of Utah and is very fit. She was recently in training to compete in a women's physique competition in Utah.

Their parents divorced when the girls were young, and it was an ugly breakup. Their father moved away, and they lost touch for a time. He failed to pay child support, and their mother struggled to take care of them. They were poor. When Jane was young, she was embarrassed to learn that her mother was taking donations from their church's food pantry.

Her relationship with her nonbiological father was difficult, and he could be mean to her and her sister. "My dad is the kind of person who likes to step on an ant hill and watch everything go crazy. If you're mad, he'll make you more mad, and then he'll laugh about it. He's just hard to get along with," says Jane.

Knowing that her biological father was out there, somewhere, helped her get through the rough times, she says. But even more than that, she knew that her sperm donor's number was 007. She could imagine that her real dad was James Bond!

"I had this fantasy. When my dad was being mean to me and we weren't getting along, I would think, *I have a real dad somewhere, and he's much nicer,*" she remembers. "I thought it was totally normal and cool, and I had this secret thing about me. Having his number be 007 helped me with my secret identity."

Jane says she used to wonder who her biological father was and imagined that one day she would find him. "I always thought about him. It was constantly on my mind. I used to think, *He'll be somebody nice, somebody better than my dad.*"

One summer day, when the girls were older, their mother read an article in *People* magazine about the Donor Sibling Registry. She told Jane about it and encouraged her to sign up on the site. Jane was nineteen at the time and home for a visit after her first semester at college. She had just had a big fight with her father.

Nina says she was always skeptical about the whole thing. She was never as curious as Jane about finding their sperm donor, and she wasn't sure that trying to find him was even a good idea. She also knew that her mother hated their father, and she thought that trying to find their sperm donor was a way for their mom to get revenge on their dad. "I said, don't tell him any stuff about us," said Nina, of the sperm donor. She was nervous about Jane giving out her personal information to a stranger.

When their parents split, their father didn't want their mother to tell the girls that she had used a sperm donor to conceive them, but she did it anyway. Predictably, he was angry when he discovered that they knew. They hadn't told him that they knew the truth to avoid hurting his feelings.

"He never talked about it," says Jane. "He said he specifically had us listed on his will as his children. He was my father, and I always called him Dad. He really didn't want us to know [about the sperm donor]. It was very hurtful to him. For men, I think it's an emasculation thing, like, if I can't have children, I'm not a man."

Later, their father complained that he was so stressed out about the Chase situation that he was getting migraines. Jane says she doesn't feel sorry for him. "He has no room to complain. I feel like it's my turn to be selfish in my life. I've forgiven him for a lot of stuff. He doesn't get to be upset. He chose to be a crap dad. He's pretty lucky that we talk to him, and we pretend the other stuff didn't happen. I'm the child, not the parent. I don't have to parent him."

Still, she says it was very stressful when her father didn't know that she and her sister had met their donor: "Now that it's out in the open, I feel great. I'm not hiding anymore."

Wendy Kramer, of the Donor Sibling Registry, said she finds that many fathers who are intimidated by their child's sperm donor tend to be people who are insecure about their own parenting. "If you're doubting yourself as a parent, you'll be threatened by someone coming onto the scene. It brings up the guilt in him that he wasn't good enough. He might think, 'I didn't do as good of a job as I should have,'" she says. She adds that sperm donors usually don't threaten confident fathers because these parents consider their relationship with their child to be solid.

Fathers who put their needs and their fears before the needs of their child are just being selfish, she says. "They should have gotten over the grief and shame of infertility before they had kids and not passed it on to their children," says Kramer.

To prevent this from happening, she believes that parents need to be adequately counseled by the sperm banks before having kids with a sperm or egg donor. It should be about what's in the best interest of the child, not the parents, she says.

Still, these are very complicated situations that can create heightened emotions on all sides. Some heterosexual couples never tell their children that they are born through a sperm donor. Children who find out later in life that they aren't biologically related to their father often have a much more difficult time accepting the situation. For Jane and

Nina, it was confusing. Since there were no rules for how to move forward with this new relationship with their biological father, they had
to make it up as they went along.

Chase wrote back, telling Jane more about himself:

No need to feel intimidated when people talk about pioneers and
Brigham Young and Joseph Smith, you are the great-great-great-
great-granddaughter of Heber C. Kimball.

It is funny you would talk about coloring. My coloring is different from the rest of my family as well. My father had fair skin,
brown eyes, and black hair. My mother had light brown hair, blue
eyes, and fair skin. My sisters are all blonde/brown, fair and blue
eyes. What is your sister's coloring?

Here's a story that might make you laugh. I was a very graceful
child, and I LOVED to dance, just silly dances I would do in the living room while listening to records and watching TV. But I loved to
watch American Bandstand and dream about the day I would be
old enough to go on the show and dance with all the other cool
teenagers. I figured when I was fifteen, I would be old enough, and
I was practicing. Then I went from 4'11" at the end of sixth grade to
6'1" at the beginning of eighth grade, so I grew about fourteen
inches in about sixteen months; and I went from a graceful boy into
a gangly awkward teen who was constantly bumping his head and
walking into walls. So no more dancing after that!

I first heard about the DSR site maybe a year ago and checked
but found nothing from any of my children. I suppose I should have
joined then, but I was too cheap I guess. I have checked it
sporadically since, and when I checked it yesterday morning, I was
electrified when I saw your post.

In theory, the whole sperm donation process was supposed to be
anonymous. Chase went to the clinic, gave his sample, and left. But
bizarrely, communicating with Jane now triggered a significant memory about their relationship. He remembered donating sperm for her
mother so that she could have another child: Jane.

Believe it or not, I remember you, sort of. I quit regular donations in about 1984, around when I started law school. I had too many Utah children and they said I had to stop, but they would call me in on occasion when someone from another city wanted me. I remember one of the very last times I went in, toward the end of law school, the nurse told me the family already had one of my children and wanted another. That is probably you.

Yes, when you decide the time is right, we can meet. Please send many pictures, but don't call me Chase, my family nickname is Kim. You can ask me ANY question you want, I decided a long time ago to live my life as an open book, and I have no guilty secrets. The fact that you are a curious person is not exactly a surprise to me.

When Chase wrote back to Jane that time, he sent her a picture of himself as a young man, and Nina immediately saw the resemblance between him and her sister.

"He looked just like Jane, but with a beard! It was ridiculous how much they looked alike," remembers Nina. That convinced her that Chase, indeed, had to be their biological father.

Jane also saw the unmistakable likeness. Seeing his picture for the first time was a revelation to her.

"He looked exactly like me. It was very strange. Now I see myself differently. I never thought I looked like my mom, so when I saw that picture, there was this connection. This mystery was solved, somehow," says Jane.

This is a common experience for those who find their donor fathers—a feeling that they have finally found the key to their identity. Yet, people born through donors can vary a great deal when it comes to this issue. For instance, Nina had little interest about who her donor was, and she was fine with not meeting him. "I thought about it a little bit, not a lot. I just didn't think it was even possible we'd find out who he was. I wasn't possessed with the need to search for someone. I was curious, but not enough to do anything about it." Many other donor children feel the same way.

But for Jane, the discovery of her biological father revealed new layers of her life and opened up a whole new world to her. Since the Mormon Church places a considerable emphasis on family and genealogy, many members can trace their ancestry back to the beginning of the church. "People really know their family history. But for me there was this big question mark. I didn't really know mine. When I saw his picture, suddenly there was no longer a question mark. His family was an old Mormon family, and he looked like me. Suddenly I had this connection with my religion. And all these things that made me not like everyone else—like my parents getting divorced, and being poor—I got to be part of it. I'd always had this feeling of being an outsider in my life. Seeing his photo helped me feel like I was part of things. Like I belonged," she says.

After receiving Chase's picture, Jane sent him photos of herself and her sister. Chase was thrilled to see that they looked like him and was happy that they were communicating. But he didn't want to scare her off. So he took his time, sending Jane emails over the next few weeks.

In one email, Chase sent more photos of himself, with this note. It read like someone who's just fallen deeply in love:

> I just can't believe it all! My head is spinning with the excitement of everything. I have to get to bed, but I wanted to send you a few pictures of me. Talk to you soon!

In another message, he noted the striking similarities in their looks:

> Yes, I would say that you and I look alike. We have the same nose, the same shape (dolichocephalic) skull and face, the high forehead, the same coloring. My head is a whirl also, but I have to get to work.

Finally, he asks if they would be willing to meet with him. But at the same time, he seeks to reassure them:

> I want to make something very clear to you. I am going to let you and your sister set the pace, and the limits. I will see you when you

wish it. I will talk to you when you wish it. You can treat me as a friend, an uncle, or some distant relative you call once a year on Christmas. Or not even that. Obviously, your real parents did a tremendous job, and it would be ludicrous for me to expect to step into their place. Not that I have any ambition to do so, I just want you to know that I know who your real parents are, and I am not one of them. Yes, I am curious about you and want to learn as much as you will let me know. But I understand boundaries, and I will respect any you set. And I repeat, you can ask me absolutely anything, I have nothing to hide, nothing.

When Chase and Jane talked on the phone for the first time, they were both extremely anxious and on edge.

"There was this nervous excitement. My hand was shaking, and there was this feeling in my chest like I was going to vibrate apart. I couldn't handle it, there was so much going on in my head," remembers Jane.

They arranged to meet in St. George, where Nina was living at the time. St. George is a small city about four hours south of Salt Lake City, on the Utah-Arizona border. It's a pretty place, with a warm desert climate, and it's close to Zion National Park. Popular for its golf courses and as a retirement destination, some describe it as Utah's Florida, with fewer hurricanes. The city first came into existence as a settlement, when Brigham Young sent Mormon settlers there in the 1800s to grow cotton. But the experiment failed and cotton farming was eventually abandoned, while the Mormons remained. In the late 1800s, the LDS church completed its third temple there, the St. George Utah Temple. Coincidentally, St. George was also home to Chase's mother—and to the girls' father, Jim.

Jane and Nina didn't want to tell their father that they were meeting their sperm donor, so they had to sneak around and pretend they were meeting a friend. They asked their older sister, Linda, who was visiting, to cover for them. It made for a stressful morning—but it was worth it, they thought.

Unlike a typical family, everything in this new relationship required a decision: Should they really be meeting their donor? Should they tell the father they grew up with about meeting their biological dad? They couldn't know what form this new relationship would really take. Even something as simple as how they should address him was a question. There are few more basic or primary words than those we call our parents—mama, daddy, mom, dad. But what is the word for this kind of father? Should they call him Dad, or Chase, or something else? Perhaps they wouldn't be able to relate to him at all. Perhaps they wouldn't even like him.

The trio decided to meet at an ice cream parlor over Labor Day weekend. It was about 90 degrees out on that Saturday, clear and sunny. Before the meeting, Nina and Jane were nervous—they didn't know what to expect.

"We worried he was a fraud, or some creep," says Jane.

Nevertheless, they drove to meet him in Nina's black Nissan Sentra and arrived at Nielsen's Frozen Custard shop on East St. George Boulevard a little early. It's an old-fashioned ice cream shop, with red vinyl booths, Formica tables with red vinyl-covered chairs, and a red neon sign out front.

The parking lot was crowded, so the sisters drove around for a little while, looking for a spot. They finally parked in the back and sat in the car, watching for this man whose appearance would change their lives. Nina thought, we already have a complicated relationship with our dad. Did they really want to add another one?

"We were sitting in the parking lot, thinking we should just drive away. We hid the car in the back so we could watch for him," remembers Nina. "He was late."

Chase doesn't remember being very late. He drove there in his dark blue Subaru Outback, arriving around one pm. He, too, was anxious about the meeting.

For Chase, this opportunity to meet his biological daughters was thrilling but also surreal. He'd waited so long to meet one of his children, and he couldn't believe it was about to happen. He'd been so curious about who they were and what they were like. He hoped they'd all get along, and that they would eventually foster a close relationship, but he also wanted to respect their wishes—and he certainly didn't want to scare them off.

"There was a certain amount of trepidation. This was a pretty unusual event—meeting two adult daughters that I'd only known for a couple of weeks," says Chase. "I was very excited, and very curious. I don't have a lot of social anxieties, but I wanted to make sure I didn't do something goofy when I met them, something that would alienate them."

Chase walked in, and scanned the tables. The restaurant wasn't very busy, even though it was lunchtime. He looked around and found the sisters sitting at a booth, not far from the door. He recognized Jane immediately from her pictures. He jerked his head back, as if in surprise (a typical Chase gesture), then headed over to them.

No one in the restaurant seemed to notice them as Chase met his two biological daughters for the first time. To an outsider, there was nothing out of the ordinary to observe—after all, it was just a father and his two daughters getting some ice cream. Except that it was highly unusual at the same time. This was a sperm donor who gave his sperm thirty-four years ago, meeting the offspring that his genetic material had helped to produce. It was a life-changing moment, for better or worse.

Meetings such as these are starting to become more common, says Wendy Kramer, of the Donor Sibling Registry, adding that there are matches on her website between donors and their children every day. "We get maybe one or two donor connections a month," she says. "I'm friends with a lot of donors and offspring who have become family. When you make a place for people to find each other, they do."

For Chase and his daughters, this meeting would be the start of a very personal journey. But each of them was coming to this from very different perspectives. Would it all work out for the best?

When Chase spotted the sisters, he walked over to them and they awkwardly shook hands. It seemed too soon to ask for a hug. He was wearing a blue Hawaiian shirt, light gray corduroy pants, and black ostrich-leather cowboy boots. He usually wore cowboy boots when he went out. A tall man, they made him appear even taller.

As Chase sat down, his daughters couldn't take their eyes off him. He felt the same way. He thought they were beautiful. Nina thought he seemed excited about being there. "It's a weird situation meeting your birth parent for the first time," she says.

Jane, in particular, was struck by Chase's resemblance to herself.

"When he sat down, I was looking at him, comparing him to me. I noticed he looked like me," says Jane. "There was this fantasy that we'd click and get along really well. But it wasn't this instant connection. I felt kind of weird. He didn't have children of his own, so I think he wasn't sure how to interact with us."

Chase, for his part, says he felt like they were already familiar to him. From his emails with Jane, he knew their hobbies and likes and dislikes. In particular, he knew that they both liked to read, so he brought each of them a book as a gift. He gave Jane a book of poetry by Federico Garcia Lorca, his favorite Spanish poet. He knew that Jane was an English major, with a Spanish minor, so he thought she would enjoy the book, especially since this copy was written in both languages. And for Nina, whom he knew loved comic novels, he brought *Joy in the Morning* by P. G. Wodehouse, another writer that he enjoyed. The sisters both appreciated his thoughtfulness.

The three of them chatted, finding out about each other's lives. It was slightly uncomfortable at first, for all of them. Mostly, they talked about themselves. Jane and Nina told Chase a little about their mother, and he learned that their "social father" also lived in St. George. (Chase refers to their father as their "social father," as many others do. Some find the term offensive. It's a way some people differentiate the biological father from the father that the child grew up with.)

Chase told them more about himself and his family. He talked about his mother and his three younger sisters (he was the oldest and the only boy) and his father, Stanley, who died in 2003. His dad had been a professor of European History and Western Americana, and he was the world's leading expert on the Mormon Trail, with numerous books on the subject. His mother, Violet, had a master's degree in English and had also been published, winning an award for her book on young pioneers.

After talking for a little while, Chase asked the girls if they'd had lunch yet. He ordered a turkey sandwich, but the girls only had soda. They were too nervous to eat, and Jane doesn't drink coffee, because practicing Mormons don't drink coffee, tea, or alcoholic beverages, nor do they smoke or take drugs. (Mormons believe that God gave Joseph Smith the law of health, which emphasizes healthy living and prohibits them from imbibing any of the above.)

As the three of them chatted, they discovered they had a lot in common: they were all bookworms, had a love for learning new things, and liked being outdoors. They were all raised as Mormon, though Jane was the only one who was still practicing. She was disappointed at first to learn that Chase was no longer a member of the church. But since her sister didn't practice either, she thought it was probably all right. (Nina believes that organized religions are patriarchal and harmful to women, and she doesn't follow any religion now.)

Jane remembers with a smile that, at one point, Chase started telling them bawdy stories about the women he'd met.

"We'd say, 'Stop, gross, remember we are your children!' He has a lot of women in his family, but sometimes he doesn't seem to know how to relate with us or how to treat us. I guess he doesn't have much experience with kids," she says.

After about two hours, the sisters said it was time to go. They were supposed to do something with their social father. They walked back out to the parking lot, and the three of them stood around awkwardly, trying to figure out how to say goodbye.

Then Chase mentioned that his mother lived nearby, and that she was dying to meet them. Would they consider going over there? She didn't live far way, and it wouldn't take long. At first, they declined.

"We were like, what if he's a serial killer? No way!" remembers Jane. "But he wore us down. That's his way. You tell him no, and he's like c'mon, please? Finally, we said, okay. We're going to get murdered, but fine."

The visit with Chase's mother and sister Kay, who was also there, went pretty well. "My mother was just enchanted with them," says Chase.

Kay had her video camera going when they walked in the door. Then, his mother and sister hugged his daughters. They all felt uneasy at first, but Kay is very social, and they talked for about twenty minutes. Everyone seemed to get along. Nina remembers that Chase's parakeets were there (he's a bird lover), and that they were very loud. Chase says his mother and sister were thrilled to meet Jane and Nina.

A picture that was taken that day of Chase and his two daughters, sitting on his mother's sofa, is one of his favorite photos. Chase is sitting to the right, with an especially pleased expression on his face; Nina is in the middle, holding a book of photographs. She's wearing a pink, vintage-style, flowered dress, and she has a half smile on her face, as though she's not sure she wants to be there. Jane is next to her sister, to the left, and she's wearing a brown top and jeans, and a long, beaded necklace, and she's beaming. Her eyes are smiling, too. Chase has several blown up images of the picture in his house. There are copies in the dining room, as well as in the living room.

When the sisters got up to leave, Chase walked them outside to their car. He put his hand out to shake their hands, and unexpectedly, Nina, the one who was least excited about their meeting, said, "You can hug us if you want." Chase didn't waste any time.

"Boy, did they get hugged after that," remembers Chase.

When his daughters drove away, he felt exhilarated. He couldn't believe it had actually come together. He was delighted to finally meet them, and especially to see how much they had in common—though he wished they could have spent a little more time together. Still, both of his daughters lived in Utah at the time—Jane was at Brigham Young University in Provo, only about forty miles from his house, and Nina was here in St. George, where his mother lived.

He hoped they'd see each other again, and he wondered what their relationship would be like.

After the meeting, they kept in touch, but the relationship wasn't always easy. The sisters were wary of Chase, whom they often felt came on too strong, despite his initial promise to let them set the pace. They wanted to take their time getting to know each other; they didn't feel comfortable becoming an instant family.

It's not always easy to get it right in these relationships. While some donors may fear the emotional stress of meeting his offspring, others, such as Chase, may yearn for the chance to connect with and get to know their children. And while some donor children might merely want to see what their donor looks like and learn about his medical or family history, others could be searching for the support and nurturing from the father they never had. For Jane and Nina, it was a little bit of both.

"I don't think I warmed up to him for a while . . . months or so," recalls Jane. "With any person you meet, you have to find how you click together. I had to figure out, who is this person to me, what is this relationship? This isn't something I've navigated before.

"I was interested in getting to know him, but I wasn't sure how to be. He wanted me to call him Dad; he wanted to see me every day. He wanted to step on the gas, and I was like whoa! I'm not ready for this. It can be overwhelming."

At first, Nina was also unsure of the relationship, but she slowly became more comfortable around him. They emailed, and he would come see her when he was visiting his mother in St. George. If she were in Salt Lake City, she would stay with him. She even went with him to see some of his friends in Berkeley, California, and the sisters visited Chase's mother when she eventually moved to Georgia.

"Meeting a birth parent as an adult is a strange thing. How do you build a relationship as an adult with your natural parent?" she says.

Like Nina, many donor children can be confused about how to move forward with the relationship. How much should she tell him about herself? How much time should they spend together?

Since Jane lived in Provo, which was closer to Chase than where her sister lived, he started inviting her out. About once a month, he would invite Jane to dinner, to concerts, or to see dance performances, since he knew she was fond of dancing. Chase could be very thought-ful when it came to those close to him.

At times, Jane wasn't sure if she wanted to meet, but she felt pres-sured by Chase to go, and she often gave in.

"He was a little bit pushy. I never had a dad relationship with him, so I wasn't sure how to interact with him, and I wasn't sure what I wanted. I was a sophomore in college, I was busy, I had my own life, and I wasn't sure how he fit in, and if I wanted to do things with him," she says.

For his part, Chase says he was not trying to make an instant family and invade their space. "I wanted to see them more often than I did, and still do, but I think it is fairly common for twenty-something women to not spend a lot of time with their parents."

Then in October, Chase called Jane and said he wanted to take her out on the Alpine Loop, a twenty-mile scenic drive that goes through two canyons and a national forest. It offers incredible views of Mount Timpanogos and other glacier-carved peaks, and it detours through Cascade Springs, a mountain spring that is accessible by a boardwalk that leads to cascading terraces. It sounded pleasant, but that day Jane was planning to attend the LDS church's big, twice-yearly meeting, the general conference. It's an all-day meeting where members of the church gather to listen to sermons from church leaders, and it's con-sidered very important in the Mormon religion. It's an international event, since the sermons are broadcast worldwide. Jane was looking forward to going, so she said no. Chase asked again, and she refused. Finally, he wore her down, and she reluctantly agreed to go along on the drive with him.

"I finally went with him, and I was so irritated. He thought I was always studying, but this was something that I wanted to do. He wouldn't leave me alone, and wouldn't listen to me. For Kim, no means ask again," she says.

During the drive, he talked to Jane about the Mormon Church, and all the reasons why he was no longer a member. "My split with the Mormon Church was not congenial," says Chase. "My parents were not happy about it at all." It had been coming for a long time—since he was a teenager—but his final separation from the church came in September 1993. It was right after the infamous September Six incident, in which six intellectuals and feminists who were members of the Mormon Church were excommunicated or disfellowshipped for allegedly publishing writings that were considered against LDS doctrine. They were also thought to have criticized the church leadership. The decision by leaders of the church to remove these prominent members shocked many within the religion, and its repercussions are still being felt today. Some of the September Six were friends of Chase's parents, and Chase was so angry about the way they were treated that he asked that his name be taken off the church membership records. That meant he was no longer considered a Mormon by the church. His parents only found out when one of the September Six, Lavina Fielding Anderson, who was visiting them, mentioned that she was proud of Chase for standing by his principles. She didn't realize that his parents didn't know what he had done. It was an awkward moment. Chase is still highly critical of the church. He doesn't discuss the issue with his family to this day.

Jane was angry at Chase's talk about her religion. She didn't want him trashing the church—especially since it was something he was taking her away from on that day. It didn't really bother her that he was no longer a practicing Mormon, but she didn't want to hear his negative thoughts on the church. "We'd only known each other a couple months at this point, and I was annoyed," she says.

When she next saw Chase, he'd come in to Provo to take her out to dinner. He chose a Thai restaurant, and over dinner she told him that she had just broken up with the guy she'd been dating. Chase was happy because he hadn't liked the sound of that boyfriend. She told him that she was dating someone else now—someone who would later become her husband. He thought this new guy seemed much better for her.

"I remember thinking that I was pleased that he was pleased. He didn't like the goofball I was dating before. And he approved of my new guy. I was glad I had his approval. I guess I was feeling more comfortable with the relationship," she says.

Relationships between donor children and their biological fathers can be fraught, and there are no guidelines for how they should behave toward each other. So what makes people want to connect with their donors? What are they searching for?

"These kids aren't looking for a dad or for money, and when these men realize this, you have more people coming forward. What that curiosity is about is for a child to know their ancestry and their medical background. And to look in the face of the person with whom they share half their genetic background," says Kramer.

But she laments that none of the donors are counseled about the needs of the people they helped to create. She says that the sperm banks need to properly advise the donors and the parents buying the sperm on how to help the children that result.

Chase always wanted the best for his daughters and was devoted to them from the start. He says of Jane: "She is my loving, agreeable angel-child, and I am pretty crazed about her."

Nina, who was divorced by this time, was having a difficult time meeting men. She was also trying to kick her drinking habit. So Chase, who lives in a fairly spacious four-bedroom house on the outskirts of Salt Lake City, invited her to come and live in his basement for a time, while she got back on her feet. He also thought she'd have an easier time meeting nice guys in the city. Chase was happy to have one of his daughters living with him. She called him Kim, but sometimes she introduced him to other people as her father, which made him especially pleased.

But it was a rocky time, as Nina was in recovery. "I was a mess," she remembers. She found it difficult to live there while she was trying to stop drinking, and she eventually moved out.

The situation was problematical for both of them. "Having Nina move in with me was not one of my better decisions. I was initially very excited about it, but the reality did not meet expectations," says Chase.

Eventually they had an argument and ended up not talking for a year. Nina said she needed some space. Was Chase trying to create something that she wasn't ready for? Was his desperation to be a father blinding him to what was good for Nina at the time?

"I needed some distance. He was trying to create this father-daughter relationship, and I felt like he was pushing it on us to fill the need that he wanted to be a dad," she says. "We had a close relationship. Then I started to feel like, this is a person I met as an adult. This is someone I'm biologically related to, but he's not my father."

Nina went to an in-patient treatment center for a month and became sober. She found a new job and a place to live, and got on with her life. Chase tried to reach out, but she told him not to contact her again. She would get in touch when she was ready. During this time, Nina thought a lot about the relationship.

It can be difficult to manage expectations when donors and their children meet and develop a relationship. For Nina, she had to be honest with herself about what she wanted out of her connection with Chase, and whether or not it was realistic.

"I was longing to have a dad who cared about me, and I tried to recreate that with Kim at first. But it didn't happen. I didn't have a dad when I was growing up. He wasn't there. When I was an adult, I thought, I'll have a great relationship with my biological father, and then I'll feel better about my past. But that's not how it works," she says.

A year later, Nina was working in downtown Salt Lake City, near where Chase worked. She was walking to work one day when she saw him across the street. She hesitated—should she go over and talk to him? Did she want him back in her life? What did she really want from this man?

Nina called out his name and went over to say hello. When Chase saw her, he became emotional; he'd thought that she would never talk to him again.

"We had had no contact for thirteen months, and I wondered if I would ever see her again. It was very painful for me. When she called out to me, I wept freely and told her I loved her and had missed her," he remembers.

She reassured him that he wasn't out of her life. "I said that wasn't the plan. I was waiting for the right time to talk to you," she says.

Now, their relationship is better. Nina finds him to be more respectful of her wishes. And while she loves Chase, she considers him to be more like an uncle to her rather than a father. But she still feels the bond between them.

Despite the complications, Chase was fortunate to have met and formed a meaningful relationship with two of his biological daughters. But for many sperm donors, the concept of having any real connection with dozens, perhaps hundreds, of offspring must be mind-boggling.

Chase also struggles with the thought of forming relationships with scores of his offspring: "I'm open to more contact with my children, but it would be a real challenge if all of them contacted me. I don't really know what I'd do," says Chase. "I'm not going to say, I don't have time for you because you're number 197."

He guesses that most of his children are as old as thirty by now, or close to it, and some may not even know that they were born through a sperm donor.

"I just hope that they're happy and successful," he says.

Still, he's enjoying having his daughters in his life. And he's delighted by the joys of being a grandfather to Jane's two young children. He Skypes regularly with her and her kids, and his granddaughter calls him grampoo. He tries to visit them in Northern California every few months. On one visit, Jane's husband told Chase something surprising.

"He said, 'it's funny but the girls are just as much like you as their mother.' I had thought that myself, but I imagined it was prejudice on my part. I didn't give it a lot of credence. But when my son-in-law says it, I do," he says.

Since meeting his daughters, Chase has also met Nina and Jane's mother, Trish, and their father.

When Jane graduated from college, she wanted Chase to be there. They met at a restaurant afterward near Brigham Young University to celebrate.

"It was awkward for a few minutes. There's nothing in your normal societal intercourse that prepares you for meeting the mother of your children for the first time. It's not a typical meeting. But I treated them like old friends, and they did the same," he says.

Trish thanked Chase for giving her beautiful daughters, and he did the same. Every Mother's Day, Chase sends her flowers with a note saying, "You made it possible."

3

The Group of 150 Kids

A Mother's Search for Her Children's Half Siblings

Two young boys were locked in a ferocious battle. They fought to see who would be victor, shifting on the floor of the bedroom for better positions. The epic clash became even more heated.

"Got you that time!" shouted eight-year-old Mark, fiercely gripping his controller while he played the Lego Batman video game. He pushed his light brown hair out of his eyes and laughed. Then he absentmindedly twirled the friendship bracelet on his wrist. It was the same one that his new friend, Eric, who was nine, wore. Mark's mother had bought one for each of them as a welcome present for Eric, who was visiting them.

Mark's mother, Cynthia, poked her head in the door to check on the boys. She smiled as she watched them play. They looked so much alike, with their high foreheads, straight profiles, and a faint blue vein running down the side of their noses. Even though Eric had blond hair and was taller, you could see the striking similarities between them. She shook her head in wonder and shut the door. More lively shouting could be heard coming from the room as she headed toward the front porch, where her guests awaited her.

Cynthia joined Susanna Wahl and her six-year-old daughter, Julianna, on the faded Adirondack chairs. The women swatted mosquitoes away as they chatted and sipped wine. Like her son, Eric, Susanna was blond and blue-eyed. She had wavy shoulder-length hair and bangs that framed a round friendly face. At forty-six, she was outgoing and self-possessed, and enjoyed meeting new people. She was a devoted member of her local Rotary Club and liked the sense of community that came from being involved with clubs and organizations. Relaxing on Cynthia's comfortable shaded porch on this hot, summer day, she felt particularly at home.

When Susanna and her kids arrived in Sharpsburg, Maryland, to visit Cynthia Daily and her son, Mark, it was a hot, steamy day in late June, and the lilacs were still in bloom, lacing the air with their scent. The American flag, fastened to the wide front porch of Cynthia's white, nineteenth-century colonial home, flapped in the wind. The peonies were staked out front, prepared for the next storm. A blackened and shiny cannonball, dating back to the Civil War, propped open the front door to let in the evening breeze. Inside, there was still a cannonball hole through one of the interior doors, a relic of the bloodiest battle of the Civil War.

That day, as the boys battled in front of their video game, Susanna and Cynthia caught up. They'd only conversed via email before and had never actually met until now. Susanna had left her husband, Larry, at home during this trip. He was their children's father in every sense of the word, except he was not their biological dad. He couldn't have children, so they had used a sperm donor. Cynthia and her partner, Emma, had used the same donor. They were all family in a very special way.

Maryland was one of the many stops that Susanna and her kids were planning to make on the cross-country journey they were taking this summer. The trio was planning to spend the next two months visiting relatives. Susanna wanted to make sure her kids met their extended family, even if some lived thousands of miles away from their home in California.

In fact, Susanna had an uncommon reason for undertaking this particular odyssey. All the relatives she planned to visit, including Mark and Cynthia, were connected to her family in an unusual but significant and very modern way. The children they would meet were Julianna and Eric's half siblings, all part of a larger group of 150 children fathered by the same man: Sperm Donor B155A.

During this unusual family reunion tour, Susanna and her kids planned to meet only a handful of their half siblings. She decided to reach out to the families that she was regularly in touch with on their shared Yahoo group. Susanna and her family had already met some of their half siblings who lived in California, but they were excited to meet more. It was a journey that Susanna embarked on with equal measures of enthusiasm and apprehension. Would the trip be a positive experience for her only two children, both of whom were born through a sperm donor? Or would they run into unpleasant situations when they met these new families? She wondered if they would be treated as the strangers they were or instead welcomed with warmth, as Cynthia had done. Yet she knew that of the half siblings who had already met, many said they felt an immediate and deep connection with each other.

Despite this strong bond, there were donor families who still didn't want any part of it. Infertility has many taboos associated with it, and the use of donor sperm to have a child is still looked on by some as immoral or wrong. There are those who are deeply religious, who feel that if a couple cannot have a child on their own they shouldn't have one, because it's against God's plan. Even those who use donor sperm to have a child may feel uncomfortable with the process and want to keep it a secret from the people who may not understand or support their choice. But for many in Susanna's group, the potential stigma had more to do with the large number of children born through a single sperm donor, and what people would think of their children if they knew about this extraordinary, yet strange, secret.

In fact, some of the heterosexual parents in the group hadn't even told their kids that they were born through a sperm donor—and weren't planning to. And there were those who *had* told their sons and daughters, but weren't comfortable with others knowing the provenance of their children because they didn't want their kids looked on as being part of some bizarre social experiment. Susanna and her kids would, indeed, meet such people on their trip.

Her kids knew that they would be meeting their half siblings on this journey, but they weren't entirely sure what that meant. Still, Susanna wasn't too concerned about how meeting all these families would affect her children's sense of their own family, because she was confident that they were secure in their relationships with her and their Dad, who they knew was not their biological father. She knew that Eric and Julianna didn't doubt their love for them in any way. But, it was hard to know what to expect on this trip.

WHEN THE HEAT and humidity became unbearable, Cynthia, Susanna, and Julianna retreated from the porch to the cooler interior of the house. While Julianna played with their cat, Cynthia and Susanna went on a laptop at the dining room table and tried to sort out the names of their kids' shared half siblings.

As the creator and manager of the Yahoo group that connects all of the families born through Donor B155A, Cynthia has a keen awareness of who the members in the group are and how many children have been born. She knew from the beginning that the group was going to be large because it grew so quickly; within the first two years, there were almost fifty kids. The group quickly outpaced other large donor sibling groups on the Donor Sibling Registry. Originally, the group connected on the DSR, through their donor number, but when the group became uncomfortable with how many people were in it (the information was available to the public), they took their names off the website and created their private Yahoo page. (Many donor sibling groups do this now to keep their personal messages and identities private.)

Susanna was relieved that Cynthia, a social worker in her mid-fifties who helps disabled children, was such a gracious host and had treated them like family. It was a great first start. They had a lot in common besides their children's biological father: Cynthia worked with disabled children, and Susanna had taught special education for many years in California, so they both understood the challenges and rewards of working with special-needs children.

Mark popped his head into the dining room. He was a stocky boy, tall for his age, with light brown hair and a wide smile. He was obsessed with hockey and video games, but he also loved animals and had a gentle side to him.

"You guys having fun?" asked Cynthia.

"Yeah! Eric is cool. Can he stay longer?"

"Maybe. We'll see."

Mark sighed.

"I feel like he's the brother I always wished for."

When he left the room, the mothers looked at each other and started to laugh. Susanna realized then that Cynthia hadn't told Mark that he and Eric were related, and clearly, Eric himself hadn't mentioned it to Mark. Susanna had started talking to her kids about their origin when they were much younger.

"Have you ever explained to Mark where he came from?" she asked Cynthia.

"I tried, but I'm not sure how much he really understood."

"Well, do you want to tell him that Eric actually *is* his brother?" Susanna gently asked.

Cynthia considered for a moment.

"Maybe. Maybe that's a good idea."

So they made a plan. They would do it that night. They'd explain to Mark that he and Eric shared a biological father—the same sperm donor.

As they continued talking, Susanna began to reconsider. She didn't want to upset the kids. And she certainly didn't want to make Mark, or her own kids, feel like they were somehow "strange" for being donor children. Common as sperm donor children had become, they were still considered unusual, an anomaly.

Her thoughts went back to the beginning of the journey that had brought her to this house, to this family, and to being a member of such a unique and sizable group of related donor families. With her affinity for community and connection, this fact became central to how Susanna thought about her family and her children's donor family. Assisted reproduction had pulled her into a murky world of familial relationships that not only lacked clear social definitions but also would have been unimaginable only a few decades earlier. Since she had no idea who the anonymous sperm donor was, trying to contact him was not an issue.

SUSANNA MET HER husband, Larry, through an unlikely connection—her parents. Twelve years her senior, Larry was a member of the same boating club that her parents belonged to. They spent time together boating with her parents, and eventually fell in love. She was thirty-three when they married.

Larry, who is now sixty, is tall, with warm, brown eyes, and close-cropped salt-and-pepper hair. When he smiles, his eyes smile, too. He's easygoing and calm, and he is a good foil to Susanna's high energy.

Susanna is the driving force in the family, and she can be headstrong, but Larry has a quiet authority that comes through when he speaks with the kids.

When Susanna married Larry, she knew they probably wouldn't be able to have children together. Larry, who was an engineering tech for Pacific Gas and Electric, had been married before, and he and his previous wife had gone through years of fertility treatments, before they realized that he was unable to father children.

"Going through fertility treatments was such an emotional roller coaster ride," recalls Larry. "I said to Susanna, 'absolutely not, I'm not going through that again.' I was ok with no kids, but I said if you want kids, we can try something else."

They considered adoption, but during a visit with her nurse practitioner, Susanna came upon the idea of using a sperm donor. Her nurse, Claire, was a single mom who had used a sperm donor to have her own baby, and she encouraged Susanna and Larry to explore this as an option.

Larry and Susanna chose to use an anonymous donor because they didn't know they even had a choice to use a known donor (meaning their child could contact their donor once he or she turned eighteen). They logged on to the Fairfax Cryobank website and invested hours trying to find the right man. Beforehand, they had discussed their preferred genetic traits. She wanted blond hair, blue eyes, and no allergies (because she had them herself and knew what it was like to deal with them). Larry wanted the donor to be smart. Of course, they both wanted their baby to be healthy, so they made sure their donor had no diseases. They also preferred a donor whose parents (preferably grandparents as well) were still alive. Having an artistic and musical child was also important because both Larry's and Susanna's families had musical backgrounds. And since their family included engineers and mechanics, they also wanted a donor with technical abilities.

"We were trying to get a donor who was as close to our background as possible—Swedish, German—so that our kids wouldn't be so different from the rest of our family," says Larry.

When Susanna talked to friends about their decision to use a sperm donor, she was candid. She told them, "Here's the truth. Boom. Deal with it."

But when it came to telling their families, they were cautious.

"We thought, how will they respond? How will they treat the kids? If they took the attitude that they're only half our kids because we used a donor, we wouldn't be happy. We didn't want any animosity," says Larry.

At first, her parents and the rest of their family were skeptical about them using a sperm donor and worried that it wouldn't work out. But they came around, says Larry, and learned to accept it. However, the couple decided not to tell Larry's parents, who were in their eighties and very old fashioned. He felt they wouldn't understand.

But when Larry told his brother and sister-in-law about their plans to use a sperm donor, they were in for a surprise: the couple had used a sperm donor to have their own two kids. They hadn't told anyone about it because they were afraid that the others wouldn't understand. Larry hadn't realized before that both he and his brother were infertile.

It WAS A sunny morning in early June, the last day of school, when Susanna and her kids hit the road from Northern California to meet their extended family. Her new slate-gray Prius was packed with granola bars, bottled water, peanut butter crackers, video games, a DVD player and movies, stuffed animals, and even a little cooler with milk.

It was more than a little hectic that day. Eric and Julianna, who were nine and six, were ecstatic to be done with classes and were running around the Ron Nunn elementary school in Brentwood when Susanna showed up. She was anxious about being on her own for so long with the children, and without her husband, Larry, who had to stay home to work this summer. She worried, what if the car broke down? What if something happened? She didn't actually enjoy driving, but she liked traveling and was prepared to put aside her discomfort to take this trip. And, she had a new car! Why not test it on the open road and take advantage of the car's excellent gas mileage of 50 mpg?

Eric and Julianna said goodbye to their friends, knowing they wouldn't see them for most of the summer. They knew what they were doing on the trip, but they weren't sure they understood exactly who these other families were, or what it meant to have a half sibling. Still, they were excited to meet some new kids and see the country.

On their way out of town, they stopped at home to drop off the kids' backpacks and books and to say goodbye to all their pets. They had taken their leave that morning from their father, who was now at work.

Susanna wondered if she'd remembered everything. She was trying to be as prepared as possible. Traveling alone with two young children for six thousand miles was no small feat. But Susanna—energetic, driven, and fearless—would not be deterred by a seven-week, cross-country trip alone with her kids. This same can-do attitude got her through a diagnosis of breast cancer when she was in her late forties: she underwent treatments, a double mastectomy, and numerous surgeries with strength and guts. What was a little road trip compared to that?

Before she left, Susanna made sure that Larry knew how to care for all their pets. Susanna was a true dog lover, and they now had three dogs, plus two more they were fostering for their local animal shelter. They also had two ferrets, a guinea pig, and a pet rat (which Larry was not thrilled about). She also checked for her "special tea" (she was on the Dr. Oz tea plan to lose weight) and for the generator she needed for her sleep apnea machine. Check.

As the group left Brentwood, a city about an hour northeast of San Francisco, and headed north on Interstate 5, the children were amped up and excited about their trip. Their first stop was Colorado, and they planned to travel through twenty-four states as they made their way to their final destination in Madison, Wisconsin, before going home. Altogether, Susanna hoped to visit seven families and meet a total of eleven half siblings. None of them had ever been on such a long car ride before, and certainly never to the East Coast. Susanna had to ask them several times to quiet down so she could concentrate on where she was going.

After driving for a while, Julianna, normally a chatterbox, became uncharacteristically quiet. She played with her long blond hair, and the expression on her face was pensive. She blinked her big, blue eyes.

Susanna glanced in the rearview mirror and frowned.

"What's wrong, sweetie?"

"I'm confused. Don't the other families have to live close by if they used the same doctor?" Julianna asked.

Susanna was quiet for a moment.

Initially, she'd told her children that she and the other moms in the group had all used the same physician when they wanted to have a baby. While she always tried to be frank with her children about where they came from, Susanna also wanted to keep the information on a level that they would understand. But now they were on a trip that would take them thousands of miles from home, and Julianna was trying to make sense of this long journey that they were embarking on. She wanted to know how the families who lived clear across the country, in New Jersey and Rhode Island, could have possibly used the same doctor?

How was she going to explain this one, Susanna wondered? She believed it was important that her children begin to learn the truth about their conception from an early age. Almost as soon as her kids could talk, she and Larry began to imprint them with the understanding that even though they were not related to Larry by blood, he was certainly their real dad.

"When the kids got older, we started talking to them about it. It's amazing how quickly they caught on and understood," says Larry. "We'd say, 'We talked to you about this before, now you can get the rest of the picture.' They understand it, and they know I was at their birth, and they don't treat me any differently. And we don't treat them any differently."

Still, was her daughter old enough to understand about donors and conception and genes? (Eric, being older, had a slightly better grasp.)

They didn't want to rush this. For example, they still hadn't really explained half siblings to Julianna, since she was only six. She and Larry were giving the whole story to their daughter as a series of incremental disclosures. She was still too young to fully grasp the concept that their donor was a living breathing person, so they were focusing on the scientific part of conception rather than trying to develop a relationship with a biological parent they would never know. Both children seemed to understand that Larry was their father in most respects—but that he hadn't contributed to their conception in a biological sense. And they both seemed perfectly fine with that information. Maybe it was because Susanna and Larry didn't make a big deal of it.

After Susanna and Larry searched through Fairfax Cryobank's online sperm donor directory in Virginia, they narrowed their choices to three donors, all of whom had good medical histories. They ordered baby pictures, voice recordings, and medical histories. Because many donors remain anonymous, the Wahls didn't choose a donor by name; they chose a number.

Donor 2080 came from a family that was musical, and his father was a minister. His baby picture was endearing.

Donor B155A's file offered a picture of himself as an adorable little boy sitting in a high chair about to eat his first birthday cake. He had golden-blond curls and big blue eyes. This donor was particularly appealing because he had living grandparents, was captain of his rugby team, had a degree in economics, and was ambitious. He seemed perfect.

Donor 1318 had a better academic background than the other two choices, but Susanna and Larry decided that his earlobes looked a little odd, so he was ruled out.

They finally agreed on Donor B155A. Susanna contacted the sperm bank, excited to be moving forward. But she was disappointed to find out that his sperm samples were sold out.

So she ordered samples from their second choice, Donor 2080. A week later, they had a call that their first choice, Donor B155A, now actually had samples available, so Susanna ordered some of his as well.

Susanna started monitoring herself every day to find out when she was fertile. For a while, there was nothing. Because Susanna was thirty-six, the doctor talked to her about using a fertility drug, such as Clomid, to get pregnant. But it turned out to be unnecessary, for she tested positive for being fertile. Although it was late in her cycle, Susanna wanted to try anyway. The fertility clinic was pessimistic about her chances of getting pregnant that time, so she decided to use her second choice, Donor 2080, and save her first-choice sperm for when she had better odds.

A few weeks later, she was thrilled to learn that she was pregnant. "We were so excited when we found out that the procedure had worked on the first try!" she says.

Nine months later, Susanna gave birth to Eric, a perfect baby boy. "When he was born, I thought, well the donor had a musical background, so maybe my son will be musically inclined, too," she says.

Eighteen months later, when Susanna and Larry decided to try for another baby, she brought out the folder she kept with information on the sperm donor. She wanted to make an appointment to be inseminated again. It was then that she looked at the picture of Donor 2080 and realized that Eric didn't look anything like him. Eric was blond, with blue eyes, a round face, and soft features. The donor's baby picture showed a boy with dark hair, a long face, and angular features.

Something wasn't right. She asked the reproductive clinician for the number of the donor she had used the last time to get pregnant. The answer was not what she expected. It was B155A. The clinic had made a mistake and given her sperm from her first choice instead.

"I said, 'Wow! I had been thinking for the last year and a half that Eric's biological father was Donor 2080!'" she says.

All her fantasizing about Donor 2080 disappeared. Gone were all her dreams of her child growing up to be a gifted musician. But with that mistake, she would later realize, Eric had inadvertently joined an extraordinarily unique group of related children. And when her daughter, Julianna, was born from that second insemination from Donor B155A, she, too, joined this unusual collection of half siblings.

When she first joined the Donor Sibling Registry, Susanna was one of the first from the group to become a member, and the numbers were still quite low. But very quickly, she watched the number of kids rise to eighty, and she realized that this group was going to be large— mind-bogglingly large. Through the DSR, she was able to connect with some of the families via email, since those who wished to be contacted posted their email addresses along with their child's name.

Susanna was comfortable with the idea of this super-extended family. She told her friends and some of her family members about it. But she still had to decide whether she wanted her kids to get to know the other children and their families. What kind of connection did she want Eric and Julianna to have with them?

As Susanna dug deeper, she discovered that the children of Donor B155A lived around the world, from the United States to England and Israel. But the idea wasn't troubling to her—in fact, she found it comforting. She thought, wherever her children went, they would have family close by. And she passed this belief on to her kids. In many ways, Susanna found herself drawn to these people.

"After all, my son and daughter are more closely related, biologically, to those children than to my own sister's kids, and infinitely more related to them than to their own father," she says.

So Susanna started emailing the other moms that she had met through the DSR or the Yahoo group. She congratulated them when they gave birth to new babies from the same donor. She wished the other children a happy birthday. She worried when they were sick.

Through their Yahoo group, Susanna found two other mothers who lived nearby, in Northern California. Long before her cross-country trip with her kids, Susanna and her children had begun to attend the other children's birthday parties, and the families saw each other occasionally for play dates. The kids knew they were related in some way, but many were still too young to understand how. The other kids' grandmothers became interested in Susanna's children and began to play more important roles in their lives. Susanna then began to check in regularly with the families in the B155A group who lived in other parts of the country who were willing to connect.

The more people that love my kids, the better, thought Susanna. *They say it takes a village. Well, this one will take a giant family!*

When Susanna first began reaching out to other mothers in the group, she felt close to them. Like her, they had each chosen to experience motherhood through a sperm donor; like her, they sorted though the Fairfax Cryobank website in search of the perfect donor. They studied medical histories and childhood photos, contemplating which was the right man to father their child, and finally, like her, they had narrowed it down to Donor B155A, the curly-headed, rugby-playing, perfect-seeming male specimen, that same biological father that Susanna and Larry had picked.

After communicating through her Yahoo group for a few years, Susanna began to long to meet more of her children's half siblings and her other "sister moms," as the mothers in the group had started calling each other. The name was reminiscent of the mothers in the polygamous Mormon sects who call themselves "sister wives." Susanna liked the expression. It summed up how she felt about the other moms. They were much more than strangers to each other.

Undoubtedly, the issues associated with having donor children weren't always easy ones to deal with. When should she tell her kids about their origin? How much should she tell them? So Susanna found a way to share advice, support, and affirmation through the virtual community that had formed with other families in the group.

But as the numbers in the group rose, many of the families began to feel uncomfortable. How were so many children being born from the same donor? Would their children be looked on as strange or even bizarre? Was there a risk these half siblings would accidentally meet and intermarry?

When the number of offspring in the group reached 150 children, the media came calling. The outsized group fascinated people. They wanted to know what it was like to have so many siblings. Did they all look alike, act alike? Did they know their sperm donor? Did he know about them?

Many parents began to pull out of the Yahoo group as a way to maintain their privacy and protect their children. No one wanted to talk to the press.

The number of children in the group didn't trouble Susanna. She considered it to be a good thing for her kids—something to celebrate. She wanted her children to meet their half siblings, and their extended family, and to have a chance to connect. This, too, she and Cynthia had in common.

Still, Susanna did have concerns about how being born into such a large family could change her children's experience of growing up. She wondered how their childhood would differ from that of their cousins, who were born into a more typical family situation. What would it mean for them to probably never get to know their biological father? Would they ever feel self-conscious about the circumstances of their conception? Would they try to find him, as other donor children have done?

It's part of the human condition to want to connect with those to whom we are related. Forming relationships with our relatives and biological parents can help to define who we are and help to explain where we came from. For many children of sperm donors, finding a half sibling or their biological father can help solve the mystery of their identity.

Susanna wasn't interested in finding the sperm donor. "Our kids have a father, so if we did find him, it would just be for curiosity. We would not want any obligation on either part," she says. But if her kids tried to find him, or wanted to meet him, she said she'd encourage it. "I'd just caution them to be careful—he might be really weird, you just never know," she added.

Larry agreed with her that it was important to connect with the other families, but he was wary about giving out too much information about themselves. Still, they didn't want to ignore the other kids and keep the matter of their children's biological origins a family secret. Susanna always believed in living in the real world. "I refuse to attempt to keep as a secret something that, after all, I believe has nothing shameful attached to it," Susanna says. In fact, she felt that any climate of secrecy could be destructive to her family.

Susanna wished she knew more about her children's donor so she could share details about his life with her kids. She believed that someday they would be curious about their biological father and would probably wonder about his motivation.

The other families in the group were also curious about the sperm donor. A few even got together and hired a private detective to try and find him. They thought he must live in the Washington, D.C., area, because he donated at Fairfax Cryobank in Virginia. But the detective was unable to track him down. Some disagreed with the decision to try and find him and consequently left the group. They didn't want to know his identity for fear it could open a Pandora's Box of problems.

In a bizarre twist, one of the mothers in the group even became convinced that she was going to find the sperm donor, and that once he met her and their child, they'd fall in love and get married. She, too, tried to find the donor, but failed. The other members of the group were disturbed by her behavior, and eventually she left the group.

WHEN SUSANNA FIRST met the other families from her group who lived nearby, she looked forward to observing the encounters between her children and their half siblings, checking for shared traits that the kids might have in common. Would any of them make strange noises like her son, Eric? Or sing like her daughter, Julianna? Eric's music teacher was impressed with how well he focused on playing his ukulele. Perhaps she would see that ability to concentrate in some of the other children? She wondered if any of the others would share Eric's reserve or Julianna's irrepressible enthusiasm? She was surprised that her kids weren't more athletic, since their donor had played rugby in college and considered himself an athlete.

At the time of Susanna's trip, the donor children ranged in age from infants to early teens (Susanna's son, Eric, is one of the oldest in the group). Many of the children are said to look eerily alike: tall, with blond hair and high foreheads. Even the children in the group who are half black, Hispanic, and Asian look like the other kids, with the same eyes, nose, and forehead.

It was this connection with the other families that persuaded Susanna to take a cross-country trip to meet as many of the other families as she and her kids could. That year, as summer approached, Susanna realized that she and her children had a unique opportunity at hand. She was out of work—her recent job as a teacher of special education children had ended—and she had nothing planned yet for her kids to do. So she decided that she would take off the entire summer and travel cross-country with her kids to meet their half siblings. She knew that the other children lived all over the United States. They could visit some of them, and along the way, they could stop in historical locales and learn about the history of their nation. It would be a geography, history, and genealogy lesson all rolled up into one. It would be an adventure.

Initially, Larry was skeptical about the idea.

"I thought it was kind of odd at first. It's nice that we know a couple of the families from the group nearby, but I don't have a huge craving to meet everyone. I didn't know what they would encounter on their trip," he says. "Being out there and not really knowing these people she'd meet and what she'd come across . . . I said be cautious about what you say. Not everyone will have the same point of view as you. I said be aware and read the people and don't bulldog them."

He also worried about her driving all those miles alone with their children, and whether she'd have mechanical problems with the car or run into some other trouble.

"It's pretty gutsy to drive cross country by yourself with two little kids. I'd probably go bananas," he says.

She finally convinced him that she'd be fine, and he came around to the idea of the trip. He realized that it would also be educational for the kids to visit historical sites and see things they'd never see again.

Susanna imagined they were like the explorers that her kids were learning about in school. Was she the first person in the world to take a journey such as this? And would it prove to be a good idea after all?

Susanna and Larry confronted head-on the question of how being born into a nontraditional family affected their children's experience of growing up. They were watching to see how their kids' unusual parentage would influence their personalities and feelings of acceptance. Would their development through childhood, puberty, and maturation differ from that of their cousins, who were born into a typical family situation?

Susanna realized that she had placed herself in a strange situation that other people—even some of her closest friends—had called "weird." They wondered how she could have given birth to children who were not related to her husband. The reason was simply that she wanted to become a mother. Assisted reproduction offered both her and her husband the wonderful gift of parenthood, as it did for many others.

As the Prius left California and crossed into Nevada, the landscape started to change, becoming arid and flatter, with rugged, snow-capped mountains in the distance, and a big sky looming overhead. Driving along Highway 50, known as the loneliest stretch of highway in the country, Susanna and her children listened to an audiobook about a man who hiked the Appalachian Trail alone.

She identified with the character, a novice hiker who was nervous about what he would encounter on the trail. In a similar way, Susanna thought, she was new to this extended sibling-family thing. They were both jumping off a cliff into the unknown, hopeful that they'd survive and optimistic that their trip would help them learn something important about themselves. And like the man in the story, Susanna was about to explore new frontiers. She wanted this trip to help her children better understand who they were and where they came from. And she wanted them to feel a deeper connection with their half siblings, as she did with her sister moms.

But there was no roadmap for how to navigate this realm, nothing that dictated what she was supposed to do—everything was unknown. She was embarking on a mysterious journey, and she had no idea how it would end.

Susanna wondered about the ancestry of all these kids as well. It didn't go up and down, it went wide for as far as you could see. It was a celebration, really, knowing all this. And what a fabulous heritage, she thought. Wherever her kids went to college, they would probably have family nearby. The whole thing was going to be unfolding. It would be up to her kids some day to carry on and have their own relationships with their relatives. The whole thing was fascinating and amazing.

She was glad that her husband, Larry, agreed with her. He thought of Eric and Julianna as his kids, and he would do anything for them. "I don't feel any different about them. They're my kids. I got them into this world," says Larry.

They both felt that letting their children know where they came from, and telling them about their half siblings, was a kind of gift they were giving them.

As the Prius wound its way from Nevada into Utah, the countryside changed yet again. From arid desert, it became greener and more mountainous. The group traversed small mountain ranges and rugged terrain, occasionally passing small lakes and rivers.

Their route took them past Arches National Park in Utah, with its spectacular red sandstone arches, and near Canyonlands, just visible from the highway, with its colorful landscape and countless mesas, canyons, and buttes.

As she drove, Susanna wondered about the strangeness of it all. These donor-conceived family communities are connected by genes but may share little else, such as religion, cultural background, or beliefs. Yet, the genetic ties between the children foster strong kinship bonds among them. After all, blood is thicker than water, she thought. She and the other mothers were more than just friends—they'd always be related. They had this bond, this incredible link, with each other.

Susanna's thoughts shifted back to Julianna's question. There were no guidelines about how to tell your daughter that she's a donor child. The rules haven't been written yet. She was on her own.

It was time to tell Julianna and her brother the whole truth about their connection to the other families.

She looked back at her daughter, curled up in the back seat, playing with her long hair.

"Well, honey. Since the other moms lived much farther away, they had to use a different doctor. But the doctors got the *sperm* from the same place."

Julianna still didn't get it.

"You know that vial that I once showed you? Each doctor used a vial just like that one. Remember, you need an egg and sperm to make a baby."

"An egg?" The children giggled at the thought of a chicken egg.

"No, a human egg. It's smaller than the smallest seed you could plant, and it was already in the mommy," Susanna explained. "The doctor just put what was in the tube inside the mommy and a baby was created."

Julianna sat still for a moment, considering the information she'd been given.

"Ok. I think I understand now."

As the group moved closer to Maryland, Susanna thought that perhaps this is what this trip was really all about: giving her children a better understanding of their place in the world.

As Susanna watched the three kids chatting happily in Cynthia's house on that sweltering, summer day in Maryland, she decided that telling Mark the truth about where he came from was worth the risk. He had a right to know.

That night after dinner, the five of them sat around the dining room table, chatting, while the adults drank coffee. Susanna gazed at the kids and thought how happy she was that she'd brought Eric and Julianna here. She couldn't believe how much they all looked alike.

Cynthia decided it was time to talk to her son about where he came from. "It's so great to have everyone here, together. But do you guys know how we're all connected?"

Eric nodded his head. Mark and Julianna looked unsure. Cynthia looked at her son.

"Mark, do you know about eggs and sperm?"

"Sort of," said Mark, a little embarrassed.

"Do you understand how babies are made?"

Julianna and Eric giggled. Susanna motioned to them to be quiet.

"I guess."

Cynthia and Susanna exchanged looks. Susanna thought, maybe Mark is too young to understand all this.

Eric suddenly chimed in.

"Let me try. We all used the same sperm donor. That's how we're connected. We have the same biological father."

Susanna watched Mark's face slowly change. He looked at Eric and just smiled. He got it.

She breathed a sigh of relief, and wondered—would their other visits go as well as this one?

Part Two

4

In the Beginning

The History of the Fertility Industry

In early times, the science of treating fertility problems was little more than a kind of magic or alchemy, with strange treatments and "cures." Women were often blamed for the inability to bear children and were disparaged for being barren. During the Roman era, priests would run through the city during the feast of Mars and flog the bellies of infertile women with goatskin whips to induce fertility.[1] Men were rarely called to blame for childlessness, and impotence was not recognized. There was little understanding of how reproduction worked, let alone how to help those who couldn't conceive.

Over time, as science progressed and the understanding of how babies were conceived became better known, real remedies for helping couples deal with infertility came into use. Sperm donation and the fertility industry have grown at an incredible rate since its early beginning in the 1950s. In this country alone, hundreds of thousands of children are now born through assisted reproduction each year.

Yet, doctors who pioneered the use of fertility treatments often felt the need to hide their work, as they risked disapproval by the public and their peers. One gynecologist, Robert L. Dickinson, who was helping women with donor sperm in the 1920s and 1930s, kept his work secret for nearly forty years because of fear of such condemnation.[2]

We think of artificial insemination, now referred to as "assisted reproduction," as a modern remedy, but amazingly, sperm donation began more than two centuries ago when a young couple who was unable to conceive visited Dr. John Hunter at his London office in 1790.

It was a time when medicine was fairly primitive, and many doctors were still using old, dangerous practices, such as bloodletting and purging. Hunter, a notorious Scot known as the father of modern surgery, was in the vanguard of revolutionizing medicine by using scientific methods rather than folk healing.[3] His house, where he also saw patients, was in the fashionable part of London, at 28 Leicester Square. Today a statue of him stands there. In a sketch from the British Library that depicts Dr. Hunter's famous home, the layout and contents are described as follows:

> The building was large and opened onto the square, which had a beautiful, well-tended garden in the center. The house was long and fairly narrow, as many London homes are, with an imposing front door that opened onto a large hall. The size of the house enabled Hunter to keep and maintain his collection of more than 500 species of plants and animals, and arrange them into a teaching museum. Hunter obsessively collected anatomical curiosities, such as preserved unborn quadruplets and various human organs and other specimens, and displayed them in his home. Many of those samples can now be seen in the Hunterian Museum at the Royal College of Surgeons in London.[4]

Hunter began his training working for his brother, William, a physician and obstetrician. Under his brother's tutelage, he learned how to perform dissections, a talent he would later put to good use. After his studies, he became an assistant surgeon at St. George's Hospital and worked his way up to surgeon, eventually becoming surgeon to King George III. Hunter was fascinated by the human body and showed an aptitude for studying anatomy. He helped provide his brother with corpses for dissection, and one estimate suggests that he helped to dissect 2,000 human bodies with his brother.[5]

Hunter's interest in examining specimens was so great that he was said to work with body snatchers who scoured London cemeteries for corpses. The corpses of executed criminals were used as well. But as a well-respected doctor living in an upscale part of town, Hunter couldn't allow cadavers to be simply delivered through the front door. What would the neighbors think? But he had a plan.

Hunter's house had two entrances: a front entrance, where patients entered, and a rear entrance that opened onto another street. It was there that he had the corpses brought in at night for his dissections and experiments. He became obsessed with examining the body of the famous Irish giant, Charles Byrne, when he died. A 2011 *Guardian* newspaper article detailed Hunter's quest to steal Byrne's body:

> When Byrne, who was 7'8", died in 1783 at the age of just 22, Hunter became obsessed with acquiring this most unusual specimen, and had some of his men follow him around. Byrne, who it was later found suffered from gigantism, was said to be able to light his pipe on streetlamps. Alas, Byrne had clear deathbed wishes to be buried at sea, specifically so that Hunter couldn't dissect his body and he wouldn't be gawped at by London society. But Hunter had other plans. He had his agents follow the funeral party, got them drunk, and then filled the coffin with rocks and stole the body. Hunter immediately boiled the corpse for 24 hours and hid the skeleton for several years until it was safe to show it. The skeleton can still be seen today at the Hunterian Museum.[6]

Understandably, Hunter was both highly regarded and greatly feared for the work he did, as well as for his temperament. He was not an easy man to work with; he was described this way by one of his biographers: "His nature was kindly and generous, though outwardly rude and repelling. . . . " Another described him as readily provoked and not easily soothed when irritated.

Dr. Hunter often conducted gruesome scientific experiments to test out his hypotheses, even giving himself gonorrhea and syphilis to prove that he could treat them (unfortunately, he couldn't). But perhaps one of his most significant experiments was one he performed on silkworms. Taking the sperm from one worm and the eggs from another, he was able to produce offspring.

Scientists had been trying to come up with fertility treatments for centuries, but until this point, they hadn't had much luck. That's because not many understood how babies were conceived. But Hunter's experiment gave him a clue to solving this riddle.

So when a couple came to Dr. Hunter with the inability to conceive, he had an idea of what to do. It was found that the husband, a cloth merchant, had severe hypospadias, a condition in which the opening of the urethra is on the underside of the penis, rather than at the tip. Because of this, the semen was escaping during intercourse. (Nowadays, this condition can be corrected with surgery.) He advised the man to collect his semen into a warmed syringe, and then inject the sample into his wife's vagina.

Not long after, the woman became pregnant and the couple had their first baby. The world's first case of artificial insemination had been a success.

Hunter always seemed unstoppable to his friends and colleagues, but eventually, his health problems caught up with him:

> Hunter dropped dead of angina at the age of 65. He asked that his body be autopsied, and that his damaged heart and repaired Achilles tendon be cut from his body and placed in jars in his collection. He was laid out on a table in his own dissection room for the procedure, which was carried out by his nephew, Matthew Baillie.[7]

His legacy extended past his medical experiments. Hunter's house, with its civilized front entrance for illustrious guests and its ghastly back entrance for the grave robbers, later inspired the home used in Robert Louis Stevenson' novel, *Dr. Jekyll and Mr. Hyde*. Some say Hunter himself was a model for Dr. Jekyll.[8]

While it may seem inconceivable that artificial insemination could have taken place so early, history shows that there had been crude attempts to artificially inseminate Princess Juana, the wife of King Henry IV of Castile, nicknamed the Impotent, in the 1400s.[9] Henry's wife was unable to conceive for many years, but six years after they married, she gave birth to a daughter, Joanna. Many historians assume that Henry was impotent, and that some form of artificial insemination was used to impregnate his wife. Later, there were claims that Joanna was not his daughter.[10]

Jewish texts dating as far back as the third century show that human insemination by artificial means was being discussed. And the Bible has many tales of couples who anguished over the inability to have a child, and whose prayers to God were answered with a son or daughter, notably Elkanah and Hannah, who went on to have six children. Abraham and Sara were also childless, and even though she was well beyond the age of childbearing, the Bible says that God gave her a son, Isaac.

Many may not realize that George Washington, the father of our country, never actually became a father. Historians believe he may have been impotent. When he married Martha, she was a widow with two small children, who George adopted and raised as his own. Despite his wish to procreate, he was never able to do so. At age fifty-four, he seemed resigned to never fathering an heir, writing: "if Mrs. Washington should survive me there is a moral certainty of my dying without issue. . . . "[11]

There are many theories about what may have caused Washington's infertility, including Klinefelter syndrome, which is typified by tall stature, testicular failure, and other problems. That could explain Washington's extraordinary height for the time—he was thought to have been more than six foot three inches tall. The average height for men in the eighteenth century was about five foot six inches.

While an understanding of the causes of impotence wouldn't be discovered for years, a key to learning how conception worked started much earlier. In 1677, a Dutch craftsman who was an amateur naturalist with no formal education discovered spermatozoa, or human sperm cells, so named from the ancient Greek word *sperma,* meaning "seed."

The work of Anton van Leeuwenhoek, who was known as the father of microbiology, eventually led the way to fertility treatments. Van Leeuwenhoek was a tradesman who had no medical or scientific background, but he had an interest in the natural world, and as a craftsman, he was able to construct his own microscopes, even learning how to grind his own lenses. Van Leeuwenhoek started out working as an apprentice to a cloth merchant and became fascinated by the simple microscopes—basically elaborate magnifying glasses— that were used to examine the quality of the cloth. He began making his own microscopes, improving upon their design. At the time, the microscopes in use had a magnification of 20x or 30x, but van Leeuwenhoek's skill in constructing high-quality glass allowed him to achieve a magnification of over 200x, unheard of at the time. He used his homemade microscopes to observe and describe single-celled organisms, muscle fibers, and bacteria. His work eventually led him to some of the most significant discoveries in the history of biology.[12]

One day, a student who was working with him said he noticed tiny living creatures with tails living in the sperm of a man who was suffering from gonorrhea. He verified his student's observation and called the cells "animalcules." He observed them coming from both a sick man as well as a healthy man right after ejaculation. He believed the sperm contained miniature humans that grew inside the womb. Van Leeuwenhoek's observations revealed to him just how many sperm were living inside men:

> I had seen such a multitude of live animalcules more than a million, having the size of a grain of sand and moving in a space . . . those animalcules were smaller than the red blood cells. They had a round body, foam in the front, terminated in a point at the back; they were equipped with a tail with five to six times the body length. They progressed in a snake-like motion helped by their tail.[13]

In a letter to the Royal Society of London for the Advancement of Science, van Leeuwenhoek said he had observed these sperm cells in the semen of dogs and rats, and said that he expected to find them in all male animals.[14]

This discovery of sperm cells led van Leeuwenhoek to a lifelong interest in the study of human reproduction. He endeavored to refute the then-current theory of "spontaneous generation," which bizarrely postulated that fertilization took place when vapors arose from the seminal fluid. Instead, he guessed that the spermatozoa penetrated the egg in a woman, but his hypothesis wouldn't be proven correct until nearly a century later when an Italian priest discovered the link.

In 1784, Lazzaro Spallanzani found that actual contact between egg and semen was essential for the development of a new animal. With this finding, he discovered how animal reproduction worked.[15]

Spallanzani trained as a lawyer, but the influence of one of his professors persuaded him to change course and study science instead. He later performed the first known successful experiment involving artificial insemination on a dog, resulting in the birth of three puppies. An unrelenting skeptic of other people's theories, Spallanzani was able to disprove the concept of spontaneous generation. He also discovered that cooled sperm became motionless.[16]

It was the discovery in 1827, by Estonian scientist Karl Ernst von Baer, of the egg cell, or ovum, that helped scientists unravel the mystery of conception. Von Baer had an interest in biology and zoology and studied the embryonic development of animals. He discovered eggs in the ovary of a dog, establishing that mammals, including humans, originate from eggs. He also introduced the term "spermatozoa," replacing what had been known as "animalcules" in seminal fluid.[17]

Two decades later, the controversial American physician James Marion Sims, known as the father of modern gynecology, reported that he was also able to impregnate a woman with artificial insemination.[18]

Sims was an Alabama surgeon who later moved to New York, where he founded Woman's Hospital, the first institution created solely for women's health. He realized that infertility could be caused by a husband's reproductive problems, just as much as it could by a wife's. Through his clinical work, he came up with a theory that was controversial at the time—that men could be sterile. He performed fifty-five artificial inseminations (he called it "artificial fructification") for six couples, but they resulted in only one pregnancy, which ended in a miscarriage. The low conception rate could be due to the fact that Sims and other doctors at the time didn't understand ovulation cycles yet. In his attempts at helping these couples conceive, Sims only used the sperm of the woman's husband, yet it still caused a stir.

Sims' experiments eventually set the stage for modern vaginal surgery, and he was credited with successfully repairing women who suffered from an appalling condition known as "obstetric fistulas." They are holes in the vaginal wall that are caused by traumatic childbirth, such as pushing too hard and for too long. (This was before there were drugs available to speed up labor.) Urine and sometimes feces would leak through fistulas into the vagina, causing infections and horrible smells. Women suffering from fistulas were so uncomfortable that they rarely left their houses. Some even committed suicide. Until Sims found a cure, women with fistulas were considered social outcasts and the condition was catastrophic.[19]

In a troubling addendum to his accomplishments, however, Sims eventually found a cure by performing horrific and prolonged experiments on slave women who were suffering from the condition. He operated on one slave, Anarcha, thirty times—without anesthesia—even though it was available at the time. It was said he gave the women little recovery time and kept them in a small makeshift hospital behind his house in Alabama.[20] Sims has been castigated for his unethical experimentation on powerless black women without their consent. He also believed that African Americans had a higher threshold for pain than Caucasians. Other reports say that Sims did not believe anesthesia was safe, and thus he never used it. And some thought that Sims was helping slave women who would have been otherwise left to deal with their horrendous situation without any remedy.[21]

Sims, the most famous surgeon of the nineteenth century, is also known for inventing a special syringe used to impregnate women and for creating a duck-billed speculum made out of pewter spoons purchased from a local hardware store. It was an early version of the speculum that gynecologists use today. He later founded the New York Cancer Hospital, now known as Memorial Sloan Kettering Cancer Center.

A few decades after Sims' failed attempts to perform artificial insemination, a little-known doctor named William Pancoast had a try.[22] A wealthy Quaker merchant and his wife who were having trouble conceiving had come to Pancoast for help at the Sansom Street Hospital in Philadelphia. The doctor, a teacher at Jefferson Medical College, examined the thirty-one-year-old woman but found nothing wrong, so he deduced that the problem had to be the husband's low sperm count. The husband, forty-one, had had a case of gonorrhea years earlier, and Pancoast believed that the infection had affected his fertility. The doctor tried various treatments, but when they failed, he took another approach.

One day, he called the wife in to his office. In the examination room, he chloroformed the unsuspecting patient, then he asked his best-looking medical student for a sperm sample. Using a rubber syringe, Pancoast inserted the medical student's semen into her uterus while six of his other students watched. No one said a word.

Nine months later, the woman gave birth to a healthy boy. It was the first documented case of donor insemination. Pancoast never told her what he had done. He later informed her husband, and they decided together not to inform his wife of the truth.

Pancoast's procedure was kept secret until nearly a quarter of a century later. That was when one of the doctor's medical students, Addison Davis Hard, visited the couple's child, by then a twenty-five-year-old businessman living in Philadelphia. Hard revealed to the young man the true story of his conception. Thought to be the "best-looking" student who had supplied the sperm, Hard later

published a letter in the journal *Medical World* detailing the procedure. The letter set off widespread debate among lawyers, doctors,
philosophers, and theologians.[23]

In the massive controversy that followed, the Jefferson Medical
College, and all parties involved, were harshly criticized for Pancoast's
actions. Some claimed that Hard was playing a joke. Others defended
him, claiming that this procedure would in fact help limit unwanted
pregnancy, while some argued against artificial insemination as gro-
tesque and absurd. But most importantly, the eugenicists were quickly
on the scene and fiercely divided the medical profession with their
claims that it was now possible to improve the genetic stock of
America.

In some ways, little has changed since Pancoast took it upon himself to impregnate a woman with another man's sperm without her
knowledge or consent. The reproductive industry has long been secretive and paternalistic, in disturbing ways.

There was the controversial and extensive use of eugenics—the
widespread and coercive sterilization of African American and Native
American women and men all over the country, as well as those who
were mentally incapacitated. Physicians commonly practiced these so-
called "Mississippi appendectomies," and the procedure was even
written into the town charter in some places.[24] The sterilization was
often performed without the patient's knowledge.

The concept of eugenics actually started in the United States in the
late 1800s by Charles Darwin's cousin, Francis Galton, who coined the
term from the Greek word meaning "good in birth" or "noble in he-
redity." Eugenics is a set of beliefs and practices supposedly aimed at
improving the genetic quality of the human population. The Nazis
later seized on eugenics and expanded on Galton's ideas, eventually
sterilizing 400,000 people in Germany. It was considered a stepping-
stone to the Holocaust.[25]

It's hard to believe that in the early 1900s, more than thirty-five
states passed laws approving sterilization. During this time, thousands
of people in state institutions who were deemed genetically defective
were forcibly sterilized. By the 1960s, more than 60,000 people had

been sterilized throughout the country. In some states, the practice actually continued into the 1970s.[26]

In 1910, a U.S. Eugenics Record Office was established to keep records on family histories as a way to encourage the breeding of "good" families. Seventeen years later, the U.S. Supreme Court took it one step further by ruling in *Buck v. Bell* that a poor woman named Carrie Buck should be forcibly sterilized on the grounds that she was feebleminded. (John Bell was the surgeon who operated on Buck.) It was a travesty of justice.

Buck had been committed to the Virginia State Colony for Epileptics and Feebleminded by her foster parents after she was raped and became pregnant at the age of seventeen. She was sent there on the grounds that she was mentally incapacitated, wanton, and exhibited incorrigible behavior. It was the same place that her mother had been sent after her husband had abandoned her.[27]

The U.S. Supreme Court justices found that both Carrie and her mother were promiscuous, and that they shared the genetic trait of feeblemindedness—though it was never proved. At the time, Justice Oliver Wendell Holmes Jr. wrote, "Three generations of imbeciles is enough."[28] Surprisingly, the Federal court has never overturned that ruling, so that involuntary sterilization of those considered unfit to reproduce is still technically allowed in the United States. The decision was seen as a victory for eugenicists. In a shocking addendum to this story, Carrie's sister, Doris, was later secretly sterilized when she went to the hospital for appendicitis to prevent the Buck family from further reproducing.[29]

In recent years, some states have proposed payments to eugenics victims, many of whom were sterilized without their knowledge. One woman in North Carolina found out that she had been sterilized at the age of sixteen when she went in to have her appendix removed. She never found out why doctors had closed her fallopian tubes.[30] In 2015, the U.S. Senate finally passed a bill to assist eugenics victims in receiving compensatory payments.

Even white, middle-class women weren't immune to the meddling of the medical establishment. Starting in the 1950s, the "120 rule" was widely used by doctors and hospitals to *restrict* sterilization of these women when it was deemed they hadn't produced enough children. The 120 rule, which was supported by the American College of Obstetricians and Gynecologists, was explained this way: if a woman's age multiplied by the number of children she had equalled less than 120, she couldn't choose to be voluntarily sterilized. So if a thirty-year-old white woman had only three children, she was not allowed to have her tubes tied. Since birth rates were declining at the time, it was thought this would keep up the population of "acceptable" white, middle-class children.

Many states at the time also had laws that prohibited the sale or use of birth control, even by married people, which was why many women turned to tubal ligation, or sterilization. Eugenicists opposed contraception because they thought that fit white women weren't having enough children compared to poor, uneducated mothers, and they bizarrely feared it would lead to "race suicide."[31]

While the eugenicists were trying to control who had the right to procreate, a scientist in Cambridge, England, was trying to help women have babies. Walter Heape learned how to successfully breed rabbits from embryos that he transferred from one mother to another. Considered a pioneer in reproductive biology, Heape had been experimenting with various animals when he conducted his first test on the rabbits in 1891. His experiment demonstrated for the first time that embryos could be transplanted from one animal to another and could lead to pregnancy—without any side effects. Because of Heape's work, Cambridge later became a leading center for reproductive studies. His successful embryo transfers eventually led to the popular practice today of using in vitro fertilization to help women become pregnant.[32]

The next few decades saw an explosion of scientific breakthroughs in the area of artificial insemination, or "AI." A Russian scientist named Ilya Ivanovich Ivanoff was the first to find practical methods for this method. He used AI to breed cattle and horses using superior bulls and stallions. Today, cattle breeding using AI is practiced in many countries throughout the world.

Yet while the scientific community was lurching forward with its advances in reproductive science during the late 1800s, political and religious leaders and ethicists were playing catch up. And not everyone was happy about the social progress that women, in particular, were making at the time.

In 1873, an influential Harvard professor and physician named Dr. Edward H. Clarke made the argument that women should not be allowed to attend college because, he believed, if they studied too much it would make them infertile. His reasoning was that the excess intellectual stimulation would divert blood away from the uterus to the brain. In his best-selling book from that same year, *Sex in Education; Or a Fair Chance for the Girls,* Clarke said that since college-educated women had fewer children, it proved his theory was correct. He also said that women who attended college would be renowned for "invalidism rather than for erudition, for sterility rather than achievement, a degenerate femininity rather than true womanliness—if she lived through the experience at all."[33]

The book set off a firestorm, with volumes of books published to refute Clarke's claims. Eventually, the controversy died down. As one historian put it, "it was becoming clear that higher education for women would survive despite the inflammatory tracts and that women were not turning into Amazons."[34]

By the 1930s, scientists were edging even closer to discovering the kind of assisted reproductive technologies being used today. In 1933, Gregory Goodwin Pincus mixed rabbit eggs and sperm in the glass top of his watch. He watched the embryo grow, then implanted it into a surrogate mother rabbit. Pincus was the first to create babies through in vitro fertilization. (*In vitro* comes from the Latin word for "in dish," as opposed to *in vivo,* or "in body.")

In an editorial in the esteemed *New England Journal of Medicine* in 1937 called "Conception in a Watch Glass," the editors of the journal suggested that the technique should be used in humans as well. "What a boon for the barren woman with closed tubes!" they said. Forty years later, the first birth from in vitro fertilization, or IVF, would take place.

But before that groundbreaking event would happen, there were more advances to be made in this arena. For the first time, freezing sperm was found to work—setting the stage for sperm banks' use of frozen sperm to impregnate women. By 1955, four pregnancies from frozen sperm were successful.

Yet, as science moved forward with these discoveries, political and religious leaders were gripped by confusion and indecision. No one knew what to make of it all—was it harmful to women, children, and society? Should the government step in? Was it a sin against God? It came to a head in 1945 when the United Kingdom announced successful artificial insemination using donor sperm. The press and politicians raised concerns, and the government tried to discourage sperm donation. The Archbishop of Canterbury called for the criminalization of the practice, and the pope declared donor insemination a sin, suggesting that anyone undergoing the procedure be sent to prison. Detractors called the babies "artificial bastards."[35]

Still, more and more people were turning to artificial insemination to have children by this time. By 1941, the procedure resulted in 10,000 successful pregnancies in the United States alone. Two decades later, that estimate more than tripled, with one-third to two-thirds of those cases actually being performed with donor sperm, though no one talked about it openly.[36]

In 1954, the courts weighed in on the practice. An Illinois court heard a case involving a married woman who had used sperm that was not from her husband. In the case of *Doornbos v. Doornbos,* the husband sued for divorce on the grounds of adultery because his wife had used donor sperm to get pregnant. The court ruled that donor sperm was adultery—even though her husband had consented. It also found that donor insemination was "contrary to public policy and good morals, and considered adultery on the mother's part. A child so conceived, was born out of wedlock and therefore illegitimate. As such, it is the child of the mother, and the father has no rights or interest in said child."[37]

At the time, the use of donor sperm was being debated around the world. In Rome, a high court also found that the use of donor sperm was adultery, while in Scotland, just the opposite was decided. Cases were going to court over a husband's right to visitation of his children after a divorce when the wife used donor sperm—and over a husband's duty to provide support for a child who was not biologically his. One New York court found that the written consent of the husband to have the wife artificially inseminated constituted a semi-adoption, giving him the right to visit his child.[38]

But social mores were starting to change. In 1964, Georgia passed a statute that children born through artificial insemination were legitimate as long as both the husband and wife consented in writing.

The government was also weighing in on a very private right—that of a couple to use birth control. Until 1938, there was a federal ban on the use of birth control. In 1956, the U.S. Supreme Court ruled that married couples had the right to privacy, including the right to use contraception. Still, millions of unmarried women were still denied birth control. It wasn't until 1972 that the highest court ruled that all citizens were allowed access to birth control, regardless of marital status.

By this time, scientists had been able to fertilize the first human egg in vitro. In 1974, the first IVF pregnancy in the world was reported in Australia, but the procedure failed.

Four years later, it worked. Louise Joy Brown, the first "test-tube" baby, was born in England on July 25, 1978, ushering in a new era in assisted reproductive capabilities. Brown was the 104th attempt by doctors Patrick Steptoe and Robert Edwards to help a couple have a baby through IVF. Brown's parents had been trying for nine years to get pregnant when they were referred to Steptoe. At first, the couple didn't understand what the doctors planned to do—the concept was so new at the time. Brown's birth attracted a great deal of controversy; religious leaders expressed concern about the use of artificial means to have a baby, and some said that scientists were creating "Frankenbabies." Regardless, Louise Brown paved the way for millions of women to undergo IVF in order to have a baby.

Meanwhile, doctors in the United States had been trying for years to duplicate Steptoe and Edwards's success, to no avail. Controversy

and limits on federal funding had caused U.S. doctors to fall behind—
by this time, fourteen other children had been born through IVF in
England and Australia.

However, that soon changed. In 1980, Dr. Howard Jones and Dr.
Georgeanna Jones opened an IVF clinic in Norfolk, Virginia. They
tried various methods until they hit on the correct protocol. Then they
found the right candidate: a young Massachusetts teacher named Judy
Carr who had had her fallopian tubes removed but desperately wanted
a baby. This time, the procedure worked, and Elizabeth Carr, the first
child of IVF in the United States, was born.[39]

Three years later, in Australia, the world's first baby born through
egg donation was announced. And in 1984, a clinic in Southern California announced the birth of a baby through an egg donor—the first
in America. Since then, more than a million such children have been
born worldwide.

In the late twentieth century, the science of reproductive technology exploded, turning the fertility industry in this country into the
Wild, Wild West, with doctors able to create and manipulate life at
will.

Soon, the practice of sperm donation would become even more
commonplace, with commercial sperm banks eventually springing up
all over the country. But it was the discovery that sperm could be successfully frozen and thawed that would one day transform the fertility
industry, creating new options for families desperate to have a child.

5

The Birth of the Sperm Bank
How Selling Sperm Became Big Business

The idea for the first sperm bank was conceived as far back as the nineteenth century, when a physician named Paolo Mantegazza discovered that human sperm could survive at temperatures below 5 degrees Fahrenheit. That gave him the idea for a central location where frozen human sperm could be stored and saved. He suggested that it could be useful for soldiers going to war who feared dying on a battlefield without a legal heir. Indeed, some soldiers during the Gulf War had their sperm frozen in case they didn't make it back. Incredibly, Mantegazza was more than one hundred years ahead of his time.

Today, any woman can go to a sperm bank's website and buy sperm. She can search for a sperm donor based on any number of attributes: from eye color to athletic prowess. Most women want a donor who is intelligent—preferably with a college or advanced degree—healthy, with no family history of genetic diseases, tall, and handsome. But these days, sperm banks will go much further than merely superficial characteristics. They'll help you find your *perfect* virtual mate. Do you have a loved one that you miss terribly? Just send the sperm bank a photo and they'll find you someone who looks just like him.

Some sperm banks, such as California Cryobank, have celebrity look-alikes on offer: always fancied pop star Adam Levine? They have someone who resembles him. They even have men available who are dead ringers for (a young) Al Pacino, Ben Affleck, or Benedict Cumberbatch. It's like a dating service for women who want a baby.

It certainly didn't start out that way.

Before the large sperm banks that serve women today were established, there were only small, boutique-style clinics run by doctors. Those physicians mainly used fresh donations from men, many of whom were medical students who understood the need for sperm by couples struggling with infertility.

By then, the medical profession had worked out when a woman was ovulating. So doctors had to get a woman into their office at the same time that a man was able to donate his sperm next door. Because sperm don't live for long outside the body, this had to be done fairly quickly. Sperm can last up to five days in a woman's body. But on clothing or other surfaces, once the sperm has dried, they are dead. In a sterile cup, sperm can only survive twenty to sixty minutes before they lose viability, depending on exposure to air and cold and other factors. At times, that made it difficult to orchestrate successful inseminations.

A major advancement occurred in 1954 when two scientists at the University of Iowa medical school made an important discovery. They found a way to advance Mantegazza's breakthrough on freezing sperm, discovering how to successfully thaw human sperm and still keep it viable.

While thousands of babies had already been born through artificial insemination by this point, the prospect of using frozen sperm was something else entirely. Until then, only fresh sperm donations had been performed. (Nowadays, the term artificial insemination is no longer widely used because of the negative connotations of the word "artificial"—now, we use assisted reproduction.) The discovery would eventually open up a whole new world of possibilities for doctors and families.

By the 1950s, British scientists had successfully inseminated a cow using frozen sperm and produced a baby calf. Their achievement led many breeders in the cattle industry in the United States, including Iowa, to use frozen sperm from champion bulls to reproduce their own cows. That gave two University of Iowa researchers, zoology graduate student Jerome Sherman and professor of urology Dr. Raymond Bunge, an idea for how to best freeze and thaw human sperm. They borrowed cryogenic techniques from the cattle industry.

Sherman had been experimenting on freezing his own sperm as a hobby when he met Bunge, a urologist who was looking to distinguish himself in the field of fertility. Sherman had read that British scientists were using glycerol, a colorless, viscous liquid, to freeze and thaw animal sperm, and that it helped to retain the quality of the sperm. The challenge was to thaw the sperm in such a way that it retained its viability and motility, or its ability to move. Sperm have a hard enough time getting to the egg without being woozy.

Most people know the basics of how eggs are fertilized, but not everyone may be familiar with the finer details. For instance, did you know that men release 200 to 500 million sperm in a single ejaculate, but only one sperm will make it to the egg in time? The force of the ejaculation helps the motility of the sperm, but then the sperm must make a treacherous journey to get to the egg in time—assuming an egg has been released. First, the sperm have to get through the thick mucus found in the cervical canal. If a woman is ovulating, she'll produce slippery mucus that has thinned and become stretchier to help the sperm along, nourishing and protecting it. However, women who are less fertile (in general) may have mucus that is thick and sticky, making it harder for the sperm to travel through. Once the sperm pass through the cervical canal, the journey continues upstream into the uterus and the sperm must enter one of the two fallopian tubes. For the next hour, the sperm go through biochemical changes in their hopeful rendezvous with the egg. An egg stays in one of the two fallopian tubes for about twenty-four hours, waiting for a single sperm to fertilize it—it is fertilizable for only about twelve to twenty-four hours, after which it will begin to break down. But the timing has to be just right. If the sperm get there too early, no egg. Too late, and the show is over. If no sperm are around to fertilize the egg, the egg moves into the uterus and eventually disintegrates, and the chance for conception is over.

Once the sperm reach the egg, the job doesn't end there. One sperm has to be the first one to get through the outer layer of the egg to reach its nucleus and fertilize the egg. As soon as the first sperm penetrates the egg, the egg undergoes a chemical reaction making it impossible for any other sperm to get in. At the moment of fertilization, the baby's genes and sex are set. If the sperm has a Y chromosome, it's a boy; if it's an X chromosome, it will be a girl. Then the zygote starts dividing as it moves through the fallopian tube to the uterus, where it implants into the uterine lining, and the pregnancy begins.

For men who don't have enough good-quality sperm, the process of impregnating a woman can be extremely challenging. That's one reason why Sherman and Bunge's work was so important—they would one day end up helping thousands of women to have babies, fulfilling their goal of helping couples to have a child. The success of their experiment demonstrated that it was possible to freeze large amounts of sperm from virtually anywhere and make it accessible to couples that were trying to have a child, says Northeastern University law professor and historian of science Kara Swanson. In her 2012 paper titled "The Birth of the Sperm Bank," Swanson writes that today's modern sperm banks would not be possible without the ability to freeze and store sperm.[1]

To be sure, at the time that Sherman and Bunge were working on their experiments, not everyone was thrilled with what they were doing. After all, it was the 1950s, and their unorthodox concept sounded disturbingly futuristic. Babies born through frozen sperm? Were women going to give birth to mutants? What was next? On April 9, 1954, the *Cedar Rapids Gazette* published a front-page story after the first babies were born through frozen sperm, with this banner headline, "Fatherhood After Death Has Now Been Proved Possible."[2]

Scientists and the public alike were skeptical of the practice of artificial insemination—especially when donor semen was used. Many likened it to adultery and said it produced illegitimate children, or bastards. When twin girls were born in 1934 to a woman through artificial insemination from her husband's sperm, her doctor, Frances Seymour, discussed using donor sperm to create "eugenic babies."[3] Even then, the concept of designer babies (back then it was being performed through the selection of donors, rather than genetics) was disturbing to many who feared what could happen if man tried to manipulate nature. The public skepticism of assisted reproduction was evident in the literature of the time; Aldous Huxley's 1932 dystopian novel, *Brave New World,* provides a disturbing vision of a future in which reproduction is taken over by the state and human embryos are raised in "hatcheries and conditioning centers." Children are then bred into one of five ranked castes, ranging from Alphas to Epsilons. In George Orwell's classic novel, *1984,* artificial insemination was also featured, but as a tool of the government: donor insemination was mandatory and reproduction was the exclusive domain of the state.

At the time these novels were being written, intellectuals such as Huxley were questioning the ultimate value of the technological advances and scientific breakthroughs that had been achieved. Huxley, in particular, mistrusted the way that science affected individuals, and he made it a theme in *Brave New World.* He said: "We are living now, not in the delicious intoxication induced by the early success of science, but in a rather grisly morning after, when it has become apparent that what triumphant science has done hitherto is to improve the means for achieving unimportant or actually deteriorated ends."

Indeed, some of the scientific advances were bringing about disturbing consequences. In the 1930s, the eugenicists promoted the use of assisted reproduction to produce superior babies. American geneticist and Nobel Prize winner Hermann Muller advocated for planned human breeding so that only the best men could be used to reproduce future generations.[4] Even Bunge, the Iowa urologist, was intrigued by the possibilities of using frozen sperm to someday produce superior humans.

Despite the public skepticism about the ethics of assisted reproduction, by the 1950s, donor sperm was already being used in most cases of artificial insemination. Those who benefited from the technique presumably didn't talk about it openly. While society may have been unconvinced about donor insemination, many in the medical community were more than enthusiastic, since it was one of the only ways they could help infertile men to have children. Eventually, Sherman and Bunge's experiment with freezing sperm would do even more to help these men. Previously, doctors had to make do with any sperm sample that men with fertility problems could provide—and many had low sperm counts. Now, doctors could instead freeze multiple specimens of a man's sperm and save only the highest quality samples for insemination into their female partners.

Sherman and Bunge knew they were onto something, but they needed test subjects. Fortunately, Bunge was on staff at an Iowa fertility clinic and he found three women who agreed to take part in the experiment. The women were inseminated with the previously frozen sperm and were promised that their identities would be kept secret. Unfortunately, the first round of insemination failed with two of the women. But the second round took, and all three became pregnant. The year was 1953.

During the pregnancies, Bunge and Sherman nervously awaited the results. Would the babies be normal? Would they be healthy and fully developed? They still had no idea if freezing sperm could affect the health of a fetus.

In the meantime, the pair had published a paper about their experiment in the British science journal *Nature*. The news that they had impregnated women with frozen sperm—creating test-tube babies—brought plenty of attention to the men, but much of it was negative.[5] They were called scientific monsters and criticized for treating humans like animals. The scientists feared the worst: If the women produced babies with birth defects or other problems, their experiment would be denigrated and they would be harshly criticized.

Sherman and Bunge kept careful watch over the women, and in the third trimester they used x-rays to examine the fetuses (ultrasound hadn't been invented yet). To the relief of the doctors and patients, everything looked fine. When the women finally gave birth, the babies appeared normal and Bunge was ecstatic. However, one baby soon developed a serious illness. Bunge feared that it would upend the entire experiment and their careers. But he was relieved to later find that the issue had nothing to do with the frozen sperm—the child became sick due to an infection that the mother had contracted during her pregnancy.

During the pregnancies, in 1953, Bunge and Sherman had submitted a paper to another medical journal, *Proceedings of the Society for Experimental Biology and Medicine,* outlining how they were creating "storage banks" of human sperm at the clinic. In effect, the pair had created the first sperm bank. They were hoping to keep the results of the experiment under wraps until all the babies were born and found to be healthy. But a reporter at the *Cedar Rapids Gazette* found out about the births and the paper published its sensationalistic story about what they had done.[6] Afterward, Bunge and Sherman were inundated with negative publicity. Bunge, burned by the harsh criticism, kept a low profile after the experience and did little to further the concept of sperm banks. It would take twenty years before commercial sperm banks became established.

Sherman, however, continued his work. He eventually became a professor at the University of Arkansas medical school and went on to open a sperm bank at the university hospital. He worked on his freezing techniques and later created the first standards for frozen human sperm banks.

Throughout the 1960s, doctors remained unconvinced about the use of frozen sperm, and many found more success with fresh sperm. At the time, university hospitals were the only places that were storing sperm— such as the one at the University of Utah, where Chase Kimball donated sperm in the 1970s. It was still a fledgling industry and few doctors even knew enough to use assisted reproduction to help patients.

That was until the early 1970s, when a Los Angeles urologist named Cappy Rothman realized there was a market for donor sperm. Rothman had been working with couples that were unable to get pregnant, and he noticed the frustration that wives felt about their situation when the fertility issue was their husband's. They could get pregnant, just not by the men they were married to. Rothman, spurred by these encounters, would go on to establish California Cryobank, now the largest sperm bank in the country.

"There was no ART [assisted reproductive technology]. We didn't even have insemination when I was seeing couples. These couples would come in, and the wife was so angry. She would look at her husband and say, 'Because I married you, I'll never be a mother.' The guy was devastated. We just didn't have the education or knowledge of how to help them," says Rothman.

That compelled Rothman to find a way to make sure these couples have a family—by using donor sperm. When he started in the mid-1970s, he was a one-man show: he recruited the sperm donor, did his own analysis of the semen, and inseminated the women. After doing this successfully for more than a year, Rothman was contacted by a local gynecologist. Rothman began sending his patients to the gynecologist for inseminations, but he continued to find sperm donors on his own, mostly through universities and medical schools. At the time, there were no guidelines or regulations on choosing sperm donors, and all the men donated their semen anonymously.

In those days, men who wished to donate sperm mainly went to doctor's offices or hospitals. Their "fresh donation" of sperm was immediately inseminated into the uterus of a woman in a nearby waiting room—with no testing done on the donor or sperm. While women chose the doctor who would inseminate them, it was the doctor who chose the sperm donor for each patient. Most of the clients were heterosexual couples, and very few of them ever told their children that they were the product of donor insemination. It wasn't until the 1980s that single and lesbian women were even *allowed* to purchase sperm (although Rothman says he never turned any women away). In a survey done as late as 1987, more than 50 percent of doctors and sperm banks barred homosexual women and single women from obtaining sperm from donors.[7]

Rothman's interest in the field of male infertility started when he was completing his medical residency in urology at the University of California at San Francisco Medical School. One of his professors assigned students one subject to study each year. His first year, Rothman studied how sperm gets from the testicle to the outside world. Next, he examined men's erections, and the culture and lore surrounding them. Rothman was fascinated with the subject matter.

"It was a wonderful field. I couldn't help everybody, but I tried," he remembers. At the time, there were very few other doctors dealing with male sexual dysfunction.

By 1977, Rothman's business had grown so big that he and his friend, Dr. Charles Sims, created California Cryobank, the first large-scale sperm bank in the country, and what he deems the biggest cryobank in the world. ("We never wanted to be the largest; just the best," Rothman says.)

Cryo comes from the Greek word *kryos* for "cold" or "frost." Sims was a pathologist who had also seen how devastating male infertility could be to his patients. While urologists deal with male reproductive organs, pathologists interpret test results in order to facilitate a patient's treatment. Both men were hopeful that their new business could help alleviate some of the suffering that they had seen in their patients. Rothman later became good friends with Jerome Sherman—the Iowa researcher who worked on freezing sperm. Both Rothman and Sims are in their eighties now, but they still go in to work every day at the sperm bank. Neither Rothman nor any of his three sons have ever donated sperm. "I have three handsome boys, but they never wanted to be donors. I'm glad—it would have been too messy."

These breakthroughs in helping men to father children were helpful in more ways than one. Men who are unable to father children can struggle with low self-esteem and a sense of inadequacy. For some, it can cause a major emotional crisis, said Dr. Patricia Schreiner-Engel, who has studied the impact that infertility can have on men. Rothman and Sims hoped that their cryobank would help some of these men by giving them the opportunity to freeze and store their sperm ahead of time. This was useful in cases where the infertility was due to planned or unplanned sterilization (such as cancer treatments that required chemotherapy or radiation). Later, these men could use their frozen sperm to father a child through assisted reproduction. Improving the lives of these men was an important part of the services that sperm banks such as California Cryobank offered. However, a survey published by the University of Wisconsin in the 1970s revealed that many doctors were actually using sperm from other donors to treat cases of male infertility.[8]

These physicians knew they were playing God, so they tried to choose donors who bore a resemblance to the husband in terms of hair, skin, and eye color. While they took donor's medical histories, they rarely conducted any tests on the donor's health or his sperm.

By the 1980s, sperm banks had begun to shift their business toward providing anonymous donor sperm to infertile couples. But doctors were still primarily using fresh versus frozen sperm, because it was thought to be more effective in getting women pregnant. Then, in the early part of that decade, something happened that would change everything.

The AIDS epidemic struck.

By the mid-1980s, doctors had discovered that AIDS was a sexually transmitted disease that could be spread through semen, and that it could take months for the disease to show up in blood tests. There were reports that six women in the U.S. had been infected with HIV through donor insemination.[9] Later, cases were reported in Canada and Australia as well. In response, the American Association of Tissue Banks encouraged sperm banks to freeze the sperm and periodically retest the donor for any sign of HIV. According to Rothman, California Cryobank was one of the first sperm banks to use frozen sperm and to quarantine the sperm for at least six months before the donor was retested.

By 1988, as a way to ensure that donors did not have HIV, the Food and Drug Administration and the Centers for Disease Control recommended that only frozen sperm be used for donor insemination, with a quarantine period followed by additional testing. Thus, sperm banks began to use frozen sperm almost exclusively for donor insemination. When the banks realized that they could store large caches of sperm and sell it all over the country, it was called "a moment of market expansion," and the sperm-banking industry exploded. The development at the time of easy-to-use liquid nitrogen tanks to freeze and store the sperm helped sperm banks to maintain their product. Once overnight delivery became available, the sperm banking industry went from being a merely local enterprise to a worldwide business. By 1995, there were sperm banks in all fifty states. That number slowly grew to 150 sperm banks in the United States alone, and they could ship frozen sperm anywhere in the world.

Today, the American fertility industry is estimated to be between $3 billion and $5 billion dollars.[10] The business grew quickly as trends toward later marriage and single motherhood spawned a greater demand for the use of donor sperm to help women conceive. Sperm banks eventually began to rely on lesbian couples and single women for the majority of their business. In Susanna Wahl's case, greater societal acceptance of using assisted reproduction—even for a married couple—gave her and her husband the encouragement to use a sperm donor so that they could have children.

At the same time, the business of sperm banking changed, essentially turning the sale of this human genetic material into a commodity, with banks marketing the most popular, "perfect" male specimens to their clients, a modern-day eugenics department store.

Millionaire Robert Klark Graham epitomized this in the 1980 creation of a sperm bank for Nobel Prize winners and other "geniuses." The Repository for Germinal Choice (originally known as the Hermann J. Muller Repository for Germinal Choice, named for the Nobel prize–winning eugenicist) became commonly known as the "Nobel Prize sperm bank." But it only had one publicly known Nobel donor: William Shockley, a Nobel laureate in physics. The rest of the recruited donors were considered future Nobel Prize winners. The bank was essentially a failed experiment and shut down in 1990, with all the sperm samples subsequently destroyed. The story of this unusual sperm bank was told in the 2005 book by David Plotz, *The Genius Factory: The Curious History of the Nobel Prize Sperm Bank.*[11]

In time, the business went global. Cryos International Sperm Bank in Denmark now claims to be the world's largest sperm bank, with the biggest selection of sperm donors, many of them presumably handsome, tall, blond-haired, blue-eyed men. Its motto used to be, "Congratulations, it's a Viking." With their Nordic good looks and strapping builds, Danish men are in high demand. In fact, sperm is now one of Denmark's top exports, along with beer and Lego. Danish sperm now accounts for a third of all the sperm that is used in the United Kingdom.[12] Cryos says it's responsible for more than 30,000 births, with 2,000 babies born each year.

In addition to becoming international, the business of sperm banking has slowly changed since the 1980s by becoming concentrated into a smaller number of large companies. The industry became corporatized, in part, because of the growing cost of recruiting and testing donors for various genetic and infectious diseases, such as HIV, hepatitis B and C, and cystic fibrosis. Donors are retested every three months.

But the industry is transforming yet again, says Rothman, with the advent of all the online genetic testing companies. Now, women are having themselves genetically tested and asking sperm banks to test the donors for any diseases that they themselves might test positive for. "This is the beginning of the public becoming aware. They're saying, I can avoid having a child with cystic fibrosis or MCAD [a potentially fatal genetic disease that prevents the body from converting certain fats to energy]," he says.

California Cryobank stores nearly 200,000 sperm specimens and processes 100 shipments of sperm every day. It is shipped in small tanks filled with liquid nitrogen that keep the vials of sperm safe for seven days. The vials are usually shipped to doctor's offices, where the inseminations are typically performed.

Despite all the things that can go wrong when genetic material is being sold, there is very little federal regulation of the fertility industry. The American Society for Reproductive Medicine (ASRM), a professional organization, and the American Association of Tissue Banks have established guidelines for sperm banks to follow, such as the careful screening of donors, but they are merely guidelines.

And while other countries, such as Britain, France, and Sweden, have placed strict limits on how many children a sperm donor may father, the United States has none—merely guidelines issued by the ASRM. Scott Brown, spokesman for the ASRM, says the government has been hesitant to get involved in reproductive issues. "When you involve the government, you let them decide who can and cannot have children, and that's not what government wants to do," he says.

The ASRM guidelines recommend that individual donors be restricted to twenty-five births per population of 800,000. But there is a loophole to this guideline (which isn't even enforceable). Since sperm is shipped all over the country—and the world—it's easy to get around this standard. The population of the United States alone is nearly 318 million. That means that a sperm donor can have around 10,000 children (if his sperm is shipped all over the country) and still fall within the ASRM guidelines. Wendy Kramer estimates that 22 percent to 27 percent of sperm donors donate to more than one sperm bank. That's sure to increase the numbers of children born to each donor.

Susanna Wahl's donor is a prime example. While he is known to have fathered at least 150 children, estimates could put that number as high as 200—with many of his offspring born in the Washington, D.C., area, which has an estimated population of 6 million people.

When the number of children in Susanna's group started to grow, some of the parents asked the sperm bank, Fairfax Cryobank, to stop selling their donor's sperm. But, they say, the bank refused. Their donor was very popular, and Fairfax wasn't required to restrict sale of his sperm, as there were no federal regulations forcing them to do so. In fact, the sperm bank wasn't even violating the guidelines set by the ASRM. California Cryobank now says it has a limit of twenty-five families per sperm donor, although Rothman doesn't think it's entirely necessary.

"There's a great difference between what's socially accepted and what is medically required. We have a lot of restrictions based on what is socially accepted, and one is to limit the donor births to twenty-five family units. But there's no scientific basis for that. Having 150 children was unacceptable, but if you look at the science, there was no harm," in terms of siblings accidentally having sex with one another, he says—because the children were spread around the country.

The dearth of regulations meant that when Donor B155A proved to be extremely prolific, the sperm bank had no reason to take his sperm off the market. After all, they were making lots of money off of him. A vial of standard donor sperm costs between $600 and $800. Most women order a few vials of the sperm in case the first one doesn't take, or they want siblings for their child. Plus, there's the cost of storing the sperm—about $70 per month, per vial, or $475 if you pay by the year. California Cryobank's donor profiles, medical histories, donor's personal essays, and staff impressions are free. But the sperm bank charges $145 for extended donor profiles (that includes a three-generation medical and genetic history) and childhood photos, and an additional $250 for "full access," that includes a facial feature report, donor conversations (in which you can hear the donor's voice), and a personality report. And two-day shipping for getting the sperm via Federal Express, in a seven-day liquid nitrogen vapor tank, will set you back about $225. Thus, assuming a woman buys two vials and stores them for a year, a sperm bank could stand to earn a total of $2,550 for one transaction.

Some women who learned of Donor B155A's fecundity actually considered it a positive thing, because it meant that his sperm was proven to work, while other parents in the group were unhappy that their donor had so many offspring. When they discovered how prolific he was, many urged Fairfax to take their donor's sperm off the market. "We sent Fairfax a letter, telling them there were over 100 births. They claimed not to know that we had that many live births, even though the sperm donor had been donating for six years. He was doing it regularly—it was like a job for him," says Cynthia Daily. However, they say, it wasn't until they threatened to go to the press that the sperm bank relented. But by then, Donor B155A's sperm was also being sold on the secondary market; that is, through doctor's offices. Doctors are able to purchase sperm directly from sperm banks, and many were using B155A's for intrauterine insemination (IUI) in their offices. One mother, who bought this donor's sperm from her doctor and became pregnant, said she later asked Fairfax for his donor profile, but they refused to release it. And some of the other children in this group were born after mothers with extra sperm in their freezers at home either gave it or sold it to other women, which is an accepted practice in the industry.

Some sperm banks, including Fairfax Cryobank, do not reveal a donor's identifying number to them, so anonymous donors such as Susanna's have no ability to check how many children they have produced. Wendy Kramer says that Fairfax has some of the largest numbers of half-sibling groups on the DSR, and the cryobank has been harshly criticized by many of the parents in the B155A group for its practices.

When I discussed the issue with Dr. Michelle Ottey, director of operations for Fairfax Cryobank and Cryogenic Laboratories, she explained that the sperm bank does its best to track how many children are born to each donor, but that it's difficult to keep accurate numbers since it depends on the mothers reporting births back to Fairfax and many fail to do so. She also said that some of the large sibling groups that have occurred are a result of what she calls the "gray market." She explained, "often times, recipients purchase excess vials of donor sperm to ensure they have enough for their procedures as well as for possible siblings. If those vials are stored off-site, meaning in a clinic, after being shipped from the sperm bank, they cannot be returned for obvious compliance reasons.

"We are aware that women have transferred ownership, sold the vials, or gave the vials to friends, and that exchange resulted in more births," she says, adding that this "gray market" means that the sperm bank had nothing to do with the sale of this sperm and is not aware of the children being born.

Ottey said Fairfax encourages patients to store on-site, so that if they don't need all of the purchased vials, they can return them. This also allows the sperm bank to better track each donor's sperm.

There have been efforts to create a National Donor Gamete Registry that would keep better tabs on who each donor is, how many offspring each donor produces, and who uses that donor, but it has stalled for various reasons. Currently, there is no regulatory agency or professional body that retains those records. California Cryobank has been leading the push for such a registry, but Scott Brown, its director of communications, says that privacy concerns have been holding up efforts to get it off the ground. For instance, how would the identity of anonymous donors be protected from being leaked or made public? What if the mothers or children tried to contact them?

Wendy Kramer, the founder of the Donor Sibling Registry, is extremely critical of the industry, including California Cryobank. "I thought it was an ethically responsible industry, but they're just money-making sperm sellers," she says. "There's no care or thought for the person being born, it's just about selling sperm and eggs. This has shattered all our illusions about what this industry was. I talk to people all the time who are just figuring that out. They're shocked when they realize that. I thought, of course, they'd limit the number of children being born, and share medical records and counsel donors and families. But they don't."

Kramer thinks there are ways to help donor offspring without breaking anonymity agreements that they have with donors. "If they at least connected people who were born through the same sperm donor, then we'd know that there were seventy-five kids in one group." She believes that part of this secrecy is spurred by the sperm bank industry's desire to avoid liability and continue selling popular donor sperm unimpeded.

"Nobody is keeping track of anything, such as who the donors are, how many kids they might have fathered, or if they have any diseases. There's nowhere to go to get any information. No one even knows how many donor-conceived people there are," she says.

Wendy and her son, Ryan, who believe that donor anonymity should be done away with, met with California Cryobank representatives a few years ago and appealed to them to stop selling sperm from anonymous donors. They believed that if California Cryobank abolished the practice, it would set the standard for other sperm banks. Thus, any man who wanted to donate sperm could do so, but with the understanding that their offspring would have the right to learn their identity when they turned eighteen (they wouldn't necessarily have to have contact with their offspring—the child would simply have the ability to know who they were). According to Wendy, they were told that the sperm bank couldn't stop selling sperm anonymously because that's what many prospective parents want. Yet it's true that some donors very intentionally do not want their identities revealed, so mandating open donation could limit the number of men donating (as happened in the UK), which would impact the amount of sperm available for the growing number of couples and single women depending on sperm availability. Clearly, it is not an easy issue to solve.

Rothman, of California Cryobank, understands Ryan and Wendy's position, but he feels that they do not see both sides of the issue.

"I think Ryan is a good looking, brilliant man who is very articulate. His mother has a mission that is not accepted by everybody, and she's managed to alienate most of the people in my profession with her dogmatic way of doing things," he says.

Nowadays, California Cryobank is expanding its horizons and has moved into the egg donor business—recruiting egg donors and selling eggs.

Wendy Kramer, for her part, cites a 2012 study of sperm donors that revealed that they are not only open to more transparency, they also agree to contact with offspring. Of 164 sperm donors surveyed in *Reproductive BioMedicine Online,* 84 percent had never been contacted by their sperm banks for medical updates, 23 percent of the donors felt they, or close family members, had medical or genetic issues that would be important to share with families, and 94 percent were open to communicating with offspring.

One of the few sperm banks that Kramer and other like-minded people recommend is The Sperm Bank of California in Berkeley. Established in 1982 as an offshoot of the feminist women's health movement, it was the first sperm bank created to provide sperm to all women, including lesbians and single women. In fact, more than 60 percent of the babies born through the sperm bank are raised by lesbian parents, and 20 percent are born to single parents. It is also the only nonprofit sperm bank in the world.

Alice Ruby has been director of the sperm bank for the past fourteen years. She believes that the way it started shapes who they are. In 1982, no sperm banks would provide sperm to a woman who wasn't married, let alone a lesbian. The Oakland Feminist Women's Health Center started a family planning clinic, offering fertility awareness classes to women. Lesbians and single women who were trying to conceive at home with known sperm donors began showing up at classes, looking for advice. That inspired the founders of the center to open the first sperm bank that would cater to these women, as well as heterosexual couples. They wanted to provide a medically safe option for women, regardless of marital status or sexual orientation.

"That's formative to everything we are as an organization," says Ruby. "We consider ourselves the ethical leader in the field. We were the first to have an identity-release program, so that children could contact their donors when they turn eighteen. That's our trademark."

Prior to the sperm bank's open donor program, most sperm donors were donating anonymously. It was considered something secretive, and families were advised by their doctors not to tell their children how they were conceived. At the time, it was believed that telling kids this information would damage the father-child relationship, says Ruby.

The Sperm Bank of California works hard to offer ethical options to its clients. It has a small, yet diverse, catalog of donors, and unlike most other sperm banks in the country, it has strict limits of ten families per donor, causing them to sell out frequently. Like other sperm banks, its identity-release donors are in high demand.

Ruby says it was the first program to provide detailed information about its donors, besides their height and racial and ethnic background. It did so in response to its clients, women who were planning to tell their kids how they were conceived, and who wanted their children to have more information about their donors when they became adults.

She says they also work hard to track pregnancies and births, requesting that its clients report back to them. Ruby estimates that 90 to 95 percent of its outcomes are reported to them—that's high compared to other banks. Wendy Kramer estimates that only 60 to 80 percent of women report live births to their sperm banks. The bank also makes sure to keep up with the health of donors and offspring, and to keep families apprised of any changes.

Because The Sperm Bank of California feels it's important to address all parts of sperm donation, it counsels families on how to talk to their kids about their conception, and advises sperm donors on how to tell their future partner or children that they were once a donor. They also have a resident ethicist on staff. Many of the staff members at the sperm bank used sperm donors themselves to have children, so they understand what it's like. Ruby, herself, is a single mother by choice who used a known donor (a friend) to have a baby (she felt it was unethical for her to use a donor from her sperm bank).

"My personal interest in nontraditional families has been going on a long time," says Ruby, whose own parents divorced when her mother came out as a lesbian. "I've been thinking about what makes a family for a while now. I'm very personally interested and committed to helping people make the families that they want," she says. "I always encourage someone who is selecting a sperm bank to very carefully read the details of the program, especially when choosing an identity-release donor. We knew we could commit to release the donor's identity, but we don't guarantee a meeting between a donor and his offspring. We want the most positive outcome for everyone."

That includes helping families of the same sperm donor connect if they wish to. So far, about 25 percent of its families participate in the family-matching program, and of those, about 80 percent have at least one match. Ruby says that some of the families are close, and the children consider each other sisters and brothers.

The sperm bank is also the only one in the U.S. that has an active and long-term research program, including a research director who studies psychosocial issues related to donor insemination and reproduction. Some of their research includes looking at outcomes among donors, donor-conceived adults, and families.

Still, Kramer longs for all sperm banks to be "ethical sperm banks." In these cryobanks, she envisions that all sperm donors would be open donors and available for contact with their children at any age, not just at eighteen. That's because adolescence is typically a time when children start asking questions about their identity and become curious about where they came from. In a perfect sperm bank, she says, donors would be mandated to share and update their health information with families. And families would be required to report any births, as well as any illnesses, their children might have. They would also be sure to allow their (donor) children to make contact with his or her donor and/or siblings. Her ideal sperm bank would also have to report the number of births per donor, and there would be strict limits on how many offspring he could have.

While it's a tall order, Kramer believes the industry can and will change as families continue to demand more accountability and regulation. In the meantime, The Sperm Bank of California represents a promising example of a new direction in the fertility industry.

6

Men Who Donate Sperm
The Story Behind Sperm Donation

BE A HERO—BECOME A SPERM DONOR

Help create families. In return for your time and commitment . . . We offer a means to supplement your income (donation up to 3 times/week . . . so that's up to $18,000/year) and receive comprehensive health and genetic screenings free of charge!

This is an ad from California Cryobank posted on Craigslist. It's accompanied by a cartoon image of a man opening his shirt, Superman fashion. There is also a silhouette of a baby crawling next to a picture of a bag of money.

Another ad, for a sperm bank in New York, reads:

GO ON SPRING BREAK
PAY FOR IT BY DONATING SPERM

Posted above these words is a photo of young people frolicking on a beach, a palm tree in the background.

It all sounds so good. Help couples have much-wanted children while making gobs of money. But the process is not that simple—on many levels.

"It's easier to get into Harvard Law School than it is to be a donor at California Cryobank. We're very strict," says the bank's founder, Cappy Rothman.

Only five out of 1,000 applicants are accepted at his sperm bank. The criteria for sperm donors are stringent at most sperm banks: donors cannot be shorter than five foot six (California Cryobank asks that donors be five foot nine or taller) and no taller than six foot six; their age must be between nineteen and thirty-eight; and they must be high school graduates. Some sperm banks, including California Cryobank, require that donors have either graduated from or are attending a four-year college or university. (Ivy League colleges are even better, and banks can charge more for PhD-level sperm.) For most sperm banks, candidates cannot be adopted or have had sex with a man in the past five years, and they must live in the geographic area. Contrary to popular lore, redheads *are* accepted—at California Cryobank, at least. Many banks recruit donors of different ethnicities, such as African American, Asian, and Hispanic men. Rothman says his bank has a need for Persian donors. "It's very dynamic. Women want to have a choice, so we try to be as diversified as we can," says Rothman. He adds that he believes he is responsible for the creation of 68,000 children through his sperm banks. Many women want to find a donor who looks like them or their partner (if they have one), with the same ethnicity or background, so that their child will resemble them.

Donors also must be in good physical shape (and not overweight), and some sperm banks even set restrictions on hair and eye color. There are also more than fifty disqualifying health conditions, including food allergies and infectious and/or hereditary diseases, such as cancer. A donor must provide a detailed medical history for his entire family, going back *four generations* (although this is very hard to check). Even then, he can still get cut. Once he's met all the necessary qualifications, he must give a sperm sample, which is tested for sperm count and motility. Donors are also required to have an above-average sperm count. While gay men are not restricted from donating, sperm banks do limit men who have had high-risk sexual activity, as defined by the Food and Drug Administration, says Scott Brown, the communications director for California Cryobank. They also screen for overly promiscuous heterosexual activity to eliminate applicants who pose a high risk of contracting a sexually transmitted disease while in the program.

And what about the cost? In 2016, sperm banks charged $690 to $790 per vial for an anonymous donor, and $790 to $890 for open donors' sperm. Each vial must contain between 10 and 15 million "motile" sperm (or sperm that is actively moving). Even though studies have shown that women can maximize pregnancy with at least 5 million total motile sperm in one go, the cryobanks like to be sure.

For an extra charge ($145), you can see a donor's childhood photos, read an extended profile, read his poetry or see his art or photography. An additional $250 will also give you the donor's facial feature report, an illustration of what he looks like, and a voice recording, so that parents may one day allow their child to hear their donor's voice.

It's not all routine details. Some profiles also include "fun facts," such as a sperm donor's favorite food, dream destination, and who they would have a fantasy lunch with (one donor chose Thomas Jefferson).

California Cryobank is a privately run company and has about 550 donors in its catalog. They are asked to donate at least once or twice a week; some sperm banks want donors to come in for a minimum of one year. In exchange, donors are paid handsomely, up to $1,500 a month.

When he created California Cryobank, Rothman quickly realized that the process of choosing a sperm donor was complicated. He remembers a particular case, early on, when a prospective donor came in to his office. He seemed like a good candidate, so Rothman marked him *approved*.

"As soon as he left the office, three women who worked for me knocked on the door," says Rothman. "They said, '*We* would never use him. He's ugly.' That's when I realized that there were other criteria to choosing a sperm donor."

Superficial or not, now all of California Cryobank's donor coordinators are women, and they have the final word on which men they accept. Rothman recalls another time when a very good-looking man came in to be a donor. He was muscular and well built, and Rothman was sure that the coordinators would approve him. But the man had an attitude and he intimidated the women so much that they felt uncomfortable working with him. He was ultimately turned down.

Located in Palo Alto, California Cryobank's NorCal branch is strategically centered near Stanford University (for recruiting purposes, sperm banks tend to have their offices near college campuses, especially Ivy League schools). From the outside, the office building looks like any other you'd find along a busy road, with its simple, contemporary architecture and green awnings. A small parking lot in front is nearly empty, but that's because most of the action is taking place in the back of the building, for sperm donors who don't want to be seen.

As you enter the front of the structure, you could be someplace as banal as an insurance office, save for the abstract paintings of babies that decorate the walls. Peek through the glass partition, though, and you see women wearing pink lab coats working on what looks like a scientific experiment. They're placing vials into a centrifuge, which spins around at a dizzying speed. At first, it's hard to guess what they're doing. I later learn that they're "washing" the fresh semen samples. As the milky vials spin round and round, unwanted dead cells and seminal fluid are discarded, leaving only pure semen.

Karen D'Amico, the brisk but friendly office manager who is in her fifties, shows me around. She takes me to a chilly back storage room where about a dozen large, gleaming tanks, about four feet tall, are lined up alongside one wall. Filled with liquid nitrogen, these tanks contain vials of semen from hundreds of donors. The vials will be stored here for three months before they are sent to the main office in Los Angeles, where they are kept for at least another three months until they are sold. The temperature in the tanks is kept to –350 degrees Fahrenheit, and one tank can hold up to 7,000 vials of semen. "The sperm can last forever in these tanks," she says, with a smile. "We just had a healthy child born from semen that was stored for twenty years!"

She doesn't seem to think there's anything wrong with a baby being born from semen that old; especially since it may not have been tested for all the diseases that semen is tested for now. Buyers are not told how old the sperm is, and in at least one troubling case, a baby was born with cystic fibrosis from twenty-plus-year-old sperm.

At Karen's prodding, the technician opens one of the tanks. Vapors rise as he lifts out a ten-inch-long, hollow, green anodized aluminium cane (it looks somewhat like a candy cane without the curved part). In its center, it can hold five plastic vials of semen, stacked one upon the other. This is how the semen is stored, indefinitely. Karen lets me keep an empty cane as a souvenir.

Then she shows me the donor entrance. Men who are members are identified through a fingerprint process, which brings up their photo. While they are waiting for a room to be available, the donors can grab a granola bar out of the snack basket and browse through a binder filled with porn DVDs, such as *Chock Full of Asians*. The men are then given a plastic cup and sent to one of four collection rooms, otherwise known as "masterbatoriums."

This masterbatorium is fairly small and nondescript, about the size of a doctor's examination room. It has a comfortable armchair, a TV with a DVD player, a stack of porn magazines, including *Penthouse* and *Hustler*, and a sink. A bottle of hand sanitizer and a box of tissues sit ready on a table next to the chair. Once the men fill the vial, they label it with their initials, using a felt-tip Sharpie. From there, it is processed through the in-house lab, first through the centrifuge, where it is washed.

For their sperm to be sold, a donor must produce at least 90 million modal sperm per donation, says D'Amico. "Modality is a biological thing; it really depends on the individual. There will always be a percent of sperm that are moving and some that are dead," she says.

The techs also examine the volume of the ejaculation and count—yes, actually count—the number of sperm in each donation. Typically, there are 24 million motile sperm per milliliter, but sometimes, says

D'Amico, donors might be rundown or they forget to abstain from sex (they are instructed not to ejaculate at least forty-eight hours before they donate—the less they ejaculate, the more sperm they produce), so their counts might be lower.

"We guarantee the total number of sperm per vial when women buy them," she says. "But not all guys are created equal." The technicians also rate the sperm's motility on a scale of 1 to 4. One means the sperm is just hanging out lazily; 4 means that most of the sperm are moving forward.

One donation can produce between one and four vials of sperm, but this depends on the man's sperm count, how viable the sperm is, and its motility, says Rothman. Once the sperm is frozen and thawed, about 30 percent is lost. Only about 8 to 10 percent of the vials collected actually lead to live births, adds Brown.

But donating three times a week doesn't mean that a donor will produce only three potential children. Wendy Kramer believes that each donation is actually broken out into eight to twenty-five vials, allowing for the possibility of seventy-five potential children for every week that a man donates. The donors, typically, are not aware of this, and subsequently have no idea how many kids they are producing. Critics such as Kramer believe that it's in the best interest of sperm banks to keep all this information secret, or donors may understandably balk at continuing to donate.

Rothman says that when he started his cryobank, there were no guidelines on the number of children that each donor could create. Then, in the early 1990s, the American Society for Reproductive Medicine (ASRM) suggested a limit of one child per donor, for a population of 800 (or twenty-five births per population of 800,000). That guideline changed again around seven years ago, he says, after California Cryobank sent out a questionnaire to its clients asking what they thought was a suitable number for children per donor. The number they came up with was twenty-five to thirty family units per donor—a number he believes the ASRM then used as a guideline for other cryobanks as well. Rothman says those recommendations were made so that the number was socially acceptable. He doesn't believe, however, that there's any chance of consanguinity among children born through the same donor.

California Cryobank has donors who are almost exclusively students and professionals. It recruits from local universities, including nearby Stanford, mainly through Craigslist and Facebook. The sperm bank also has offices in New York, Cambridge, and Houston, and works hard to recruit donors from elite universities such as Harvard, MIT, UCLA, and New York University. The Palo Alto office has around thirty active donors who usually go in at least once a week to donate, although the bank prefers that they donate three times a week. The men must have fifteen to twenty vials of sperm banked with the company before they are allowed to appear in their online catalog.

"We have donors come in who are so cute that I'm sure their sperm will sell immediately, and then they don't," says D'Amico. "For years, we had an adorable man whose sperm didn't sell for some reason. It depends on the search criteria that people use."

As mentioned earlier, the screening process for prospective donors is rigorous. When men come in to the office for the first time, they are given a physical, then their blood is tested for infectious and genetic diseases. They must return every six months for another physical and are paid $60 for each visit. The men also have to give a comprehensive family health history. Each sperm donation earns a man $125, so if he donates, say, three times a week, he can make up to $1,500 per month. If you're a struggling college student, that's welcome money.

Not surprisingly, D'Amico is a cheerleader for the business. She talks about the women who come back to the office to show off their babies. "We had one woman who brought in her two-year-old baby and she started to cry because she was so thankful. These children are so wanted—they're not born by accident. People want these children so badly."

Of course, sperm banks *are* helping women who otherwise wouldn't be able to have children on their own. And these women are having babies with sperm from what are surely superior specimens of men. But is this search for a perfect child a form of eugenics, a way to produce uber children? There seems to be something wrong with this scenario. Still, who wouldn't want to give her child the finest characteristics and the best start in life, when given the choice?

When Chase Kimball donated sperm in Utah in the 1970s, he was young, tall, handsome, and athletic, and working on his second graduate degree. He was also very musical and able to play the piano at a concert level (and he was a Mormon, which was undoubtedly appealing to other Utah Mormons seeking to have a baby). He's not sure how many kids he has, but he estimates it could be in the hundreds. Undoubtedly, he was a donor who was sought after.

So what makes some sperm donors, such as Chase and Donor B155A, the one with 150 children, so popular? The latter was tall, blond, blue-eyed, and smart. He was athletic, in good health, and had living parents and grandparents. As an economics major in college, he donated for four years at Fairfax Cryogenics. And while we don't know his identity, we do know quite a bit about him personally: he played the guitar and was captain of his rugby team; his favorite color is green, and he likes lasagna. He is very altruistic and likes to help other people. He has brothers, living grandparents, and a good medical history. In a picture of him as a child that many of the mothers were able to see (for an extra fee), the donor is a little boy of about a year old, sitting in a high chair about to eat his first birthday cake; he has blond curls and big blue eyes. He's adorable.

Many of the mothers, like Susanna, were able to purchase a personal essay by him, recorded on an audio CD. A counselor at Fairfax Cryogenics described him as "tall and muscular" with "sort of a baby face." The counselor said that he is "a nice guy," and one who "always seems to be in a fairly good mood."

Donor B155A is six foot two, weighs around 215 pounds, and works as a financial planner. One staff member at the sperm bank said he looked like the actor Ian Zeiring (who appeared on *Beverly Hills, 90210, Dancing with the Stars,* and *Sharknado*).

He's also responsible. When two children in the group were born with serious health problems, the donor returned to Fairfax Cryogenics to be tested (he was negative for the illness).

But why did he donate sperm? What makes someone a serial sperm donor? Is it just for the money? Perhaps he did it as a way to help others have the child they always wanted. Does he have any idea how many children he has fathered? Since Fairfax does not give sperm donors their identifying numbers, it would be difficult for him to obtain any information on his donations.

So how was this donor able to produce so many children? For one thing, his sperm probably had very good motility. One woman who used his sperm said it was practically jumping out of the vial. When doctors consider how well a man can create babies, they look at both his sperm count and his sperm motility. The sperm count is easy to understand: it's the simplest measure of a man's reproductive health. It is the number of sperm found per milliliter of semen with each ejaculation. A normal sperm count is anywhere in the range from 15 million to 150 million per milliliter. Various factors can impair a man's sperm count, such as a viral infection, environmental factors—such as hot weather—a hormone imbalance, or even infrequent sex.

While a man might have a normal sperm count, his sperm motility is also an important factor in getting a woman pregnant. Motility is the way sperm move. People talk about "strong swimmers" making the best sperm, and in a way, they're right. Sperm with healthy motility are the straightest, fastest ones. Scientists grade sperm from A to D, with A being the best swimmers and D for sperm that don't move at all. In between are sperm that are sluggish or travel in circles. If less than a third of a man's sperm don't swim forward progressively, his motility is considered low. Of course, it only takes one Michael Phelps–style swimmer to get a woman pregnant.

The World Health Organization developed the values for normal sperm count and motility after studying semen from 4,000 fertile men. Studies have shown that while low motility caused by genetic or physical issues can't be corrected, there is strong evidence that low motility can be improved by changes in a man's diet and lifestyle, such as losing weight, not smoking, limiting bike riding, and avoiding use of car seat heaters. But some doctors say that the best thing a man can do to improve his sperm motility is to have frequent intercourse. This leads to increased testosterone production and more rapid sperm production. And according to a 2009 Australian study, the more frequently a man has sex, the better the quality of his sperm—including its motility.

So what makes a man become a sperm donor? Many do it just for the money (sperm donors can earn anywhere from $1,000 to $1,500 a month), as Ryan Kramer's sperm donor did. For some, it could be an urge to spread his genetic material far and wide, especially if they think they may not have children of their own, as was the case for Chase Kimball. For others, it might be purely altruistic—a way to help families who are otherwise unable to have a child.

In a study that looked at the motivations, views, and experiences of sperm donors, conducted by Wendy Kramer of the Donor Sibling Registry, and two other researchers, it was found that of the donors surveyed, their primary reason for donating sperm was to help other families, followed by payment for their donation. The study, published in 2012 in *Reproductive BioMedicine Online*, a journal on reproductive health, surveyed 164 sperm donors. The least popular reason given for donating was that they knew they might not have children, so they wanted to pass on their genes. But this study and other similar ones found that men often have multiple reasons for donating, and age, marital status, and already having biological children of their own can have an impact on their motivation.

In the study, many said they had decided jointly with their partners to donate, and that some of their wives or girlfriends had been very encouraging about their decision. One man said, "At the time that I donated, my wife knew about and encouraged donation and that was part of the decision to donate." Another said his wife had "actually accompanied me to the sperm bank . . . to help with the donations on occasions." Most of the donors (85 percent) said that their wives were open to meeting their offspring, and a third had already told their children from their own family, while others said they planned to wait until their kids were older before they told them about any other offspring.

But what of the children who are produced through these donations? There's much more to sperm donation than just going into an office and *dancing with yourself*, as Billy Idol once so aptly put it in his popular song. These men are creating living, breathing human beings. It's easy to forget that, with all the technical talk about sperm count and motility and insemination. I was curious to know how many sperm donors think about their offspring. Do they feel they have any moral obligation to maintain relationships with their biological children? Do they even want to get to know their offspring or act as a father to them, as Chase Kimball did?

Chase spent quite a lot of time thinking about and searching for his offspring and was thrilled to meet them and form a relationship with his daughters. He remarried in 2015 and hopes that he and his new wife will have their own children someday, but he'll never forget the biological daughters he's come to know and love.

Many sperm donors say they think often about their biological children and hope to eventually meet their kids. In the *Reproductive BioMedicine* survey, 97 percent of the men surveyed said they thought about the children they had helped to create. They were mainly curious about how many children they had, whether they were healthy and happy, and whether they shared any physical characteristics.

One respondent said, "I'm very curious and hopeful they are well, healthy, and happy." Another said, "I often think about who they are, are they happy, and what are they doing with their lives." One donor said, "I wonder how they look, if I would one day see a child that looks like me and ponder if they're genetically related." Still another, "Yes I think about them and pray for them on a regular basis. They may not be my family but they are still part of me."

The responses from the survey also showed how complicated these relationships can be, and how difficult it was for many of the donor's wives and partners to understand their connection with their offspring. Many said they found this to be the most challenging aspect of connecting with their biological children.

One donor commented: "She has concerns that my desire to contact or meet my offspring is a sign that they (my wife and my daughter) are not enough." Another said, "My long-time girlfriend is ambivalent. She is supportive of me with respect to the one family that I have met but is extremely concerned about long-term implications of establishing/maintaining contact with multitudes of donor kids." Another man said, "She still does not 'get' the complex emotional issues that connect the children to the donor and vice versa."

Feelings of resentment were also described. Said one donor, "Managing the relationships at home . . . I learned that my wife had feelings of jealousy when I would spend time online chatting with my donor child's mother."

There were also challenges to the relationships when secrecy was involved, or when the offspring's mother was a single woman. The donors who had multiple offspring also had to deal with the understandable challenge of trying to meet all their children. One donor said, "It's still early, as most kids are so young. I foresee the most challenging aspect being the sheer volume of potential people to connect . . . maintaining communications with sixty-plus kids, in addition to parents, is daunting."

One sperm donor discovered on the Donor Sibling Registry that he has seventy children and now keeps track of them using a spreadsheet. He finds it overwhelming, especially since he says that the sperm bank promised him low numbers of children. Every once in a while he finds out about a new child or even twins.

When donors start, they sign an agreement that outlines the cryobank's right to use his sperm, says Rothman, adding that when a donor has asked his bank to stop distributing his sperm, they have taken it off the market. He says California Cryobank has done this at least three times, for donors who became religious or famous, or who died (it was taken off at the family's request). But he says it's very rare for donors to ask this.

There are some troubling stories of sperm donors with multiple children. Kirk Maxey, a physician, claims he may have fathered up to 400 children in the sixteen years that he donated sperm. He was a medical student at the University of Michigan in the 1980s when he began donating sperm, at the urging of his wife, who was a nurse at a local fertility clinic. They had recently had a son, and she thought that helping others to have kids would be a generous thing to do. Because few clinics used frozen sperm at the time, Maxey was sometimes called in at inopportune times to donate. Once he had to produce the donation in the car on the way to the clinic—he said it was an extremely risky thing to do. Several years ago, Maxey became curious about the biological children that he helped to produce and tried to find some of them, in part so that he could provide them with his medical history. When he realized that the doctors weren't keeping track of his offspring, Maxey says he began to panic that some of them might accidentally start dating one another and have sex. This was especially worrisome since Maxey's sperm was used in a concentrated geographical area—the region surrounding Ann Arbor, Michigan. But because sperm banks ship sperm all over the country—and the world—they believe that any cases of accidental incest among offspring of the same sperm donor, in the same geographical area, would be extremely rare.

Maxey says he's troubled about what he sees as the prevalence of deception in assisted reproduction—especially in the way that sperm banks deal with their donors. For instance, he was given very little information about the number of children he helped to produce. "I think it would astonish people how it pervades a field in which actual lives and the health of unborn children can hang in the balance," he says.

Most of the sperm donors that I spoke to were open to some level of connection with their children. And the *Reproductive BioMedicine* survey overwhelmingly backs that up; 94 percent of the donors said they welcomed contact with their offspring, but the type of contact they were interested in varied greatly.

Most were willing to answer any questions the children might have or supply medical information. About 80 percent were open to email contact, sharing photos, and having a meeting, while a third of respondents said they didn't feel comfortable inserting themselves into their lives as parents, and that their offspring already had parents. About 20 percent had already been in contact with their biological children, and many of those donors said that it was important to keep boundaries on both sides. One donor said, "I keep reminding myself that it's supposed to be about her, it's not about me." Another donor said, "My kids feel familiar and comfortable to be around. I feel connected to them, but it's unlike any other relationship I have ever had."

One sperm donor who posted anonymously on the Donor Sibling Registry believes his children should be able to find out about him. He wrote:

One thing is crystal clear for me. That is that the interests and well-being of the children—all of them—are paramount. Regardless of what the legal framework was at the time of my being a sperm donor, I believe that I do have responsibilities to the children born as a result of my sperm donations. At the very least, those children have a right to know what my part of their genetic heritage is . . . I will be more than happy to get in touch, if and when they do desire. I think about them often and wonder who, where, and how they are, and what is happening in their lives. I think that if one day some of my unknown offspring do make contact with and meet me it might be—for them primarily and for me too—a wonderful "jigsaw" experience!?! I only donated for a period of about eight months! All of that said, the prospect of it actually happening is a little daunting, in some ways. What if they do not like me, or I them? What if they feel unhappy with my having contributed to their creation but then taken no responsibility for them—especially if they have had an unhappy life? How will my own family react to and view them? On and on my thinking goes. However, at the base of all of this, I am quite clear in my mind that these wonderful children do have a right to know what they want to know about me—because in them, there is a part of me.

John, thirty-six, donated sperm five years ago as an open donor. He says it's a myth that men don't want to think about the fact that they've donated sperm and go about their lives as if it never happened.

"Once you're five or six years out, you realize you might have some kids out there. You start to get curious. That part was unsettling for me," he says. "But I felt good about it. I looked at it as a way of helping people who were in need of assisted reproduction for some reason. I made peace with that."

He decided to be an open sperm donor so that he could one day be available for any children who might want to find him.

"I felt a responsibility that if a child wanted to find out something about me, that information would be out there," he explains. "I'm keeping a journal, so if a child looks me up one day, they'd know how I felt about them. That I'd be there to help if they needed me."

"Now my goal in life is to have my own small family and one day meet my offspring," he says.

Some donors go even further with such intentions, making it a point to get to know their offspring. Michael Rubino has formed unusually close relationships with some of his children. In fact, he has changed his will so that all of his belongings will one day go to his donor children. An artist based in Los Angeles, Rubino donated sperm in the mid-1990s after he and his wife were unable to have children of their own.

Rubino was married in 1985, but in the early 1990s he and his wife realized that her fertility issues made it impossible for them to have kids. They attended support groups for couples like themselves. It was harder on his wife; although he'd wanted kids, Rubino hadn't been looking forward to the early years, with the sleepless nights and round-the-clock diaper changes.

Once they heard the stories of others who couldn't have children, Rubino's wife encouraged him to donate sperm. So he did. He thought it would be a great way to help others to have children, and also be a part of the gene pool, especially since he didn't think he'd ever have kids of his own. Rubino also liked that there were no financial or legal responsibilities involved with fathering these children. He was thirty-three when he began donating at California Cryobank as an open donor (which meant his offspring could contact him when they reached eighteen years old). Rubino was a popular donor: he was handsome, with his dark hair, blue eyes and long lashes, and cleft chin. He was also tall and slim, and he spoke fluent French. On his profile, he wrote that he was an artist who wanted to help those who were infertile.

What made him even more desirable as a potential father was that he'd graduated from the University of California at Berkeley with a 3.75 GPA.

On an audiotape that he recorded for the sperm bank, he talked about his love of art, his penchant for traveling, and his fondness for the Italian opera composer, Puccini. Though he loved classical music, he also enjoyed singers Billie Holiday and Roy Orbison. He also talked about his and his wife's own fertility problems, and how disappointed they had been. "I'll probably never have a child of my own," he said. "I feel privileged to help someone do that."

Who wouldn't have wanted this guy to father their child?

For the next two years, he donated sperm twice a week, making about $400 a month. He was told that he would not receive any information about any children he had fathered. Curious, he'd often ask how many children he had? They told him they couldn't give him that information. When he turned thirty-five, California Cryobank retired him as a donor, saying they had enough sperm from him.

He and his wife later divorced, and Rubino expected that he wasn't going to meet any of his offspring until he was in his fifties, when his kids were at least eighteen. A few years back, when he was in his early forties, he had contacted California Cryobank to let them know that he had moved, in case any of his donor children tried to contact him. They said they'd put a note in his file. He continued to work as an artist, painting portraits and oil paintings with political and environmental themes, and living a Bohemian lifestyle. He did not remarry and never had any kids of his own.

One day, his sister called and said, "Check out the Oprah Winfrey show—they're talking about donor children meeting their dads." Wendy and Ryan Kramer were on the show discussing the Donor Sibling Registry. He went on his computer and clicked onto the website, but he couldn't remember his donor number at first. That was the only way he would know if any of his offspring were trying to reach him. He finally remembered it, Donor 929. He checked the site again and was excited to find that there was, indeed, a note for him. He couldn't believe it. It was from a woman named Anne Gerry. It read:

Message to donor: THANK YOU! These children are the greatest gift of my life. They are beautiful, brilliant, talented, kind, absolutely delightful. . . . We are very open to contact with the donor and/or siblings. . . . If my donor sees this, I don't want anything. I just want to thank you for my wonderful, perfect children.

Rubino was moved to tears. He couldn't believe that he had two children. So he decided to contact Gerry. They talked on the phone, and he learned that she was a psychotherapist who lived in Massachusetts, a single mother by choice, and that with his help, she had given birth to two amazing children: Madeline, who was four, and Joseph, who was seven. She had been thinking about him for a long time.

They kept in touch, and the kids wrote him Christmas cards addressed to "Daddy." He sent the children presents—fossils and minerals that he had collected. A few months later, Gerry and her kids came out to see Rubino and stayed for a week with him in his tiny apartment that was attached to his art gallery. The visit went well. They went to Disneyland and the beach, and Madeline and Joseph bonded with their biological father as they spent time together. Gerry was especially thrilled that her son, Joseph, was able to spend time with Rubino. She worried that he hadn't had a chance to bond with a man. Their visit was profiled in a *Washington Post* article that was published in 2005.

For his part, Rubino referred to Joseph and Madeline as his children and asked that they call him "Dad."

What sperm donors call their kids, and what the children call their biological fathers, varies greatly and can bring joy or create heartache. Rubino loved it when his kids called him Daddy, and he calls them his children. Ryan Kramer's donor, Lance, says he doesn't consider Ryan and the others his "children"—they're his offspring. "They're someone else's children. I have no more right to have an interest in their life than a stranger," he says. "But I'd be interested to keep track of how my other offsprings' lives turn out."

Chase Kimball calls his biological daughters' dad their "social father," a term that some find offensive, but which others use to differentiate between biological fathers and the fathers they grew up with.

While Rubino loved being called Dad and spending time with his kids, he told Gerry that he didn't ever see himself as a family man, or as having a family in the conventional sense.

"I was sour grapes on the whole kids thing. I thought, 'I don't need kids.' I wasn't sure I even liked kids," says Rubino, of the time before he met his offspring. "I was an artist. It was all good. I thought, 'I'll meet these kids when they're eighteen and we'll have lunch.'"

Through a group called Single Mothers by Choice, Gerry had been in touch with another mother who has used Rubino as a sperm donor. Lena lived in San Diego with her young son, Adam. Though Gerry was tempted to keep Rubino to herself, she told him about this other child that he had. So before she and the kids left, Lena and her son drove up from Southern California to meet everyone. Adam was six and a half at the time. His mother introduced Rubino as a friend—she didn't feel ready to tell her son that he was meeting his father.

Adam loved dinosaurs, so the group planned a visit to the La Brea Tar Pits, a popular tourist site in Los Angeles where the skeletons of mammoths and other prehistoric creatures have been found. The families all had a great time, and Rubino was surprised to find out how much he enjoyed being with his kids.

"By the time my wife and I split I was thirty-five, so by then I figured I'm not having kids. The weird thing is that I fell in love with these kids immediately. I didn't expect it. I'm not much of a fuzzy-wuzzy type. But each of my kids trips me out. They're all healthy, good looking, and funny, with great personalities," he says.

Since those early meetings with Joseph, Madeline, and Adam in 2005, Rubino has met more of his offspring—one or two each year. He now has made contact with seventeen of his children, though the cryobank says he has eighteen kids all together. His kids live all over the country, from Hawaii to the East Coast, and they are all very different. Rubino has had a chance to visit some, and others have come to see him. There are about half a dozen kids that he has yet to meet, but he is in touch with most of them through email or Facebook. All of the kids are about twenty years old now.

"I get along great with everybody. It's been kind of amazing," he says. "For me, there's an instant bond thing happening. And I think with them, too. It's all good. It's actually been really easy."

It's very unusual for a sperm donor to have this kind of close relationship with his offspring, and Rubino is remarkable for the openness and warmth he displays with his children and their families.

"Michael is the type of donor any mother and/or donor-conceived person would be happy to connect with," says Wendy Kramer. "He's kind, respectful, and willing to step in as a family member—only if that's what families are looking for."

He believes that he has a stronger bond with the children he met when they were very young, such as his daughter Marie, who lives in Hawaii. They refer to him as "Dad" and keep in touch, calling occasionally to say hello. Rubino says that those he first met when they were sixteen, seventeen, or even twenty years old are wonderful, and they're happy to meet him, but they don't call him "Dad." Maybe that's because they were already (basically) adults and some of them already have fathers. Many of the kids come from same-sex couples and have two parents.

Rubino believes that his children all look similar to him and to each other. "It's kind of cool. They all have certain features. This one has my eyes or my jaw. Three of them definitely look more like me," he says. As an artist, Rubino expresses himself through his work, so he has taken to painting his kids' portraits after he meets them—then he sends the paintings to his children. So far, he has painted five of them. In one painting, he is giving one of his sons a piggyback ride. They are on the beach, and Rubino is wearing sunglasses. They are both smiling and look very happy in the portrait.

He has been fortunate with his family's reaction: Rubino grew up in San Francisco, and his family is very open and liberal. Rubino says they've been very receptive to his offspring—especially since both his brother and sister were married and divorced and never had kids. His mother was delighted to meet four of her grandchildren before she passed away. "My sister gets a kick out of it. She's the aunt, and she's on Facebook with them all the time," he says. "I'm only sorry that my father died before he had a chance to meet my kids."

Rubino's friends think it's great that he has been able to connect with his children, and he says that some are even a little jealous. One friend who has two kids tells him he has the best of both worlds—he gets to enjoy his kids, and yet he doesn't have any of the responsibilities of having children, such as paying college tuition.

In fact, over the years, Rubino, who is now fifty-six, has become extremely close with his son Adam, and Adam's mother, Lena. A few years after they met, Lena, a single mother who worked as a paralegal, moved up to Los Angeles with her son. Since he was an artist without a set schedule, he offered to take Adam after school sometimes and during the summer. They would hang out and go to the beach together. Then, two years ago, Rubino decided to sell his property in the city. He and Lena had become good friends (they've never been romantically involved), and he knew that she was renting her place, so one day he approached her with an idea: "I said, 'why don't we buy a house together?'" So for the past two years, they've been sharing a house with their son, Adam. Rubino is pleased that he gets to spend so much time with his son, who is now eighteen.

"Adam is like the perfect kid. We've never had an argument, and he's doing great in school," he says. His son is now in high school. Once he graduates and goes to college, Rubino believes he might then sell and move out. Or stay. "We do like the house."

"I'm a loner and an artist. I like being alone. And for a long time, I was very happy like that. I went from this quiet and not super social life to this huge extended family. I'm communicating with someone every day and I love it," he says.

When he first started meeting his children, he felt a little anxious about the whole experience. "I thought, 'how am I going to meet all these kids?' I was worried about it, and briefly took my name off the DSR list to get a breather. I was worried that five more kids might show up," he remembers. "But then I thought, 'it's not fair. I don't know how much I'll be in their lives, but these kids have a right to know their father.' So I put my name back on the list, and I'm so glad that I did." He was worried about 150 or 200 kids contacting him, but fortunately, the number has stayed at eighteen.

When he began donating sperm, Rubino had no idea about limits or finding his kids. He actually became friendly with Cappy Rothman, the founder of California Cryobank, when Rothman came to visit his art gallery once. Rothman told Rubino that there was a limit to the number of children he could father, and that it was twenty. "At one point, I said 'how many kids do I have?' They said they couldn't tell me. They were secretive about it. I just wanted a number." It wasn't until years later that Rothman told him that he had eighteen children.

The only thing that gives him a little heartache is when his children ask him to visit, and he's unable to because of lack of time or money. He has flown to the East Coast half a dozen times, give or take, to visit his children there, and they keep asking him to come back. Once, a daughter in New Mexico invited him to her high school graduation. He bought tickets and planned to go, but a problem with the airline made him miss his flight—and, unfortunately, her graduation. He was devastated.

His next trip will be to visit his daughter in Hawaii. Rubino also has a daughter in the Cayman Islands, who was born to a black mother. "That makes me feel cool," he says. "She's beautiful."

And so this man who never had children of his own will one day leave behind a legacy: eighteen human beings who will always remember him for giving them life, and more.

Since they've developed a relationship, Anne has actually changed her children's last name on their birth certificates to Rubino-Gerry, because she wants them to have their father's surname, and she plans to change her will so that he would have custody of the children if she dies. Rubino has already revised his will so that everything he has, including his house and his paintings, will be left to some of his children.

"I didn't expect to meet all my kids, but I'm really glad that I did," he says. "It turned out that the whole sperm donor thing was the best thing I ever did."

Part Three

7

Donor Children and Identity
The Search for Self in an Anonymous World

Dear ******,

I am not even sure how to begin. I was the result of an artificial in-semination procedure on June 26th, 19**. This is possibly the most surprising experience of my entire life (other than being told that my dad was not my biological father).

23andMe provided an opportunity to know more about my potential health risks and possible half siblings . . . I never expected "Father - 50% match" to show up when I opted for the close relative search.

I'm having a hard time sifting through the emotional whirlwind, but I know for certain that I would like to get to know you better. If you're open to this, please let me know. Hope to hear back from you soon.

Sincerely,

******

A donor-conceived woman wrote this letter to her biological father. She desperately wanted to meet and get to know the man whose sperm helped to create her.

Andrew Solomon, author of *Far from the Tree: Parents, Children, and the Search for Identity,* says there's a real impetus toward understanding how you came to be.

"I think children and adults search for their identity to get a sense of who they are and how their experience of life or their world differs from that of other people. They're looking for a community where they can find other people who share aspects of their identity," he says. "I think everyone starts out not knowing their identity. It's a journey of discovery. I think it's hard to feel secure and confident if you don't have a clear sense of your identity. It's difficult to succeed in relationships or school or work if you don't have some degree of clarity about who you are. People say, just be yourself, but it's hard to do that if you don't know who yourself is."

Solomon notes that the idea of know thyself comes from the Bible. But know thyself is actually very hard to do, he says. People tend to try by putting together all the external information that's available about themselves. That's why we're all checking our genealogy online—we all want to understand where we came from. When he thinks about his own ancestors, who were farmers in Eastern Europe, he says he feels disconnected at some level from those distant origins. "I find it almost impossible to reconcile my experience of life now with that life. Are they people like me who were doing those things and leading that life? What are the things that I do that are derived from them? I think in a way we're all curious about the larger question of where the world came from, where humanity came from, and it's all connected to the mystery of 'where did I come from. Now that I'm here, who am I? What are the characteristics by which I'll be seen by the world?'"

Feelings of lost identity can vary greatly from child to child, even between siblings. Some donor-conceived children will feel perfectly fine not knowing who their biological father is, and never have any identity issues. For instance, Chase Kimball's daughter, Jane, was intensely curious about the identity of her donor and what he was like, and she fantasized about meeting him. Yet her sister, Nina, rarely thought about her donor and had little interest in meeting him, although she was happy to get to know Chase when they finally met.

Then there are others, like Ryan Kramer, who from an early age had an insatiable curiosity about his biological father and couldn't rest until he found him. Ryan was lucky to track down his donor and meet him when he was an adolescent, a time when kids are forming their identity and are most interested in finding out where they came from.

Self-identity is the way in which a person views themselves and their role in the world. Kids with a strong sense of self and a feeling of belonging to a family or community tend to be emotionally resilient and better able to deal with challenges in life. It also gives them a good foundation for learning and development. Beginning at birth, children's relationships with family members, friends, and their community help to form their identities. Adolescence is the most important period for children to create a sense of identity. That's when they begin to explore what makes them special, and that identity is constantly being formed and reformed through their experiences and their interaction with the world.

"This stage of development helps us to figure out who we are and why we do what we do and what we believe," says Jenna Slutsky, PhD, a clinical psychologist and researcher at The New School's Center for Attachment Research.

Renowned developmental psychologist Erik Erikson helped us to understand the stages and challenges for building self-identity, with his theory of psychosocial identity development. Erikson, who was famous for coining the term "identity crisis," had his own identity issues as a youth and grappled with them for much of his life. That was probably because, like some donor-conceived children, he never knew who his biological father was. His mother, Karla Abrahamsen, was from Denmark and became pregnant with Erikson while she was estranged from her first husband. It was thought the father was an artist or photographer. Abrahamsen later married her son's pediatrician, a man named Theodor Homberger, who adopted the boy and gave him his surname. But because he did not know who his real father was,

Erikson experienced serious identity confusion as a young man. He also didn't look like anyone else in his Jewish family—he was tall, with blond hair and blue eyes. In school, Erikson was teased for looking too Nordic, as well as for being Jewish. He didn't know who he was.

His mother had tried to avoid the scandal of having a baby out of wedlock by moving from Copenhagen to Frankfurt before he was born. When he was young, she told him that his real father was Homberger, but Erickson always suspected that something wasn't right. His mother waited until his late childhood to tell him the truth—but the identity of his biological father was always kept a secret, and he remained bitter that his mother and stepfather had lied to him.

Erikson spent his late teens and early twenties wandering throughout Europe, searching for himself. He sketched and painted for a time and eventually met a friend in Vienna, who introduced him to Sigmund Freud's daughter, Anna. Through her, Erikson began his career as a psychoanalyst, mainly of children. He later met a Canadian-American woman named Joan Serson at a Viennese masked ball and fell in love. They married and had children, and were happy in Vienna for a time. But with the advent of Hitler and the Nazis, they decided it was best to leave Austria—especially since Erikson was Jewish. First, they went to Denmark to try and find work, as well as traces of Erikson's biological father. However, the Danish government would not give him a work permit, so they left and the family moved to Boston, where Erikson gained a strong reputation as a child analyst. He went on to work at various universities, including Harvard and Yale, despite never having attended university. Before he became a naturalized citizen, he decided to change his surname from Homberger to Erikson (as in, *son of Erik*), as a way to recognize his birth father, whom he believed also had the given name of Erik. He kept Homberger as his middle name to honor his adopted father; his wife and children also later took the name Erikson.

Erikson's work on the stages of psychosocial development has since become central to psychology textbooks and to many of the self-help books that some of us read today. In his books, such as *Childhood and*

Society, Erikson helped us to understand how children develop a sense of who they are from birth, and how our relationships with family members help to mold our identities.

He theorized that children develop in stages and that development is influenced by one's environment, with a crisis at each stage that must be resolved. During the adolescent phase, children begin to ask existential questions about who they are and who they can become, and their families play a role in helping them to define themselves. This is one reason why some children who don't know the identity of their fathers, like donor children, can have difficulty in fully creating their sense of self. According to Erikson's theory, if the "crisis" at one of the stages is not worked out, then the child's development can be adversely affected. Throughout adolescence and early adulthood, children grapple with mental and physical changes, and their sense of identity continues to shift.

While many donor-conceived children are perfectly content with their origin, some, such as Alana Newman, have a difficult time accepting the basis of their conception.

Newman grew up with a mother and a father, but found out when she was quite young that she had been born through a sperm donor. She was confused and lonely as a child and did not get along with her stepfather, who she said was abusive. Newman has an older sister who is adopted, and she says that her mother has always been open with both of them about their origins, which she appreciates. Surprisingly, when Newman was older, she went on to donate her eggs—twice. She believes that donor-conceived children are more likely to sell or donate their own gametes. She's critical of egg donation now, but at the time, she needed money, and the concept of using assisted reproductive technology to help others have babies was something she had grown up with.

"At the time, I thought, there needs to be more open identity egg donors and sperm donors, so I volunteered myself as open ID so that the kids could contact me whenever they felt like it," she says, adding that egg donation was very difficult. "It's extremely painful; your whole body is almost locked at the end, you lose all flexibility in your abdomen and core, and you have menstrual pain like you've never felt in your whole life."

Now in her late twenties, Newman speaks of the harmful aspects of being a donor child, and advocates for donor offspring to have input in future regulation of the fertility industry. She started a website in 2011 called Anonymous Us (anonymousus.org) that allows donor offspring to write anonymously about their experiences (the letter at the beginning of this chapter appeared on her website).

"I started the website because, through my own experience, I'm trying to speak out. I know there are other donor-conceived people out there who are dealing with a lot of painful issues," she says. "We want to be considered when [the government is] reviewing the fertility industry for regulation, even though it means directly insulting or betraying our families or loved ones. There's a huge barrier for donor-conceived people to come forward because it threatens our relationships with their loved ones. But I think regulation is on its way, and we need the kid's perspective to regulate it in the right way."

Newman, who is also a singer-songwriter, lives in Louisiana and is married with two children. All the stories on the website appear anonymously because, she says, "Anonymity in reproduction hides the truth, but anonymity in storytelling helps reveal the truth." The site is a story collective, with various categories of storytellers: donors, parents, adoptees, and fertility industry professionals, as well as partners, friends, and others. It's a place for people to tell their deep, dark secrets, she says.

Here's an excerpt from a story, "Ambiguity of Identity," that appeared on the site on March 14, 2014. It's written by a young man who was donor conceived:

> My experiences make me wonder about the role of family and its socially constructed nature for the donor conceived. We are made to feel like we have no choices and to accept things as they are. This conflict that I have experienced over the course of my life makes me feel very alone and sad for the loss of my biological father. Yet this feeling of loss is not accepted by contemporary

society and the donor conceived are made to suffer in silence while the fertility industry that assisted in our creation continue to espouse the virtue of anonymity. So many of us have spoken about how important the right to our genetic identity is to us. Not a day goes by that I don't sit and wonder about who he is and whether he has a family of his own; and the question of whether he would embrace the idea of meeting me or at the very least acknowledging my existence.

As I stare into the eyes of the man whom I believe to be my biological father I wonder if it is worth going down this path of emotional self-destruction that I have experienced on so many occasions. So many times I have believed that I've found him only to be crushed when I discover that one piece of information that rules him out as a candidate. I have a list of names that I continue to attach notes to. I've had my DNA tested multiple times and I've scoured libraries and medical licensing records to narrow down the very few men who could be my biological father. Every time I reach this point of both happiness and intense fear I ask why offspring such as me are forced to endure this never-ending psychological torture. Sometimes I question whether it is worth continuing to put myself through this. The possibility of being rejected by my biological father is high and this makes me wonder whether the results may end up being worse than not knowing. I do not know if I would be able to handle that. Reality eventually sets in and this initial feeling of happiness can instead turn to bitterness and anger. That is the ambiguity of identity that I face. I am stuck between two realities and my desire for the truth is lost among them.

Here's another story, "Forever Searching," from June 17, 2015:

I have been actively searching for my paternal biological family for 2 years. The DNA sites, Facebook groups, and other groups online are very helpful. It is just SO VERY exhausting to search. Every day I search; it has become a routine of mine, and each day it gets more exhausting. Sometimes I wish I could simply forget about it or stop searching. I know some donor-conceived people who don't search and seem perfectly happy living their life. I wish I could be like them. But I can't bury this. Even if I tried, I would be reminded everyday by looking in the mirror and seeing familiar qualities in strangers. Besides that, "donor conceived" is already so much a part of who I am and my identity (or lack thereof) that I cannot extinguish it.

To be sure, not everyone who is donor-conceived struggles with his or her identity. Many are content with their families and their place in the world. Here's a story from the Anonymous Us site, dated April 7, 2014, titled "Identity":

I've never wanted to meet my donor, and I haven't come across many other people who feel the same way.

I love my moms. I love them with all I've got, and I know that they love my brother and me more than anything in the world. My moms, my brother, and I. That's my family.

My donor is not my family. I understand and respect my moms' decision to use a donor, and regardless of his reason for donating, I'm glad he did, but I have very little, if any, desire to meet him.

I've always felt that way, and I think I always will. Being a donor kid is part of my identity, but my donor's identity is not.

In addition to questions about identity, even knowing what to call one other, or their donors, can be fraught for those who are donor conceived.

"If adopted people meet their biological father, they get to call them their father. Yet donor-conceived people don't get to call their donor their father. People will say, 'that is not a father, it's a donor. It's not a person who raised you,'" says Wendy Kramer. "Other families will say, 'how dare you use the word sibling?' when they are talking about half siblings. They think it implies that these people are family. People are very threatened by the use of sibling, sister, brother, or father. But if you say donor, you may offend donor-conceived people."

Kramer adds that some children with heterosexual parents will say, he's not my father, he's just a donor, while some kids in LGBT families will say their donor was just a cell and nothing more.

Ryan Kramer's donor, Lance, was clear about what he called his son and his other donor kids: "I should clarify that they aren't my children. They're my offspring. They're someone else's children. I have no more right to have an interest in their life than a stranger."

There is very little research on the topic of donor-conceived children and the issue of identity, since the subject is so new. But the studies that have been conducted are illuminating. In a study that looked at why some donor-conceived children want to know the identity of their sperm donors, researchers found the reasons included wanting to prevent medical risks, avoiding accidentally having sex with a brother or sister, connecting with one's roots, understanding where one's traits come from, discerning one's characteristics, and mapping out one's family history.[1]

The 2013 study "Donor-conceived children looking for their sperm donor: what do they want to know?" was published in the journal *Facts, Views & Vision in ObGyn*. It compared the need to find the identity of one's donor with that of children who were adopted. Over the past several years, adoptees have argued that they had a right to know their birth parents because it was important to their identity, family, and private life. Previously, not knowing who one's parents were was thought to be a common cause of "genealogical bewilderment," meaning a state of confusion and the undermining of one's identity due to not knowing at least one genetic parent.

"Some kids are haunted by it every day, and some don't care," says Wendy. "It's just like an adoption. Everyone has different levels of anger and frustration, peace and contentment. Adolescence is a time where there is the most curiosity about your family. It's important to fill in the pieces for our children."

Ryan used to wonder where he got his aptitude for science and math; even his facial features were a puzzle to him. There are donor children who are curious to know if they inherited their musical ability from their father, or more seriously, many want to know their medical and genetic backgrounds.

Naomi Cahn, a law professor at George Washington University who has written extensively about the fertility industry, says studies show that when people search, they're searching not for a father, but for their genetic identity and their own sense of history. "It seems to give people more of a place in the world when they understand where they've gotten their genes, and when they see people who share the same characteristics that they have," she says.

In a 2016 study that looked at how adolescents integrate their donor conception into the development of their identity, Jenna Slutsky, of the New School, and fellow researchers found that children who were securely attached to their mothers were more accepting of their donor conception than insecurely attached adolescents.[2] The study suggests that the quality of mother-child relationships influences a child's feelings about donor conception.

"Our research is looking at how adolescents integrate early knowledge of who they are," says Slutsky. "While they might have different information to integrate into their sense of identity, there is currently no evidence to suggest that the process of identity formation is any more difficult for a donor-conceived child than it is for any other child."

Still, Margaret Somerville, founding director of the Centre for Medicine, Ethics and Law at McGill University in Montreal, says that some donor children grieve over not knowing where they came from.

"They talk about being genetic orphans and say, 'Not only do I not know where I came from, but my child won't know where they came from,'" she says. "I had someone say to me recently that they thought knowing who your genetic relatives are is important because it's the only bond you couldn't renounce. You can reverse a marriage, agreements, whatever, but this is so fundamental."

Said one donor-conceived man from Australia who has not been able to find out if he has any half siblings because he doesn't know the identity of his donor: "Personally, I am deeply traumatized that there could even be one half sibling that I have never known and will never get to know, let alone the fact that there could easily be dozens. While never being able to know your own family is emotional enough, the fact that there may be numerous half siblings is deeply disturbing on a level akin to being manufactured to appease the masses. We are human beings with biological and social families, yet the ability to produce so many siblings is actually dehumanizing."

In a study that looked at the psychological impact on seven-year-old children conceived by gamete donation, researchers examined the secrecy surrounding families who used sperm and egg donors. (A gamete is a cell that joins together to begin making a person.) The 2011 study appeared in the *Journal of Family Psychology* and was funded in part by the National Institutes of Health. It also compared this issue with adopted children who were not told by their parents where they came from:

> It has been argued that secrecy will have an adverse effect on family relationships and, consequently, on the child . . . research on adoption has shown that adopted children who are not given information about their biological parents may become confused about their identity and at risk for psychological problems. It is now generally accepted that adopted children benefit from open communication with their parents about their adoption and information about their biological parents. Family therapists have also argued that secrecy may jeopardize communication between family members and result in a distancing of some members of the family from others. In relation to donor insemination, it has been suggested that keeping the circumstances of conception secret will separate those who know the secret (the parents) from those who do not (the child).

The study also looked at the mother-child relationships in donor families, and found that mothers who did not tell a child about their

donor conception had less positive interactions with their kids, suggesting that families benefited from being open about their children's
genetic origin.

Secrecy is a fraught issue within the donor-conceived community.
Until recently, heterosexual couples seldom told their children that
they were born through donor sperm or eggs, since they didn't have
to. Finding out in your twenties or thirties, or even later, that your father isn't, in fact, your father, can be a traumatic experience. In some
cases, everyone else knew this "family secret"—everyone but the child
in question. That can feel like the ultimate betrayal.

Lisa discovered when she was thirty-four that the man she'd always known as "Dad" wasn't, in fact, her biological father. When
she was about to get married, she decided to have a genetic test done
through 23andMe. She wanted to find out if she had any genetic diseases she might be a carrier for before she and her fiancé had kids.
She asked her parents for a saliva sample, too, and had them tested.
After receiving the results, Lisa was shocked to learn that her dad
didn't show up in her list of known relatives. She couldn't believe it.
Lisa told the genetic testing company that they must have made a
mistake. So she had another test done with a different company—
but the results were the same. With that second test, she realized
that her parents had been lying to her all her life about who her father really was.

"I had to accept it, but it was very strange. You think you know who
you are . . . " says Lisa, who lives in the Salt Lake City area. "I felt like I
didn't recognize myself in the mirror anymore."

She decided not to tell her parents, since her father was elderly and
wasn't able to handle emotional discussions well, and her mother was
suffering from late-stage Alzheimer's. But she talked to some friends
about the news, and it somehow got back to her father. He was furious
and threatened to disinherit her.

Later, Lisa found out that her father had had a vasectomy after having four sons with his first wife. He claimed he didn't know that she
wasn't his biological daughter, and he said that her mother must have
gone to a sperm donor behind his back. In a way, she was relieved to

find out that he wasn't her father because all her life, they'd had significant differences of opinion and he'd been critical of her, so this explained a lot, she says. There was a time when she thought she might have been adopted, but she looked so much like her parents that she thought it couldn't have been true. Now, she realizes that her mother chose a donor who looked like her "social" father so that no one would suspect that he wasn't her real father.

"The discovery gave me some validation, so it was a mixed bag. But I'd rather know the truth," says Lisa.

Soon, Lisa became curious about who her father really was. She didn't think her mother had had an affair, so she started looking into sperm donors. She went onto the Donor Sibling Registry website, where she found two donors who seemed to be a match with the year and place where she was born, as well as with their ethnicity and characteristics. She knew from her genetic test that her ancestry was mainly Western European and British Isles. In 1982, when Lisa was born, frozen sperm was rarely used, so she surmised that her parents must have used fresh sperm. She knew that they lived in the Washington, D.C., area at the time, so it had to be a man who lived nearby.

The first donor that Lisa contacted was very nice, but she soon discovered that he was not her father. They're actually still in contact and he has been supportive of her search. Then she tried the other donor. He turned out to be the one.

"We were both in shock," she remembers. "He'd been waiting six years for someone to contact him on the DSR website, but he was also very cautious about meeting me."

Her biological father had been a prominent figure in Washington at one time, so he sent her some books about himself so that she could decide if he was someone she wanted to get to know. After communicating for a few months, she unexpectedly received a message from him one day saying that they would have to end their conversations. He discouraged her from getting in touch again. Lisa was devastated. She tried to write him again, but there was no response. Then, a few months later, she read online that her biological father had been diagnosed with terminal cancer.

"That was so upsetting to me. I just discovered him, and to find out that he was dying . . . " she says.

She asked Wendy Kramer to contact him on her behalf. He responded and said he was sorry for hurting Lisa in any way, and that he was proud of her accomplishments, and that he believed she would contribute great things to the world. She wrote him back, thanking him for what he had done for her mother.

Sadly, he died last April, before she ever had a chance to meet him.

Through Facebook, however, she was able to get in touch with one of her biological cousins after her father's death. It turned out that her donor had a brother and sister, and Lisa found out that they and their children were receptive to meeting her. She discovered that her biological father had been gay and had never married nor had any kids of his own. He had kept a photo in his room of a little girl that he called his daughter, she was told. She's not sure if it was of her. Lisa hasn't been able to find any donor siblings that she might have.

Lisa has decided to wait until her "social" father (as she calls the father she grew up with), who is ill, passes away before she meets this new family, to avoid hurting him. "I feel like I have this other branch of family in my life. It would be nice to get to know them," she says.

With this knowledge about her biological father, she says, "I feel more certain of my sense of self, and my identity. I feel more supported because I know my donor's family. I'm grateful to have found out who he was."

Most experts today agree that it's best for parents to tell kids from an early age that they are donor conceived. While the field of research into donor-conceived children and identity is still quite new, what has changed dramatically is that over the past ten to fifteen years, more parents *are* telling their kids about their origin, says Slutsky.

"As more donor-conceived individuals are told of the nature of their conception, the larger the population that can participate in research so that we can listen to, understand, and share their experiences," says Slutsky. "It used to be similar to adoption; it used to be more secretive. But with time and shifting concepts about assisted reproduction, it's become more accepted and more readily discussed."

Kramer strongly advocates telling donor-conceived kids the truth about their conception when they are very young. In her book, *Finding Our Families: A First-of-Its Kind Book for Donor-Conceived People and Their Families,* she said, "Children who know the truth and seek out their genetic relatives report having richer lives, more sources of moral support, and stronger relationships with the parents who have raised them." She believes that knowing about your origins is a right for all donor-conceived people, and that disclosure is in everyone's best interest.

That's something that Mary knows only too well. When she was thirty-seven, she discovered that she was donor conceived. A family friend told her as her father was dying of Alzheimer's; her mother had passed away years earlier.

"She said she thought I should know that he wasn't my biological father. It was quite a shock. At first, I didn't know if it was true . . . " she says. "That was twenty years ago, and I didn't know where to go or how to find any resources. I didn't know how to move forward at all."

There wasn't any way for her to verify it, since the Internet was still so new at the time. Mary, who lives in Utah, had two older siblings, but they knew nothing about it. They were her father's biological children. She learned that her mother had Rh-negative blood, which was a serious issue for women who wanted to give birth in the 1950s. If women who have Rh-negative blood become pregnant with a baby who has Rh-positive blood, and the blood mixes, the mother's immune system will create antibodies that may harm the child. This usually doesn't happen until delivery, so the first baby is normally fine. But with each pregnancy, the antibodies that are now in the mother's blood could make the baby very sick. The problems get worse with each pregnancy that is Rh-positive. Nowadays, doctors are able to prevent the mother's antibodies from harming the baby.

Her mother had told Mary that when she came along, she was her "miracle baby," but she never gave her any details about how she had conceived her.

The more people she talked to, the more Mary came to believe it was true that she was donor conceived, and she began her quest to find her biological father. In the beginning, she had very little luck, and she says she was even threatened by doctors from the sperm bank that her mother had used. No one was willing to give her any information. According to Mary, one sperm bank employee told her, "You had better stop this, or else. This is none of your business. It was your parents' choice, and you better let it go."

At the time, Mary had young children and thought it best to suspend her research. She was in touch with some other donor-conceived people through a support group that she had found, so she was able to talk to them about her concerns. Then, three years ago, she and her sister decided to have DNA tests performed on themselves. She found out that they were, in fact, half sisters. With that knowledge and her test results, Mary resumed her quest to find out the identity of her donor. By now, her kids were in their twenties, so she felt it was safe to look into her past.

Through an ancestry site that she used, Mary, now 55, discovered a first cousin on her biological father's side. This woman's father was the brother of Mary's donor, who had been a medical student when he donated his sperm, and he had Rh-negative blood. Unfortunately, her donor died in 2000, before she had a chance to meet him. He was from a small town in Utah, attended the University of Utah, and was thirty-six when she was conceived. He eventually became a doctor in Utah. Mary finally met her cousin, but she seemed hesitant to give Mary much information about her father.

A year later, Mary met another cousin on her father's side, and they became good friends. Through this woman, she was able to meet her donor's ninety-three-year-old sister. She gave Mary pictures of her biological father and told her all about him, including many stories about his life.

"It changes everything and nothing at the same time. It's good to have this info finally, at my age. I never thought I would figure it out. But you're still not with family; you're still an outsider. Although they were warm and kind and told me about their summer camping trips, and a maternal grandmother who was a pianist, it was bittersweet. My social father and I were not at all close. I think he had real issues with [using a donor]. It was a secret that he planned to never tell me. I still feel anger about that. I guess they were doing what they thought was best," she says.

Just recently, Mary had another match on an ancestry site from someone who might be related to her and her donor. She turned out to be her biological niece. Mary believes that she was born to her donor's son.

Learning that her parents lied to her and her sibling has been hard on her sister as well (her brother has since passed away). "The biggest issue has been that we thought we knew our mother, and for her to keep this huge secret was shocking to us. I believe that she had opportunities to tell me. I feel strongly about parents telling their children the truth. I wish I had heard it from my parents, not a stranger. It was really devastating to me," she says.

Mary's parents might not have told her the truth about her origin because when she was born (in the 1950s), fertility doctors were advising couples not to tell their children about their conception because they believed it was for the best. Back then, no one could have envisioned the emergence of DNA tests that would tell someone who their biological parents were—or were not.

Finding out that you are donor conceived is one thing, but for some children, learning that they now have dozens of half siblings can be quite another. Some children may find the shear numbers are daunting in terms of making sense of their identity and what "family" means for them. This is particularly an issue in the United States, which essentially has no limits on how many children a donor can conceive, merely guidelines that suggest the number be capped at twenty-five children per donor (per population area of 800,000). Of course, we know this number is not realistic, since there are already donors with seventy-five and even 200 children now. So what does being one of so many unknown offspring do to a child's perception of himself? What does it do to someone's individuality? For a child to develop a positive sense of who they are, says Slutsky, they need to feel they are unique individuals, with their own life story. They need to understand that they are different from others, with their own interests and talents.

"By not having limits (on sperm donors), we are asking people to struggle with making sense of their own identities amid kinship networks in a way that no one in human history has ever had to do before," said Elizabeth Marquardt of the Center for Marriage and Families, Institute for American Values.

When Slutsky and her fellow researchers asked children in their study how they felt about having multiple siblings, they were given a range of responses: a few kids who had a lot of half siblings said they liked it. They were happy to be able to pick and choose who they wanted to be close to within their group. Others, with smaller groups of around six children, said they had become their own family unit. Very often, the donor siblings all got along, she says, adding that none of them said it confuses their sense of who they are. But, she says, having seventy-five siblings is a very different experience from having ten.

"A lot of people are feeling their way through this territory. It's interesting to see how they're conceptualizing these other people," she says.

That's what Amy is doing. She used one sperm donor to have her daughter, now eighteen, and another one to have her son, who is now twelve. She knew that her daughter had a few half siblings, but she was curious about how many half siblings her son had and speculated that the number could be high. She believed her son's donor was extremely popular—he was a doctor, tall, with blond hair and blue eyes. She knew of a few other women who had purchased her donor's sperm, but she didn't know the total number of children he had produced. Amy worried that the number could be high—as many as one hundred or 150 kids. She was nervous about finding out.

We met at a local bar to talk about her experiences using sperm donors. An attractive blond who is 51 and gay, Amy had been open with her kids right from the start about where they came from. Before they were even old enough to understand, she had begun using language like "donor" and "conceived." As her kids grew, the idea that they had been born through a sperm donor seemed like no big deal to them. Her daughter had connected with a few of her half siblings on Facebook, and they had an uncanny resemblance to each other, but she wasn't really interested in meeting them or pursuing a relationship any further than occasional online messages.

While we sat together sipping cocktails, Amy decided to visit the Donor Sibling Registry website to find out about her children's siblings, but she had forgotten the donor's identifying number for her son's donor. There were eight other parents who had used the same donor who were in a closed online group, so she instant-messaged one of them on Facebook for the donor number. It was tense as we waited for a response.

"I can't believe I forgot his number!" she said, sheepishly, adding, "If someone told me that I had a hundred half siblings, it would make me feel so disconnected from my identity."

Her eyes were teary as she thought about what this would mean for her son. When she had chosen her son's donor from Fairfax Cryobank, she wanted the best candidate she could find to father her child. She even paid a premium for the sperm, based on the donor's education—the fact that he attended medical school. "If you're going to have a baby, you want the best sperm that you can get, right?" It turned out that she had even looked into buying sperm from Donor B155A, who had a similar profile (Fairfax sold sperm from both donors), but had settled on a different one. Amy was initially disappointed because she wasn't able to purchase more of her daughter's donor sperm for her son. But now, she says, it doesn't matter. "I wouldn't have them any other way."

So why do people spend so much time and effort (and money) trying to find their family and their biological relatives?

Bryan Sykes, the Oxford University geneticist, has a theory: "There's a very deep feeling about finding your ancestors. I think it goes back to the fact that most of our evolution was spent in different circumstances," he says. Thousands of years ago, when our ancestors were hunter-gatherers, we depended heavily on our families to survive. Sykes believes that our genes evolved to create an extremely strong link between relatives, thus the inherent desire to find our family members.

Certainly, Sykes' theory is bolstered by the business end of this impulse, at least anecdotally. In 2012, for instance, the website Ancestry.

com was sold for $1.6 billion. The site has more than 2 million users and has grown in popularity since it launched in 1996. Anthropologists believe that our interest in ancestry relates to evolution. Since family members share genes, helping your kin to reproduce is a way to pass on your genes, something known as "kin selection."[3] And finding your ancestors lets people feel more connected in an otherwise large and crowded world, where social media can make you feel like a number.

While we were at the bar, Amy found an answer to her question about the number of siblings that her daughter had: it was thirteen. That didn't seem too bad. But then she found out the number of half siblings her son had: forty. She didn't seem to know how to react to this information—it was more than she had hoped for, but less than she had feared. She would get used to it eventually, she said, but she still found forty to be a disturbingly large number.

While Amy was troubled at the thought of dozens of half siblings for her kids, many mothers who used sperm donors, such as Susanna Wahl, don't feel that it's a problem. In fact, Susanna thinks it's a good thing for her children to have family all over the country—and the world, for that matter. She plans to visit Cynthia Daily's family in Maryland again soon, so that her son, Eric, and Cynthia's son, Mark, can further cement their close relationship. She believes that by knowing who his half siblings are, Eric will one day better understand who he is.

8

Suddenly Sisters

Accidental Meetings and the Health Risks of Anonymous Donors

When she was twelve, Zoe was excited to go to sleepaway camp for the first time. She hoped she'd make some new friends and looked forward to being away from her home in San Francisco and exploring someplace new. As soon as she got to camp, she met another girl in her cabin named Remy. They gravitated toward each other, becoming instant friends.

One day, while the campers were hiking in the Yosemite Valley, Zoe started telling her friend her life story, including that she had been born through a sperm donor. When they got back to their cabins, Remy had a message from her best friend back home. That got her synapses firing: she realized how much her two friends had in common. They both had sandy blond hair, light blue eyes, and similar mouths and skin tone. The two girls even acted alike—they were both adventurous and brave.

Remy told her new friend that she reminded her of her best friend back home. She recognized her friend in Zoe's face, and in her energy. Even their mannerisms were similar. She kept saying, "You remind me of my best friend!" Then she remembered that her friend had also been born through a donor. Could they possibly be sisters? She wondered. . . .

When camp ended and they were saying goodbye, Remy asked Zoe for her number. As the girl began writing her phone number, she shouted, "Your donor number!" She wanted to find out for herself if the two girls were sisters. Zoe's mother had had her memorize her donor number just in case she ever met a boy that she wanted to date, who might turn out to be a half brother.

"My daughter knows her donor number for this very reason," says Zoe's mother, Susan Frankel, a fifty-something single mother who has long, strawberry-blond hair and a warm, friendly way about her. "She's been in school with numerous kids who have donor (fathers). She's had crushes on boys who are donor conceived. It's part of the sex-ed here in San Francisco."

As soon as Remy's mother picked her up, she blurted out her news and begged to be taken to her friend's house right way, so she could confirm her suspicions.

When they arrived, Remy found that her friend was distracted by her new baby brother. After a few minutes, she couldn't take it anymore and blurted out, "Sophia, I think I found your half sister!" At first, no one said anything. Then, Remy told her Zoe's donor number. Everyone looked shocked. Sophia had also memorized her donor number. She ran to one of her mothers and yelled, "I have a sister!" She was thrilled. As soon as Remy arrived at home, she called her new friend and left her a message.

"Within an hour of getting off the bus, I had a phone call from my friend. She said, 'Zoe, I found your sister!' I didn't believe it at first. I thought, there's no way it's possible. I was shocked, but also super excited to have a half sister my age," says Zoe.

These two girls who, until a few days before, had no idea of the other's existence, were indeed half sisters. When Susan brought Zoe to meet her sister, the mothers just stared at the girls, for they looked so much alike. Sophia said there was an immediate bond and she felt as though she'd known Zoe for a long time.

Zoe says the meeting was awkward at first, but after a little while, they relaxed. "We obviously looked really similar. We have the same hair color, the same shape face and eyes, and even the same mouth and nose. I remember it being really awkward and really cool at the same time," she says. "Now, I call her my sister."

The story of Zoe and Sophia's meeting is remarkable. To think that two half sisters—two girls born through the same sperm donor—could meet each other is incredible.

There have been other cases of half siblings meeting accidentally, including two half sisters who met in 2014 while searching for a roommate at Tulane University in Louisiana. They both had similar backgrounds—lesbian moms who had used a sperm donor—but more importantly, they looked a lot alike. Both girls have long, curly brown hair, identical noses, and dimpled chins. They also had comparable interests, and the same taste in clothing. After joking for a semester about being "sisters," they finally asked their moms for their donor numbers and found out that they actually *were* half sisters. Their mothers had used a Colombian sperm donor who they said was "handsome, athletic, and intelligent." Now, the girls are getting used to the idea of being sisters.

Families are meeting accidentally in all kinds of ways. Cynthia Daily, whose son is part of the group of 150 children, says there were a few parents from her group who met by chance while working for the same company in the Washington, D.C., area (the sperm was purchased nearby, in Virginia).

Yet there is a darker side to encounters such as the ones above. The fact that children have to be taught to memorize their donor numbers to avoid accidentally dating or having sex with a half brother or sister is chilling.

Accidental incest among half siblings could have disturbing consequences, leading to genetic abnormalities and other serious health problems. While experts say the chances of half brothers and sisters having consanguineous relations with each other by accident are quite slim, there is a very real fear among some donor-conceived children that it could happen to them.

Still, there are many who say that limiting the number of children born to each sperm donor would help to avoid the problem of accidental incest among half siblings, cousins, or other relatives. Wendy Kramer says that donor limits would also make it less likely that donors and siblings would have the challenge of meeting and getting to know a large number of relatives. The biggest donor sibling group on the DSR (Susanna Wahl's group) is now believed to be at 200 children, and there is a donor listed on the site who has so far connected with seventy-five of his offspring. There is little tracking of births by sperm banks and clinics (mothers are asked to self-report births to the clinics, but not all do so), so no one is keeping count of how many children each sperm donor is producing. Kramer believes there may be donor sibling groups with even larger numbers of children than Susanna's—many of the big groups have taken their names off public websites to avoid an invasion of privacy. Some women who used sperm banks have been shocked to find out how many offspring their donors had produced.

Andrea chose a sperm donor through New England Cryogenic. She knew that he hadn't donated for long, so she expected low numbers of children. But when she went on the DSR a few years later to check how many offspring he had, she was horrified to discover that her daughter's donor-sibling group consisted of sixty-one children. In fact, only six of the sixty-one children were conceived using her sperm bank; unbeknownst to her, the donor had also donated multiple times each week for years at Fairfax Cryobank in Virginia. She was able to contact her donor, and she expressed her concern over how long he had donated sperm.

"He said that he was a popular donor and that the clinic had too much financial incentive to set limits. Clearly, he understood that the numbers of conceived children could get very high, yet he hadn't thought through how it might impact the children," she says. "I am so outraged by the lack of clinic regulations."

Andrea believes that her donor wasn't honest with the sperm banks when he was asked if he'd donated previously.

"I have a three-and-a-half-year-old daughter. I will honestly answer any questions from her, based on what seems appropriate, developmentally. I can't even imagine what it might be like for her to learn the truth about how many children were conceived using the same donor. We have met two families, though of course I haven't tried to explain the relationship. Over the years, I have had email contact with other families as well. It helps to have the advice and support of those who have gone down similar paths, as well as to share pictures and stories about our children," she says.

Critics say this country's five-billion-dollar fertility industry is largely unregulated, with an "anything goes" attitude. It's disturbing to think that these companies are in the business of making human beings and playing with the genetic consequences—and no one is watching them. With no real limits on how many offspring a sperm donor may have, one sperm donor can father dozens, if not hundreds, of children, as in the case of Donor B155A. The American Society for Reproductive Medicine, a professional organization, has issued guidelines recommending that individual donors be restricted to twenty-five births per population of 800,000—but those are merely guidelines. No one is enforcing them.

Arthur Caplan, an outspoken and influential bioethicist, has been complaining about the lack of regulation in the reproductive industry for the past twenty-five years. "Handling reproductive materials requires much more oversight and control than we have in place now," says Caplan, who leads the Division of Medical Ethics at New York University Langone Medical Center, and is also a professor there. "When it comes to whether or not people are passing on problems to their children, the question is, whose interest should come first? Normally, the court puts the interest of the child first, but with this technology, we're in a difficult bind. Is any disability so bad that it's better not to be born at all? The courts and legislators don't want to go there. If you're asking is it better off not to be born, then you're in a thorny disabilities discussion."

There are few restrictions on how often men may donate sperm, so serial donors can go from sperm bank to sperm bank, making money by selling their sperm. Most commercial sperm banks don't track who the donors are, nor how much of their sperm is being sold, nor how many children each donor produces. The only way they keep tabs on the number of offspring now is by asking women to report pregnancies and live births to the clinics, but they aren't required to do so and not all comply.

Kramer believes that only 20 to 40 percent of mothers inform the sperm banks about their births. No one even knows how many children are born each year through assisted reproduction, since there is no government entity that keeps track of that, either.

"We thought this was an ethical, responsible industry. But they're just money-making sperm sellers. There's no care or thought for the person being born—it's just about selling sperm and eggs," says Kramer, a fierce critic of the industry. "It's always about money. And liability. They're afraid that if we connect people (donor siblings) they'd know there were seventy-five kids. The more secretive they can keep it, the more liability they can protect."

There are now more calls for legal limits on how many children a sperm donor may have in the U.S., as many other countries already do. Naomi Cahn, a George Washington University law professor who specializes in fertility issues, says it's time for the industry to be regulated. For instance, she believes that children should be able to find out who their donors are, just as adoptees are starting to gain more rights to information about their birth parents.

"There's been an incredible movement toward openness in the adoption world. States are moving toward complete disclosure with respect to children's birth certificates. Now, people can try to find out who their birth parents are," she says. In New Jersey, adopted people are now allowed to obtain their original birth certificates containing information about their parents, under a new law that went into effect January 1, 2017.

Cahn believes the U.S. should move in the same direction as other countries, such as Britain, France, and Sweden, which have strict limits on how many offspring a donor may have. In Britain, the birth of the first "test-tube baby" in 1978, Louise Brown, sparked a debate over the future implications of in vitro fertilization. So a committee was formed, led by Mary Warnock, a noted English philosopher, to examine the use of assisted reproduction and the issues involved. The landmark Warnock Report recommended the formation of a government agency to regulate the sale of human sperm and embryos. It also suggested that strict limits be imposed on the number of children that a donor could have.

Warnock says that during the committee's research, they came across some bizarre examples of sperm donation, including one man, a postman in Leicester, whose sperm storage lab was his own kitchen refrigerator and who supplied all the sperm himself, charging a hefty fee for it.

"We had a lot of evidence to support regulation of AID (Artificial Insemination by Donor) as well as IVF. The risk of siblings unknown to themselves marrying and having children round Leicester was very high. This in itself carried health risks, and of course no one had any idea what faulty genes the postman and others like him might carry," explains Warnock, who is now in her nineties.

Many critics of the U.S. industry believe that the UK system could be a model for assisted reproduction practices here. The Human Fertilisation and Embryology Authority (HFEA), set up in 1991, licenses and monitors all UK fertility clinics, including those that provide IVF treatments, artificial insemination, and storage of eggs, sperm, and embryos. It also oversees all research regarding human embryos and maintains a database of every IVF treatment, as well as the use of all donated sperm and eggs.

Under the authority, sperm donors may not donate to more than ten families (the families may have more than one child using the same sperm), and sperm donors are only paid thirty-five British pounds for each visit, or about $50 (about a third of what U.S. donors make). The authority regularly reviews and revises its laws: in 2008, the HFEA decided that both partners in same-sex relationships should be recognized as legal parents of children who were conceived through assisted reproduction. Any changes to a donor's health are also updated in his or her profile, so that families may access this important information. (This is also supposed to be done in the U.S., but donors don't always provide updates.)

And in 2004, the HFEA ruled that all donor-conceived children in the UK could access the identity of their sperm, egg, or embryo donor, including their name and last-known address, once they turned eighteen. That means that there are no longer anonymous sperm donors in the UK—something that has become a contentious issue in the U.S.

So far, donor anonymity has been banned in Austria, Finland, Germany, The Netherlands, New South Wales, New Zealand, Norway, Sweden, Switzerland, the UK, and Western Australia, according to the DSR. In February 2016, the state of Victoria in Southeast Australia took the unprecedented step of allowing *all* donor-conceived people there to gain access to identifying information about their donors and heritage, no matter when they were born. That means that even donors who believed they were donating anonymously twenty years ago will now be known to their offspring (as long as the information is available). The Victoria Legislative Council says that all donor-conceived Victorians should have the right to information about their heritage.

Fertility industry spokespeople in the U.S. say that both donors and parents continue to ask for donor anonymity. But wouldn't most donor-conceived children rather have a choice as to whether or not they'd like information on their donor, or the ability to contact him when they are older? And while some say that an end to donor anonymity could lead to a shortage in donors, Wendy Kramer and others do not believe that to be the case. She says that figures kept on sperm donors by the UK's HFEA shows that in 1992 there were 375 sperm donors there, but by 2013, there were actually more: 586. Anonymity for sperm donors there was ended in 2005.

Perhaps more importantly, the issue of donor anonymity may soon become obsolete. Since Ryan found his donor a decade ago, more and more donor-conceived children have been able to identify and contact their sperm donors, often with the help of the Donor Sibling Registry.

"I can't help but wonder when the sperm banks and egg clinics will start acknowledging that there is no such thing as guaranteed donor anonymity," says Wendy.

She believes that the fertility industry has done its utmost to keep donor offspring and their biological fathers from getting to know one another, adding that some clinics will refuse to give donors their identifying donor number, so they can never contact their children, even if they want to. Wendy also thinks that some sperm banks will sometimes not connect donors and offspring, even when they both request it.

Susan Frankel and her daughter, Zoe, were lucky; they were able to meet some half siblings, as well as their donor.

After Zoe connected with her half sister through her camp friend, they stayed in touch. In fact, the girls became very close, and their families are now extended families for each other. Sophia's family lives just across the San Francisco Bay, and both girls are Jewish with mothers who are lesbians. When Zoe had a bat mitzvah, she asked her sister, Sophia, to participate as a family member. The half sisters are only six months apart in age, and they have a lot in common: they both love soccer, roller coasters, being adventurous, and laughing a lot. They also like to draw, and even went to camp together. They're both thrilled to have the sister that they always wanted.

Susan, who is a marriage and family therapist in San Francisco, had Zoe with her former partner. She felt it was important to help her daughter find her donor siblings, but she believed that meeting one's half sisters and half brothers was less complex than meeting one's donor. Yet, Zoe did think about him a lot. When she was six years old, she wrote her donor a letter on Father's Day. And every year at school, she would make an art project for him on Father's Day and keep it in a box in her room, for the day she would finally meet her biological father and give it to him.

"I'd always been curious about him and read his [donor] profile a million times when I was younger," says Zoe, who is now twenty-three. "My mom and I would flip through the pages together."

Her mother asked the sperm bank if they would pass on the letter, and also if he would answer any questions that her daughter might have. Susan believes they passed on the letter, but says that afterward, they cut off all communication with her.

Soon after, Susan happened to be reading an anonymous posting by a donor on the Donor Sibling Registry, and she suddenly had the feeling that this was her donor. He had written about the quandary that he found himself in: he wanted to meet his offspring, but he felt like he couldn't because he was married, with kids of his own. He wrote that he was interested in talking to other donors about the issues they dealt with.

"I just had a gut feeling that it was him, based on the language that he used," says Susan. "I chose him as a donor because in his profile, he wrote lovingly about his interest in children and how becoming a father would change his life."

She contacted Wendy Kramer to ask if she could confirm that he was her donor, based on her donor number. Wendy told her, "Don't hold your breath. I have fifty women who called and asked me the same thing." But fifteen minutes later, she called Susan back and said, "Are you sitting down? He *is* your donor." Susan remembers thinking, "I was like, 'Oh my God, Yes!' and, 'Oh my God, No!'"

Through Wendy, her donor agreed to receive a letter from Susan. He wrote back, tentative at first, because he knew his wife was uncomfortable with the situation. Susan remembers that he was one of the older donors on the site, and that he seemed mature.

For nearly two years, they corresponded with each other, but Susan didn't tell Zoe. She decided to keep it to herself until her daughter was ready to connect with her biological father herself. Susan also wanted to gather information on him, just in case something happened. She speculated that his wife must have agreed to his decision to donate, but that, like all good things, it was nice in theory—until the kids he had helped to create grew up and wanted access to him.

When Zoe turned thirteen, she traveled to Israel, and Susan thought it was a good time to try and meet her donor—without her daughter present. "I was anxious about it. We were breaking the rules (about when they could meet), and I didn't want him to have any paternity access to my daughter. I wanted to avoid a lot of heartache," she says. He was an open donor, but she had agreed when she purchased his sperm that her daughter wouldn't contact him until she turned eighteen.

Susan and her donor, Randy, decided to meet at a café in San Francisco, where he also lived. The meeting was both wonderful and strange, she remembers.

"I didn't know what to say, except to thank him for the gift he gave me. I was very grateful to him," she says. "I think he's a good guy. He wanted to do something wonderful for other people."

She was surprised to find that she didn't see her daughter reflected in her father. And though she found him to be warm and pleasant, she wanted to be sure that they maintained their boundaries.

Randy says he began donating sperm in 1990, after his first son was born. He was a cute little boy, who even made it onto the cover of a few parenting magazines when he was young. Randy and his wife were living in San Francisco, and he was working as an artist, so money was tight. Some of their friends were lesbian couples who had used sperm donors to have children, and they encouraged him to donate. At the time, he was thirty-eight and had no idea how the process worked.

"At first, I thought, 'No way.' But once it was explained to me, and I understood that I'd be helping infertile couples and lesbians, it became more understandable," he says.

He went through all the necessary testing, including psychological testing and physicals. Then he had to write a statement about why he planned to donate his sperm. He said that his child was such a joy to him that he wanted to help others to experience the same thing. He found that his sperm count was pretty high—the sperm bank employees told him he was going to be a popular donor.

At the time, Randy's wife was fine with his decision to donate.

"Both of us didn't really think of what was to come. None of the men donating sperm at the time thought about the women who were buying their sperm, or what the kids might feel," he says.

They treated him well at the sperm bank, giving him a pat on the back each time he came in. Randy went there twice a week for the next two years, making $40 to $50 each time he donated. The extra income—about $400 a month—was helpful, especially with a small child to care for. Since the bank was mainly using fresh donations back then, there were times that he would cross paths with the person who was purchasing his sperm—even though he was supposed to be anonymous. He believes they divided up each of his donations into twelve to fifteen separate samples as a way for the bank to increase its profit margin.

When he was forty, he was told to stop donating because he was too old. He and his wife had another son, and he didn't think much about his sperm-donation years. He didn't imagine there was anything further he could do. Then he learned about a website that could connect donors and their offspring (the Donor Sibling Registry) and that brought it all back into his consciousness. After connecting with Wendy Kramer, he found out that one of the mothers who had bought his sperm wanted to contact him. It was Susan Frankel. After exchanging emails for a while, he agreed to meet her.

"She told me that her daughter, Zoe, had a psychological need to know who her biological father was. I was in shock. But I was feeling like, if I could put an end to her pain, I would do that," he says.

He decided not to tell his wife, who was starting to develop some issues about the whole sperm-donation experience. He doesn't remember much about that meeting, but he was curious to meet his daughter, Zoe.

Susan was cautious. "We both had a lot to protect—our families." They decided that when Zoe returned from her trip, they would let her decide if she wanted to meet her father.

"I came home from school one day, and she told me that she'd found my donor and that we could correspond. Ever since I was young, I'd been interested in finding out who he was," remembers Zoe.

So she and Randy emailed for a little while, until they finally arranged to meet—at an ice cream parlor in the city. Susan recounts how it felt at first:

"It was awkward. He just stared at her—he didn't know what to do with her for a long time," Susan remembers.

Zoe remembers feeling uncomfortable during the meeting. But she could tell that they looked a lot alike: they had the same curly, dirty-blond hair and blue eyes. "It was strange meeting someone who made me, and I didn't know him," she says.

Zoe had brought the box of things that she'd made for him for every Father's Day since she was two years old—all the cards and art projects—and when she gave it to Randy, he suddenly began to cry. "I remember it felt good to give it to him, and I left wanting to see him again," she says.

Randy remembers feeling overwhelmed by emotion at the encounter with the daughter that he'd never known before. He noticed similarities in their looks—she had his eyes, and his curly hair, and a mole on her face.

"I just fell in love with Zoe. I didn't know I'd have this reaction to meeting her in person . . . just knowing that I'd created her, I had this emotional bond," he says. "She gave me some of the things that she'd made since preschool, and it hit me. Even right now, talking about it, it's an emotional moment. I still have the box she gave me—I keep them in a safe place." He gets choked up as he talks about it. "It was very emotional. Here was my kid, and I felt like her father. And even though we only lived a few blocks away from each other, I hadn't played a big part in her life."

That night when he went home, he cried, overwhelmed by the emotion of it all. "I thought, what am I going to do now? This was all unknown. I couldn't be a part of her life. I thought, wow, this could be a problem if I have a busload of kids or more. Just trying to remember all their birthdays. . . . "

They met a few more times, but Susan found it uncomfortable because she knew that Randy was keeping it a secret from his wife. "It felt like an affair," she remembers. "Then it became a big mess."

When Randy finally told his wife about Zoe, it was the beginning of the end of their marriage.

She felt threatened by this new person—his child—in her husband's life. Randy was overcome.

"She said, 'If a kid shows up here, I'll kick them down the stairs.' That was not acceptable to me. But she's entitled to feel that way. It would be difficult for any woman to find out her husband has forty kids out there, and that some of them want to know me. It's a big thing to ask," he says. They had been assured by the sperm bank that the children he helped to create would never reach out to him or want a relationship with him. Obviously, that wasn't the case, he says.

Then things became even more complicated—and strange.

At the time, Zoe was occasionally emailing her father photos of herself, at his request. One day, his youngest child walked by while he was looking at one of her pictures, and said, "Why do you have a picture of Zoe on your computer?" It turned out that Zoe had been his son's camp counselor. San Francisco, it seemed, was a *very* small place.

Zoe had taught at a local circus summer camp for a few years and remembers a little boy there who everyone said looked just like her. They had the same curly, blond hair and similar looks. In fact, the other campers and counselors would joke that they must be brother and sister, but Zoe would laugh it off. She never imagined that her donor would have his own children who lived nearby; she thought any of her half siblings would have moms who were single or lesbians, like hers.

That's when Randy finally told his children about Zoe. And she discovered that, in addition to the half brother she already knew, who was several years younger than her, she had another half brother who was five years older. Eventually, they became friendly, and he even started to treat Zoe like he was her older brother for a time, inviting her and her mom to his school play and keeping in touch.

Randy says his boys had an easier time than his wife did with the whole situation. "It's the adults who have the problems. The kids seemed OK with it all," he says. Growing up in San Francisco, his boys had several classmates who were donor kids, so they were used to the idea. He thinks the news about Zoe even made them feel a little special.

Because Randy's wife was so unhappy about Zoe's presence in his life, the situation became complex, Susan says. Zoe backed off, trying to give Randy and his wife some space to work things out. But they couldn't, and, eventually, they divorced.

Since going to college, Zoe and her father talk to each other only occasionally, keeping in touch on Facebook. But they rarely see each other, which makes him sad. Zoe understands this.

"He's someone I care about, and I'm interested in his well-being, but I wouldn't think of him as a family member," says Zoe. "Meeting him satisfied my curiosity. I never expected him to be a father to me—I didn't desire a father figure. I just wanted to know who he was and what he looked like and if we had similarities. It was interesting to see what piece fit in his puzzle."

She was curious to find out where she got her curly hair and blue eyes and was surprised that they both have a "weirdly similar laugh." Meeting him answered questions she had about herself, but it didn't change her life.

It can be hard not to be disappointed when you meet your biological father, especially when there are so many expectations, says her mother, Susan. "I think he was very touched and wanted a relationship with her, but it was very complicated. He was very moved that his progeny wanted to meet him. In theory, it's one thing; but in reality, it's another. I felt sad that his circumstances were so complex for him that it made it difficult for him to develop a relationship with her. He kept saying, 'I'm so sorry I can't see you, and that I can't invite you to this.' He felt guilty. I finally had to say, stop saying sorry. He's a good person, with a big heart. I think it's important for her to know that, and she does. She knows where he is if she needs him."

Since meeting Zoe, Randy has met two of his other offspring— daughters who are close in age to Zoe, including the half sister Zoe stumbled across through sleepaway camp. His boys met these new half sisters as well. Randy believes that all of his offspring are great kids, with no issues. He found out through Zoe that he probably has children in Mexico as well and was shocked to learn that the sperm bank had sent his genetic material all over the world.

And while he doesn't have any regrets about donating sperm, Randy does regret that it caused the breakup of his marriage.

Now sixty-four, he would tell any man who is considering becoming a sperm donor to think very carefully about what they are doing. "There's no way they can ensure your privacy any more. It's easy to find out who you are. Your identity will be known much sooner than you think . . . And what you feel now may change. You may find out, like I did, that you have emotions for these kids. These emotions may be one-sided, and that's a painful thing to find out. It can complicate your life much more than you'd ever imagine," he says.

He *is* unhappy that he and Zoe aren't closer. "She's something else. I wish we had more contact, but now she's building her life."

As a therapist, Susan understands Randy's feelings about her daughter. Eventually, Zoe started to connect with and meet some of her other half siblings, and even went along when one of them wanted to meet their father. The relationships that Zoe has developed with them are much more straightforward. There's either chemistry or there isn't.

"With the sibling relationships, there's so much more possibility. It's a win-win when there's a small group—there's a lot of love to go around," says Susan. She and her daughter have become close with a few of the families, celebrating holidays together, going to the movies, and even taking trips to Hawaii.

"The discovery of her siblings was quite wild. The kids would just stare at each other and compare their hands and their feet. A couple even have a bent finger," says Susan. "I like that she has options, since I didn't give her a sibling, and my brother doesn't have kids. But it was cozy when we knew about ten or fifteen half siblings—I don't want there to be fifty or a hundred."

Currently, Zoe has twenty-eight reported siblings and has met fourteen of them. She keeps in touch with most of them on Facebook but is still close with Sophia, the sister she met through camp. "It's strange to think that I have a bunch of genetic siblings out there, and that I could run into them at anytime—especially since it's happened to me twice already!" She feels that twenty-eight siblings is plenty.

"We used to have get-togethers with our half siblings, and I felt like eight kids was a lot! I think it's cool to have all these half brothers and sisters, but it's definitely not the norm," she says, adding that when people hear how many half siblings she has, they're pretty shocked. Still, growing up in San Francisco has inured her to thinking that her life is strange in any way, especially since some of her friends were also born through sperm donors.

Susan and some of the other parents in her donor-sibling group were upset, however, when they learned that some of her donor's sperm had been sold through a sperm bank in Mexico, even though they had been promised that the number of children would be kept low.

"It's so unethical, what the banks did. It's one thing if they told us that they would use the sperm however they chose, but they lied. They told us there would only be ten families. But then there were fifteen families. Then they started selling his sperm as if he was an unknown donor. It's a big money-maker, and we all know why they're doing it. These kids don't want to have thirty siblings. Even my daughter, who is very extroverted, doesn't want that," she says.

Susan believes the industry should be regulated and that offspring of sperm donors should be limited to ten families. She also thinks that sperm donors should not be anonymous, and that it's not fair to make decisions for children about these things before they are born. As a therapist who has counseled families who used assisted reproduction, she believes that sperm banks need to better prepare sperm donors and those who use them to be aware of the issues they may be dealing with.

For instance, there is growing concern among parents, donors, and medical experts that genes for rare diseases could be spread more widely through the population through sperm donation. Today, men are donating sperm with little genetic testing performed on them, so that babies are being born with serious genetic illnesses, such as cystic fibrosis and autism.[1]

Even with the industry's current comprehensive health screenings for prospective donors, genetic diseases can go undetected. Take Sharine and Brian Kretchmar of Yukon, Oklahoma. Sharine had trouble conceiving a baby, so their doctor advised them to try a sperm donor. They carefully looked into various sperm banks and donors until they found the man who they believed was the right fit for them: a family man who was a Christian, with a clean bill of health. The couple purchased his sperm through the New England Cryogenic Center in Boston, and they were reassured that their donor had been tested for any serious genetic conditions.

Under the Food and Drug Administration, sperm donors are required to be tested for communicable and infectious diseases, but, surprisingly, testing for genetic diseases is *not* required. Donors are screened at the discretion of the sperm banks for common genetic conditions, such as cystic fibrosis and spinal muscular atrophy, as recommended by the American Society for Reproductive Medicine. The banks generally screen the donor, but not his sperm. Still, sperm banks have no obligation to test its donors, and the degree of genetic testing that's performed varies.

Critics of the fertility industry say that genetic testing should be mandatory for all donors, and that medical testing should be consistent for all sperm banks. That makes sense.

Many donor families are asking for more information on the health of their donors, as well as on the other children conceived with the donor's sperm. Some have discovered that their donors weren't honest when they reported their health histories to their sperm bank, including failing to tell them about cancer or other serious illnesses in their families. Others believe that their sperm banks failed to inform them when their sperm donor was ill or changed his medical profile.

After Sharine Kretchmar gave birth to their son, Jaxon, in 2010, the couple was ecstatic. But soon, the baby began to show signs that something was seriously wrong. When he failed to have a bowel movement in the first couple of days after being born, he was rushed in to surgery. The news wasn't good: the doctors believed that Jaxon could have cystic fibrosis.

Sharine and Brian were devastated.

"We knew at that point in time that we had bigger problems," says Sharine. "We knew there wasn't a way around denial at that point. I'm a nurse, so I kind of felt like I knew too much. But I don't think you ever realize . . . until it hits you. Until you actually live it out each day."

They couldn't believe that the doctors could be right, because they knew that their donor had been tested for cystic fibrosis. They were wrong. It turned out that Jaxon carried the genes for cystic fibrosis, and that he had inherited them from both his mother *and* his donor. Sharine did not know that she was a carrier. Their donor, they discovered, probably had not been tested for the disease because the sperm was so old—it had been donated at Rocky Mountain Cryogenics, a sperm bank in Wyoming, twenty years earlier. When that sperm bank closed, the gametes were sold off to New England Cryogenic Center. The Kretchmars were never told that their sperm had come from a different sperm bank, nor that it was so old. A New England Cryogenic Center (NECC) spokeswoman said that her bank had been given proof that the donor had been tested for the disease, but that she believed that the testing had been faulty. The Kretchmars sued the sperm bank and have since settled. Sharine says she was shocked by what she learned about the industry:

"We learned that although our claims could only be with NECC, this exact sort of thing continues to happen with other cryobanks. We left NECC in a regulation chokehold of sorts. We know it's impossible to prevent all genetic illnesses, but it will never be in their interest for a child of their donors to be born with anything that is neglectfully preventable. We learned that there are nearly no laws in place to protect families like us, or children like Jaxon. For an industry whose basis is assisting the creation of life, they have very little regard for life. My son is only viewed by them as a bad business transaction," says Sharine.

Jaxon's illness has been devastating to the family. Now six years old, he has to take around forty pills each day to help deal with his disease. For three to four hours each day, he has to wear a special vest that shakes his airway and helps to loosen the thick, sticky mucous that settles in his lungs. His parents give him several nebulizer treatments daily, plus inhalers, and nutritional supplements and a multitude of sinus rinses and sprays. He's had to undergo six surgeries; two in the past year due to sinus polyps and infection related to his disease. Cystic fibrosis is a progressive disease; the life expectancy for those with the disorder is usually about thirty-seven years.

"Jaxon is doing well and he works very hard to stay that way. Cystic fibrosis definitely takes its toll on him, and we couldn't be more proud of the little person he is becoming. Jaxon loves playing soccer and is a green belt in tae kwon do. Staying active helps to keep his lungs healthy. He is very responsible with his routine. It has just become a way of life for him." Jaxon often wears a mask at school to cut down on germs. He isn't scared of blood draws, x-rays, or shots. Sometimes he will show the nurse right where to put the needle. He did give his parents a bit of a scare recently when he so very calmly told his teacher he couldn't breathe and his chest hurt. He was very quickly developing pneumonia. They worked around the clock doing treatments every few hours for two weeks in order to avoid a hospital stay. "That was a bit of a stressful time. His lung function decreased dramatically and we are still working to fully regain it," says Sharine. "Brian and I still work opposite schedules so one of us can be home with him. We also try to have a somewhat normal life, but that just isn't our reality. Managing his CF is definitely a consuming full-time job itself."

Sharine says another mother who had a child through a sperm bank, who now has cystic fibrosis, has contacted her. "She cried for hours when we first talked. She was so grateful that she wasn't the first and she wasn't alone like I was. Although she wished she had known earlier, she was still very grateful that we put ourselves out there enough to be heard. It just reaffirmed to me that my heart wasn't settled and more awareness needed to be raised," she says.

She and her husband have been working to do just that, with the hope that they can prevent another family from going through what they have, and to save a child from living a life of medical hardship. They travel throughout their home state of Oklahoma, speaking and fundraising for research into the disease, and Sharine has attended national conferences with the Cystic Fibrosis Foundation. In 2014, Jaxon was named the 2014 Oklahoma Child Ambassador for the Cystic Fibrosis Foundation.

"We more than obviously proved that testing wasn't being done on their products, but it wasn't until we were able to prove that they intentionally changed documents to better market their products did they actually take us very seriously. The industry as a whole thrives on getting away with as much as they possibly can, covering up what they can, and hoping for just a slap on the wrist if they get caught. Until they are truly regulated and more standards are put in place, children and families will pay the price.

"Building a good case against NECC was like having to invent the wheel for our attorneys, they did just that and made it spin. Now as new cases arise, at least they can continue to make it spin, hopefully a little easier for the next family," says Sharine.

Unfortunately, there are other cases like that out there. Children are inheriting serious genetic conditions from their sperm donors, including heart defects and spinal muscular atrophy. One family is dealing with Long QT syndrome, a rare genetic condition that can be deadly. It can lead to Sudden Arrhythmia Death Syndrome, otherwise known as SADS. So far, a mother and two of her young children have the gene, which they believe they inherited from a sperm donor. The family is trying to find the sperm donor so that they can alert him, and any other children that he had, about the serious condition.

Hundreds of cases of children inheriting rare genetic diseases from their sperm donors have been found, and some experts believe there could be thousands. And the more children there are in a donor-sibling group, the more likely it is that a genetic disease will be able to spread through those families, and subsequently, through the population. In Susanna Wahl's group of 150 children, there are several kids with autism. It's still not clear if autism is a heritable disease, but a 2015 UK study of twins found that there could be a link.

There have also been cases of children inheriting rare diseases such as neurofibromatosis type 1, which can cause benign tumors in nerves in the skin, brain, and other places, and can increase the risk of cancer. In another donor-sibling group, at least eight children have inherited a deadly heart defect from their donor known as hypertrophic cardiomyopathy. The donor was found to be a carrier for the disease, which can cause sudden cardiac death. One child from the group has died from the disease, and at least two of the children had to have pacemakers installed.

In an international case, a Danish sperm donor was found to have passed on a rare genetic condition to at least nine of the forty-three children that he fathered, causing Danish laws on donation to be strengthened. Nordisk Cryobank's donor passed along the NF1 genetic disorder to his offspring; his sperm was sold to women in ten different countries. The condition affects neurologic functions.

In another disturbing case, three families have sued a Georgia sperm bank, Xytex Corp., for selling them sperm from a donor they later found out had schizophrenia, a criminal record, and had falsified his education. At least twelve more families were also planning lawsuits relating to their Donor 9623. There are allegedly thirty-six offspring from this donor. The families found out the identity of the donor through a donor-sibling group and discovered that he had lied about his background. The women who purchased his sperm say they were told he was the bank's "best donor," who was known for his great health, high IQ, and university degrees. Now, the parents are anxious that their children may one day become schizophrenic. According to the suit, the donor also allegedly lied about having college degrees. It also says that Xytex never tried to verify the information that he provided.

All these horror stories beg the question, why isn't the fertility industry better regulated in this country? Why is no one keeping these children out of harm's way? One answer may be that very few people actually want more regulation of assisted reproduction.

The couples that desperately want babies don't want regulation, nor do the fertility doctors who have successful practices—and the sperm banks certainly don't want more oversight. That leaves the donor-conceived children, and now, many of these kids are now coming of age and demanding their rights. In the U.S., the UK, and Australia, groups such as Anonymous Us, Tangled Webs UK, and the Donor Conception Network in the UK are campaigning for change through Internet campaigns and at conferences, and acting as support networks for each other. These groups are also trying to raise awareness for those who might use sperm or egg donors so that potential parents are conscious of the effects that assisted reproduction may have on their offspring.

In June 2015, the first conference for donor-conceived people was held in Melbourne, Australia. There were calls for national laws to allow access to donor information; the state of Victoria, in Australia, has already passed laws that allow those who are donor conceived to find out about their donors.

The laws giving donor-conceived people the rights to more information about themselves have been incremental; in 2011, a law was passed in Washington State, effectively banning anonymous sperm and egg donors. It requires all egg and sperm donors to release identifying information if one of their children requests it once they reach the age of eighteen. It also gives these children their donor's medical histories. But the law does allow donors the choice to opt out.

Many donor-conceived people have been following a landmark case in British Columbia, Canada, that banned anonymous gamete donations. But the government has appealed that law.

Another issue is whether Congress would want to step into the quicksand that surrounds regulation of this industry. Caplan, the bioethicist at NYU, thinks not. "Politically, it becomes a super-heated hot potato, because every disability group and right-to-life group will say this is on the road to eugenics, and we can't do this. People will say, I lived with cystic fibrosis, or sickle cell . . . " says Caplan. "The chances of the FDA gaining that kind of control (over the industry) is zero to negative a large number."

As for the testing of donors, the Donor Sibling Registry has called for mandatory whole genome sequencing of sperm donors by all sperm banks, especially those that ship sperm to countries around the world, such as the large U.S. and Danish banks. This now costs less than $1,000 to do. While sperm banks tend to test some donors for some diseases, it doesn't rule out the rare genetic diseases that some men are passing on to their offspring.

In the meantime, families may request an open donor and have themselves tested. Cappy Rothman, the founder of California

Cryobank, says that more and more women are having themselves genetically tested through companies such as 23andMe, then asking the
sperm banks to make sure that their donor isn't a carrier for any of the
same genetic diseases that they might be carriers for.

"The dynamics are changing. People are becoming more aware,
and genetics are becoming more popular. They're saying, 'I can avoid
having a child with cystic fibrosis or other diseases,'" says Rothman.
"All of us have a recessive trait. It's not a problem unless two people
have the same trait."

The fear of inheriting genetic diseases has made companies such as
23andMe and Ancestry.com immensely popular with women and
couples planning to have children. Then there's the future, with companies such as GenePeeks.

Created in 2014 by Lee Silver, a Princeton University geneticist, it
could forever alter our approach to having children. GenePeeks has
the ability to weave together the DNA of a man and a woman and create a "virtual child." That avatar will be able to tell them important information about what their real child would be like if they had one.
Effectively, it will allow parents to see into the future to "meet" their
child, while he or she is still just a hope in their eyes. For now, the
company's goal is to use this virtual child to screen for heritable diseases. "We're able to predict a child's risk for genetic disease, such as
cystic fibrosis or even autism, before that child is ever conceived, before a fetus even exists," Silver explains.

Silver's partner in his endeavor, Anne Morriss, knows intimately
what genetic illnesses can do to a family: her own son, born with the
help of a sperm donor, was diagnosed at birth with MCAD, a rare and
potentially fatal genetic disease that prevents the body from converting certain fats to energy. She learned too late that she was a carrier for
the disease, as was her sperm donor. Now, she and Silver hope that
their company will be able to prevent situations such as hers.

A Harvard MBA business consultant, Morriss says their company
isn't about designer babies and creating perfect human beings, as some
critics have charged, but rather about detecting genetic diseases before
a baby is born.

With GenePeeks' genetic analysis as a standard part of reproductive health care, Morriss says the company could significantly and non-invasively reduce the number of children born with devastating conditions. It could also reduce the number of abortions performed in response to prenatal indicators of a severe genetic illness.

For practical purposes, GenePeeks will help couples make decisions about their children before they are conceived. For instance, a couple that discovers their child will probably be born with the deadly Tay–Sachs disease may choose to adopt instead. Or a couple that finds out their baby will almost certainly become autistic may choose to go ahead with the pregnancy and practice early intervention on the child. In some cases, parents who do proceed with a pregnancy will have advance warning for diseases where early intervention can make a difference. For some diseases, what is done in the first forty-eight hours of a child's life—before testing can give you a definitive answer about a disease—can make the difference between life and death.

GenePeeks' technology is already being tested on women who use sperm donors. It has the potential to revolutionize the sperm bank industry by finding safer ways for women to choose their donors—and possibly to spare a child from inheriting genetic illnesses.

"This is about lowering the risk for devastating conditions," says Morriss. "I think in our lifetime everyone will know the risk, and we'll get to make meaningful choices to protect our family."

9

The New Normal
Changing Families

It's early on a Saturday morning when I arrive at the Brooklyn Marriott, within spitting distance of the Brooklyn Bridge. The wind off the water is fierce as I struggle to open the door to the hotel. A group of young Japanese tourists passes by, guidebooks in hand, heading off to see the sights.

I step inside the hotel. It's much like any other Marriott I've been inside. Bland, slightly upscale furniture, dazed tourists wandering around, brisk hotel workers looking busy. A friendly employee directs me down the hall to my destination.

A large white sign reading SINGLE MOTHERS BY CHOICE 30TH ANNIVERSARY CELEBRATION points me toward a large auditorium where the conference is being held. It was on the Single Mothers by Choice (SMC) website that I'd originally learned about the super-sized donor-sibling groups.

Because of the enormous response for this 30th anniversary celebration—more than 300 women are expected—it's being held for the first time at this Marriott. I realize how incredible it is that it's been more than thirty years that single women have been consciously having babies on their own.

Outside the room, groups of women with babies and small children sit on the carpet, chatting about breastfeeding, babysitters, and playgroups.

Not a man is in sight.

"What do you do when a stranger asks, 'what does your husband do?'" asks one mother as she sits cross-legged on the floor, breastfeeding her baby. The other women nearby nod their heads. They've heard this question before. "I tell them it's none of their business!" says a woman wearing a long skirt, her brown hair plaited down her back. The other women smile and clap.

Nearby, representatives from sperm banks hawk their wares as though it were a trade show for the latest computer gadgets. There's California Cryobank, and a few others—Fairfax Cryobank of Virginia and RMA sperm bank of New York. Single women and lesbians are now the biggest customers for sperm banks. According to California Cryobank, single mothers account for 50 to 60 percent of all sperm purchased at its sperm bank; lesbians for 25 to 30 percent, and heterosexual couples 15 to 20 percent. It's a far cry from the early days when sperm banks actually refused to sell to single women and lesbians, catering mainly to heterosexual couples struggling with infertility. I wonder, are these the same sperm banks that once turned away women such as the ones here today?

The sperm banks offer brochures and even donor catalogs, but California Cryobank has the best giveaway: a pen with a light-up center that contains small white blobs shaped like sperm. As you turn the pen upside down, the "sperm" move up and down in the liquid contained inside. Each time you click the pen, the sperm change color: red, blue, green, multicolor. My kids were going to love this.

In one corner, a woman sells a children's book she's written, *Nan's Donut Dilemma,* about a little girl who is sad when her school holds a "Donuts for Dads" day, but she doesn't have a father to bring to the event. Sales of the book appear to be brisk.

Finally, I meet Jane Mattes, the founder of Single Mothers by Choice. A tall, big-boned woman in her sixties, with short brown hair and an easy smile, she reminds me a bit of Julia Child. Mattes is a New

York City psychotherapist who founded SMC in 1981 after having her son, Eric, the year before.

"I started Single Mothers by Choice because I didn't want to be alone," says Mattes. "I needed the support of other moms who were in the same situation as me."

From its modest beginnings as a small support group for single moms in New York, the organization now boasts more than 30,000 members—mostly women in their thirties and forties—who comprise SMC chapters throughout the U.S., and in countries such as Australia, England, and Canada.

ABOUT 41 PERCENT of all babies in this country are now born to unmarried women. As society becomes more accepting of women having children on their own, and the technology for doing so becomes more sophisticated and more widely available, there will be even more of these new kinds of families, consisting of single moms and their kids. In fact, there are now 11 million single mothers in the United States, and that number is growing steadily. About 39 percent of those women are forty years old or older, and since 1990, the birth rate among these older women has tripled.[1]

Single parenting has become a norm in this country; in 2006, 12.9 million families were headed by a single parent, and around 80 percent of those were headed by a female. For the first time, there are now more single women than married women living in this country.[2]

The phenomenon has even made it into popular culture, with *The Switch,* a romantic comedy starring Jennifer Aniston, about a woman who uses a sperm donor to have a baby on her own, and *The Back-up Plan,* featuring Jennifer Lopez as a single woman who meets the man of her dreams shortly after being artificially inseminated. Lesbians who use assisted reproduction to have children are also featured in films, such as *The Kids Are All Right,* about the children of a gay couple who seek out their sperm donor father. And there are quite a few celebrities who have become single mothers by choice, providing inspiration for women everywhere, including actress Kristin Davis, who starred in the popular TV show *Sex and the City,* and adopted a child;

actress Charlize Theron, who adopted a son; the actress Connie Britton, who starred in the TV show *Friday Night Lights*; actress Diane Keaton; actresses Mary-Louise Parker, Meg Ryan, and Sandra Bullock; and the singer Sheryl Crow.

Of course, it all started with TV's *Murphy Brown*, who had the temerity in 1992 to have a child on the show without being married. Vice-presidential candidate Dan Quayle blasted Brown and single mothers by choice everywhere for "mocking fatherhood" by having a baby out of wedlock. His attack became a major campaign controversy that year and sparked a debate over the decision by women to have children on their own. Fast forward twenty-plus years, and that debate has largely disappeared. More than half of women under age thirty are having babies without getting married. The unconventional has become the conventional. The women at this event don't seem bothered about what's conventional anymore, and neither does Mattes.

Despite her rather formidable appearance, Mattes is warm and friendly and promises to introduce me to other single mothers. Her son, Eric, now in his early thirties and recently married, is also here. He is tall, with curly brown hair and boyish good looks. His mother proudly puts her arm around him as she introduces him.

Mattes had her son on her own when she was thirty-six. She had been casually dating a man in New York City, where she lived, when she found out that she was pregnant. She thought it was an amazing opportunity, since she wasn't sure she'd even have children, and she had many friends who had difficulty conceiving. The man she'd been dating didn't feel the same way.

"He said good luck, I think you'll be a very good mother. He was a great guy to date—smart, interesting, and nice. But he wasn't interested in a family or children. After a while, I lost track of him," she says. "I thought getting pregnant was a gift, it was a miracle. It was so unexpected."

The year was 1980, and at the time, there were very few women having children on their own—by choice, anyway. Still, Mattes wasn't deterred. After a brief moment of shock, her family was supportive and encouraged her to go through with having the baby. "My mother said, 'Oh, what am I going to tell my friends?' Then in the next breath, she said, 'I'll finally be a grandmother like all my other friends!'"

But Mattes, who is a psychotherapist, didn't know any other professional, older women who were having a baby on their own, without a father. When her son was around a year old, she thought it might be nice to form a little support group with other women in the same situation, so she asked all her friends if they knew anyone around her age who was going to have a baby on their own, or was thinking of having one. Mattes suggested they come to her house for coffee and cake, and waited to see if anyone would appear. A few weeks later, seven women showed up at her house; two were pregnant, one had a newborn baby, and one had adopted a child on her own. The others were thinking about having a baby. The group proved to be a lifeline for all of them.

"It was amazing, because no one else could understand how wonderful and how stressful it was. It was a miracle for us to have children, but no one could understand the pressures of always being the one on, 24/7," says Mattes. "We shared all our feelings, and we talked and talked. We actually had very little in common besides this," she remembers, adding that she didn't even know about sperm banks until she met the other women. "We didn't intend to be anything more than a little group in my living room."

When their group of single mothers was written about in the *New York Daily News,* and then picked up in the *New York Times,*[3] and then that article was syndicated, they started getting letters and mail from women like them all over the country—Chicago, Boston, San Francisco. Soon, they started giving the women who lived in the same cities each other's names. While Mattes had her baby the old-fashioned way (though she didn't marry the man), most of these women were having children with the help of sperm donors, though it was barely talked about at the time. Once the Internet came along, the group was deluged with email. Eventually, they started to organize some more, and in no time Single Mothers by Choice was born. Like Mattes' first group, most SMC meetings are comprised of "thinkers" (women thinking about having a baby on her own), "tryers" (women who are trying to have a baby), and mothers.

The SMC groups started in big cities on both Coasts, but now there are chapters everywhere, including in the Midwest and in the more conservative South. It's not unusual anymore to meet a single mother by choice in places such as Louisiana, Alabama, Georgia, Texas, and North Carolina.

For Mattes, the group was a lifesaver. It was a way for her son, Eric, to have friends who had the same kinds of families as his: families without a father. Now, it's much more common, but in the early 1980s, it was a new phenomenon. Her son had teachers who had never seen this before, even in New York City, and they didn't know what to say to the children. When more single mothers by choice began to appear, elementary schools in the city began inviting Mattes to come talk to the children, as well as teachers and staff members, about these new mothers.

"I would help them understand, depending on the age of the children, that you don't actually have to have a mommy and daddy to have a baby. A doctor can help a mommy to become a mommy," she remembers.

Her son would ask her from time to time about his father. "It was a little hard for him to understand why someone wouldn't want to be part of a family," she says. (She has completely lost touch with her son's father.) But being with the other families helped, especially when they took vacations together. The women started by renting cabins together in upstate New York once a year. Now the groups meet for holidays a few times a year, in destinations all over the country. And on this day in October, they will meet at a conference where hundreds of other single mothers by choice will gather.

I HEAD INSIDE the cavernous auditorium and am astonished by what I see and what Mattes has created: here in this room, where insurance agents with PowerPoint presentations normally meet, sit row upon row of single women at long conference tables, some with babies on their laps or breastfeeding, and some with children in nearby strollers. They are all in their thirties and forties and come in every size, shape, and ethnicity; there are Asian and African American women, white women, gay women, and straight. Some wear hippie-style clothing, with long hair and sandals, while others look like they just stepped off Wall Street.

The women chat and smile, relaxed that they are finally in a place that fully accepts them for who they are, where no one judges them for choosing to have a child on their own. They love that no one here asks, "Where's your husband?" or questions their children about his or her father. These women decided they didn't need a husband in order to have a child, and for the most part, they are content with their choice.

I am struck by this hidden subculture and wonder, are there groups of women such as these meeting all over the country, quietly shifting the demographics of American motherhood?

Standing out in this crowd of single mothers is a slightly nerdy-looking older man, with glasses, gray hair, and a paunch. On his faded green, slightly stained t-shirt is a nametag that reads, "Sperm Donor in the 1980s."

Other women at the conference eye him curiously. Today, for better or worse, sperm donors are selected for their height, athleticism, and good looks as much for their genes and intelligence. It's the rare woman who would intentionally pick a short, average-looking man to father her child. A woman nearby whispers to her friend, "*That* guy was a sperm donor?"

His name, it turns out, is Robert Koral, and he's a tax lawyer in New York. He says he donated sperm for eight years while in law school, over thirty years ago. So what's he doing here, at the Single Mothers by Choice conference?

"I never had kids of my own, so I'm hoping they can help me find some of my donor children," he says. "I donated twenty times a month for years, so I figure I must have a bunch of kids out there, and I'd like to meet them."

Most of the panelists today are single mothers, and some have even brought their grown children to speak. A speaker tells of bringing her young daughter to a playground, where they saw a father playing with his young son. The two watched, mesmerized, as the dad playfully chased his son. Finally, the girl pointed to the young father and said, "Mom, can I touch him?"

The audience heaves a collective sigh at this anecdote. Being a single mom is not easy, they all seem to say with their eyes.

Most of the women in attendance today had their children through sperm donors; the rest through adoption. They're eager to share their questions and concerns; they worry about what to tell their kids when they ask who their father is, whether they'll be able to access their donor's medical information. They wonder if they were right to use an open or a closed donor.

A woman in the back raises her hand. She's disturbed because she has discovered that her son has eighty-one half siblings. Although she used an open donor, she wonders if her son will ever get the chance to meet his father now.

"I worry about the donor's reaction," she says. "My child isn't first in line to meet him. I thought when it was up to twenty offspring, it was unseemly. Do you feel this is an appropriate number of offspring for one donor to have? I expect the number of kids will be up to one hundred soon."

Women in the audience chatter about the question. "Eighty-one half siblings! That's ridiculous." "He'll never meet his father."

The members of the panel, which is titled, "Looking for Genetic Roots," don't seem to know what to say. Finally, Wendy Kramer stands at the podium. She's heard this question before.

"Unfortunately, these high numbers of kids *will* make the donor less likely to come forward," she says. "Most experts agree that ten kids per donor is the optimal number. We hope that someday, with regulation, we can make that number the legal standard in this country."

IN THE THIRTY years that Mattes' Single Mothers by Choice has been around, remarkable changes have occurred. Once, it was mainly women in their mid-thirties who were having babies on their own, but now Mattes says she's seeing women in their late twenties doing this as well. They're starting earlier, says Mattes, so they can have two children, rather than just one.

"If they don't start now, it will be difficult fertility-wise to have two kids. They're planning it more . . . it's not some wild, desperate last chance to have a baby. It's become one of the options that people are considering," she says. "That's what I hoped would happen—that this would become an alternative for people. I just didn't know it would happen so fast."

The phenomenon is reflected at the other end of the age spectrum as well. Increasingly, says Mattes, women in their mid- to late-forties, who previously might not have been able to have children, are using both sperm *and* egg donors to get pregnant. There are also more fertility resources available now that allow older women to have kids, such as more effective fertility treatments, and the ability to freeze their eggs when they're younger.

Deb Hordon understands these women intimately, because she is one of them. A professional woman who lives in Boston, she had a baby at the age of forty-seven. Deb dated through her twenties and thirties, but when she didn't find the right person to settle down with by the age of forty, she decided to try and have a baby on her own.

First, she froze six of her eggs. But she would find out later that the technology at the time wasn't advanced enough to work for her. Then she tried intrauterine insemination with donated sperm, several times, but none of the procedures worked. When she was forty-five, she had her eggs thawed and tried using them to create embryos. She was able to get one healthy embryo, but unfortunately the pregnancy didn't take.

"I was so emotionally devastated and distraught after the failures," she says. "I grieved the losses."

But she wasn't ready to give up on having a baby, so Deb started looking into adopting a child or an embryo. This is different from using a donated embryo, because those who use these embryos must go through a process similar to adopting a child, including psychological testing and home studies. And through a formal adoption process, the parties involved decide what the child's relationship will be with the originator, that is, the person who had the embryos created.

Reproductive endocrinologists estimate that there may be more than a million frozen embryos in storage facilities across the country. Some are from cancer patients, hoping to have a child after their treatment, but most are leftover from couples who had several embryos made but already used one to have their own children.

"It's an amazing development in the fertility world," says Deb. "It's more affordable than using a donor egg, or going through an IVF cycle."

She decided that adopting an embryo was her best bet and started looking into those that were available. Deb wanted an embryo from a donor who looked somewhat like her so that her child wouldn't have to answer too many questions about her origin as she became older. So she searched for donors who had olive skin, and dark hair and eyes, and discovered a woman in Spain who fit the description. She had just had a baby boy through one of her embryos that she'd had created and did not plan to use the others, so she offered them for adoption. Deb decided that she wanted to adopt the woman's other embryos, so she underwent psychiatric and financial evaluations, as well as physical exams to make sure she was still healthy enough to have and care for a baby at her age. She didn't have to pay for the embryos, but spent $8,500 in total for everything else. The cost usually includes the procedure, the agency fee, shipping the embryos, a home study, legal fees, and medical screening.

Miraculously, Deb became pregnant. But, she says, it was a difficult pregnancy. She had preeclampsia toward the end and had to have a caesarean section. Women who are over forty are considered high-risk for pregnancy, as are women who undergo IVF, and she was both. Fortunately, the baby was healthy, and now she has an adorable little girl, born in January 2016. Deb is ecstatic.

"It was a spiritually profound and beautiful experience. It's been the best thing ever for me," she says. "I've been trying for so long—it's so unbelievably fulfilling. I'm so blessed."

She says that, despite being in her late forties, taking care of a newborn on her own hasn't made her feel tired at all, though she admits that it could be the euphoria she's experiencing from finally having a child. "For people who are younger and have babies, it's so normal. If I'd had a child in my thirties, I wouldn't have experienced this so deeply," she says.

And while she regrets that she doesn't have a big family around to help her with her baby, Deb says she's surrounded by incredible people in both her personal and professional life.

"People have been so encouraging and supportive of me, including men that I've worked with," she says. "The age thing never bothered me. I never thought, 'I'm too old to do this.' And I've never had anyone say, 'You're too old to have a baby.'"

She has a few other friends who are single mothers, and she is also a member of a local SMC chapter, but she feels like the group was more useful at the decision-making stage. Also, she doesn't entirely agree with the group's moniker.

"I would call it, 'Single Mothers by *Second* Choice.' I think that many of us would have loved to do this with a partner, but we didn't find one in time," she says. "I still believe that I will find the right person."

It was a long, difficult process to come to the decision to have a baby on her own, she says. "First, I had to give up and grieve and accept that I wouldn't do this with a partner. I hung on to that wish for years. I kept looking and it didn't happen. It was incredibly hard, and it took a long time to accept."

She also had to embrace the fact that she would do this on her own, without a big family network to help her; sadly, her mother died when Deb was twenty-four. So she waited until she felt like her career was stable and secure enough for her to afford to have a baby on her own. Now, she feels like she's at the pinnacle of her profession and starting to find success. "The world is totally out of sync with women's bodies. Unless you find a partner, it takes a long time to establish yourself in the labor market to the point that you can even afford to have a child."

If the numbers are any indication, soon we'll be seeing more women like Deb who are choosing to have babies on their own, says Rosanna Hertz, author of *Single by Chance, Mothers by Choice: How Women Are Choosing Parenthood without Marriage and Creating the*

New American Family. She says that more men and women are choosing to wait to get married, and so more women are remaining single—but they still want to have kids. Because it's so easy to order sperm on the Internet, says Hertz, a professor of sociology and gender and women's studies at Wellesley College, more women are able to have kids on their own. And that change is partly what made single women the biggest customer of sperm banks today—more than half of all sperm is purchased by these women. Hertz says there's been what she calls a "queering" of reproductive gametes, with more lesbians purchasing sperm now as well, and a steep decline in heterosexual use of donor sperm.

Amy, whom we met in Chapter 7 and had two children through two different sperm donors, says that at the time she had her first child in 1998, she and other gay women felt like they were pioneers. When her daughter was born, she and her partner tried to get both of their names on their child's birth certificate, but they weren't able to do that. Now, that's become much easier. Amy says she knows lesbian couples in which both women became pregnant using the same donor so that they could both have children who were related.

While single women and lesbians have become the main clients of U.S. sperm banks today, their counterparts in other countries are still discriminated against. In France, Sweden, and Switzerland, both single women and lesbians are not allowed to undergo artificial insemination by a sperm donor. Many countries are struggling with the complexities of assisted reproduction. While same-sex marriage is legal in France, only heterosexual couples are allowed access to gametes. That causes some women to order sperm online from other countries. To make the situation even more complicated, says Hertz, their child could technically be denied French citizenship.

"Every country in Europe has different regulations, and there's no attempt to unify or universalize them," she says.

Finding a place where single women can adopt a baby has become more limited, too. They are no longer allowed to adopt children in China or Russia, making it even harder for some women to have a child.

One reason why fewer straight couples are buying sperm these days is that a new IVF technique was developed in 1995 that made it easier for infertile men to have children. Intracytoplasmic sperm injection allows clinicians to inject a single viable sperm directly into an egg. This was a game-changer for heterosexual couples, says Hertz.

Despite the selective laws and stigmas against single mothers that exist in some countries, there is greater acceptance of single mothers here and abroad. But there's another reason why their numbers are growing. According to Hertz, there have been various studies over the past several years showing that two-parent families aren't always better for children than single-parent families. That research has helped to sway many of these women to go ahead with having a baby on their own.

In a study comparing the parenting quality of single mothers by choice with that of two-parent families, it was found that there were no differences between family types. Both groups had children conceived by donor insemination. The February 2016 study, led by Susan Golombok, director of the Centre for Family Research at Cambridge University, looked at maternal well-being, mother-child relationships, and child adjustment, and found that single motherhood didn't result in psychological problems for children.

Amy's eighteen-year-old daughter, Maya, has no problem with her parentage. She was raised primarily by one mother because her mothers split up when she was a toddler—though her second mother remains an important part of her life. An artistic high school senior, she is well-adjusted and happy. She is tall, lanky, and pretty, with long brown hair and dark eyes. She plays field hockey, basketball, and softball in school and plans on becoming a graphic designer one day. Her mom started telling her when she was very young that her biological father was a sperm donor.

"I don't have a first memory of when she told me. I think she was always open about it and wanted me to know. I have lesbian parents, so it was pretty obvious. I remember her telling me I had a sperm donor. She said, 'You have a dad, but we don't know him,'" she says. "I have two moms and they are my parents. He's someone who donated his sperm so my mom could have me. I call him my sperm donor, not my father."

When she was younger, Maya attended a Catholic school in Maine and felt self-conscious about being born through a donor—she feared other people's reactions. She knew her friends' parents weren't accepting of her situation. But now, she says, she's at an age where she's not embarrassed about it and doesn't mind telling people. In fact, she thinks it's pretty cool. And, she has a very close relationship with both her moms.

"I haven't had a bad experience from it. I see my moms as my parents, and I know they wanted to have me. I was a goal for them," she says, adding that coming from a family like hers keeps her open-minded. "It makes me more accepting of other people and their situations and families."

Maya's donor was anonymous, and she has never met him. She says she's somewhat curious about what he might be like and thinks it would be interesting to see where she came from, but she's afraid that she might not like him. She also worries that meeting him could change her perspective on him: "I feel like once I met him, I'd think of him as my father, and I don't want to see him that way. I don't see him as someone who raised me."

Still, Maya says she would like to know if she inherited her athleticism and her artistic ability from him, since she doesn't think she inherited them from her mom. She'd also like to see where her features came from, as she doesn't really look like her mother.

Maya has two half sisters that she knows of, but she hasn't met them yet. One of her sisters was born four days before her, and the other is a year older. They message each other on Facebook and have become online friends. Since they live far away—one is in Michigan and the other is in California—it's been difficult to set up a time and place for all of them to meet. "If they want to meet me, I think it would be cool to do that. It's interesting. It gives me something to look forward to. There's an excitement and mystery to meeting them," she says.

Hertz, the Wellesley sociologist, says that having these extended families, including half siblings, is a new and positive development for the children of single moms and lesbian mothers. For some of these children, donor siblings have become enormously important, giving them a chance to get to know their genetic relatives, and to see what they look like. That's especially significant when they may not have a chance to meet their anonymous donors.

Still, that's changing, too. More new sperm donors are donating under "identity release," or as open donors, these days. That's because of market demand, says Hertz, since more women want to give their children the option to connect with their biological fathers when they are older.

Stacy, a single mother by choice who lives in California, says she chose an identity-release donor for that very reason—she wanted her daughter to have the ability to find out about her donor if she was ever curious. She has a group of friends who are also single moms, and she says that they have all chosen identity-release donors as well, citing studies that found it's in the best interest of the child to have access to their origin information.

One study that looked at families who used identity-release donors found that almost none of the parents regretted using an open donor, and that telling their child that they could one day obtain their donor's identity had a positive impact on them. The 2004 study, published in the British journal *Human Reproduction,* included lesbian families, single women, and heterosexual couples, and found that the experiences were relatively the same in all kinds of families.[4]

Almost all the children surveyed said they did plan on obtaining their donor's identity one day. According to the study, "The youths did not seem to be looking for a father in the donor, instead their interest stemmed more out of a strong curiosity about him, likely because they felt learning more about him would help them learn more about themselves."

Stacy struggled with infertility for eight years and now has two daughters who are both two years old, but a few months apart. One was born through a sperm donor and a surrogate, and the other was adopted.

"On the very same day that my gestational surrogate became pregnant, I got a call from a woman who was newly pregnant and had a baby she was willing to let me adopt. I hit the jackpot two different ways," she says.

Because of the many issues she'd had trying to get pregnant—she'd had five miscarriages and an emergency hysterectomy—she decided to go ahead with both options, just in case anything went wrong. Fortunately, it didn't, and she was blessed with two children instead of one. The girls don't look anything alike: one has red hair and blue eyes, and the other has dark hair and dark eyes. When people ask questions about the girls, Stacy doesn't get annoyed. She understands their curiosity.

Stacy, who is forty-five, is thrilled with her children, though she admits that raising two babies at the same time as a single mother has been incredibly difficult at times. Fortunately, she has family nearby to help. She also has a wonderful relationship with her adopted daughter's birth mother, who lives nearby. "She's surprised and grateful that I keep in touch with her. As far as I'm concerned, that's a high priority for me. I want my daughter to have access to her birth family when the time comes. Adoption has been so amazing for me," she says.

A tech worker in Silicon Valley, Stacy says that she initially encountered resistance to her plan to raise a child on her own while she was trying to conceive, and even lost a few close friends over it. When she announced her first pregnancy (she ended up having a miscarriage), she realized that some of her more religious friends were having a hard time with it. Three of her friends eventually stopped speaking to her, but she has since reconciled with one of them. "Once the babies are here, it changes everything. You can't shut out a cute baby. I feel surprisingly accepted now that they're born," she says. Even her father, who raised her and her siblings on his own, was disapproving at first. But he has since come around, and even generously helped her out when she was having financial difficulties. "My dad raised us alone,

and he considered parenthood an onerous responsibility. He was beg-
ging me not to do it. Now, everyone in my family is on board with it.
Who could not love my children? They're adorable!"

She hasn't told her colleagues at work about her children's origin,
but she knows they are curious when they see photos of her daughters
on her desk. When her second child was born, she says she got push-
back from her boss about taking maternity leave again, but eventually
she was allowed to split her leave between both babies.

When people ask about her girls, and if she's single or married, she
just says she's single, rather than a single mother by choice. "Before, I
felt like I had to stand up and be counted as an SMC. And I didn't want
people to assume that I was a weird flakey-flake who went and got
knocked up. I wanted people to know that this was a conscious choice.
I also didn't want people to think that I had an ex somewhere who was
paying child support. Don't compare me to them," she says. "But now I
just say, 'I'm a mom.'"

Her sister and her family actually live next door and have been
helpful, but, she adds, "there's an illusion that if you have a lot of family, that burden won't be as heavy on me. When push comes to shove,
the burden is all on me. Having family nearby doesn't lessen that at
all," she says.

Stacy points out another strange reality of single motherhood—she
feels that moms like her, single by choice, are not given the right to
complain. "If I just want to complain and get some sympathy, I get,
'Well, you chose this,'" she says. "As a single mother by choice, you
don't get a right to have a bad day and vent. People echo that back to
me all the time, but they never say that to married people who choose
parenthood."

Fortunately, she has a large and active local Single Mothers by
Choice group that she *can* complain to. The group is comprised of
well-educated professional women who could afford to have a child
without a husband. And while her career in the tech industry has en-
abled her to afford to raise two children on her own, she's had to sacri-
fice by giving up her dream of owning her own home. Stacy also says

that she probably would have chosen a different career path if she didn't have children to provide for, but she doesn't regret her decision for a moment.

Still, she admits that she would like to get married one day and complete her family. "When I made the decision to have children, it was hypothetical. But now that I've brought them into the world without a father, it weighs on me sometimes. There will come a day when they realize that they don't have a father because I made a choice to have them on my own, and they might be sad about that. They might feel like they really missed out," she says. "I was raised by my dad, and I never knew my mom. It was a big hole in my life for me."

In the meantime, her extended family has actually grown to include three other donor-sibling families that she has connected with— all who used the same sperm donor. Like many other groups of their ilk, they keep in touch through a private Facebook page, sharing pictures of their kids and keeping each other up to date on how the children are doing. Their babies are all still very young, but they plan on meeting up at some point soon.

"I was excited to meet these other people—it's been really wonderful," she says. "It turns out that we click really well as people. We have similar values; two others are lesbian couples, and we're all in the same ballpark in terms of progressiveness. And we don't have any families who are hiding it from their kids."

While it's become more socially acceptable for women to have kids on their own, those who had children years ago regularly faced the indignity of being treated differently from others. Ramona, who had her daughter in 2005, remembers being pregnant and trying to prepare for the birth on her own. "It was pretty socially unaccepted at the time to go to Lamaze or birthing classes by yourself as a single mom. I went alone a lot, but sometimes I tried to bring a friend. Then, if you tried to be part of a mom and baby group, it was hard, too."

Ramona, who lives in Atlanta and has two daughters through sperm donors, made the decision to have a baby on her own in the late 1990s, when she turned thirty. She'd been in the Navy and had married young, but sadly, the marriage didn't work out. She dated but didn't find the right guy. Eventually, her mother suggested that she have children on her own if she hadn't met someone by the time she turned thirty. "My mom planted that seed for me. She really encouraged me," she says. "When I made the decision to have a baby on my own, I felt like I was the only one in the world doing this. You think you're all alone. This was especially true for those of us who have older children who were born before social media."

After several attempts at getting pregnant, she had her first daughter in 2005; she was overjoyed. But later, she started to feel guilty that she had chosen a donor for her daughter who wasn't identity-release. At the time, she didn't have much of a choice—there were very few open donors back then, and those that were open cost more money.

"I chose a donor because I liked his medical history. But I feel like I robbed my child of the chance to meet her donor, of ever knowing her paternal heritage," she says.

When her daughter was one year old, she decided to try to have another baby. It ended up taking thirteen months of trying, with nine IUI's and four different donors, before she became pregnant again.

"You have your heart in your stomach when they don't take and you're out of vials," she says. "It's a roller-coaster ride of trying to conceive . . . there are highs and lows."

Her second daughter was born when she was in her late thirties. Ramona says it's more popular now among her other single mother friends to have a second child, in part because it's become more socially acceptable for a woman to have a baby on her own.

Mattes also recounts how difficult it was sometimes, raising a child as a single mom more than thirty years ago. When her son was very young and attending public school in New York City in the 1980s, there was a "bring your father to school" day. Worried that the boy would be upset about not having a dad, she suggested that he bring his godfather to school that day instead.

"He said, 'Now why would I want to do that?' He was so fine with not having a dad," she remembers. "The nuclear family in the traditional sense is so rare these days. People who don't like single moms are the same people who didn't get it thirty-five years ago. They thought it was a statement against marriage, against men, but it was simply a desire to be a mother. The rest was secondary. I never regretted it. It was the most wonderful and hardest thing I've ever done."

Pam, who works for a university in California, had her daughter on her own in 1999. While she was fortunate that her friends and colleagues accepted her decision, she worried that her church might not be as understanding about her choice.

"I'm part of a Catholic community, and the Catholic Church doesn't believe in reproductive technology," she says. " I didn't feel like I'd get fired or banished from my church, but I was concerned about how it would be received. In the end, my church and pastor were very supportive."

Like many single moms, the early years were the hardest for Pam. Her daughter was a colicky baby who cried every night. She was lucky to have good friends who would stop by at night and bring her dinner, or just help out.

She believes that her daughter has always been comfortable with her origin. Pam told her from an early age that she was born through a donor. In fact, she practiced telling her the story as soon as her child was an infant. When people would stop her daughter, who has darker skin than her mother, they would say, 'Your skin is so beautiful.' Her daughter would reply nonchalantly, "Thanks, I got it from my donor.'"

Pam remembers being flummoxed when a student in her daughter's day-care class asked what her daughter's dad looked like. She answered, "I don't know." Her daughter always seemed at ease with the story of how she came to be.

"When my daughter was in first grade, another child was asking her about her father and said, 'You have to have a dad.' [My daughter] just said, 'I don't—I have a donor.' I think it's the kids who were lied to who are the ones who are pissed off."

Of course, despite all the advances that single women have made, they still face intolerance and ignorance. One single mother that I know has her young daughter in ballet class. She was recently told that at her child's upcoming recital, all the fathers would be asked onto the stage to dance with their daughters. When she heard that, she burst into tears. Fortunately, her teenage nephew said he'd be happy to dance with his cousin. That made her day.

10

Families of the New Millennium

*How Donor Families Are Rewriting
the Dynamics of Kinship*

Susanna Wahl hoped that the remarkable cross-country journey she and her kids were taking to meet their half siblings would teach her children about so many things and give them a better sense of the country they called home.

As a teacher, she wondered how meeting their half siblings on this trip would change her children's view of the United States. When they learned geography in school, would they associate a state with a half brother or sister that they visited? With half brothers and sisters living in California, Colorado, Kansas, Illinois, Wisconsin, Pennsylvania, New Jersey, Rhode Island, New York, and Hawaii, their familial connections covered a map of the whole country.

But during the trip, Susanna realized that what her children were really learning was that family is one of the most important things in life.

"Like it or not," she says, "they will always be connected to the people who make up their family tree."

Kansas is a world away from Susanna's home in Northern California, and the Southeastern part of the state is flat and slightly drab, with little to distinguish itself besides the prairies and forests that dot the landscape. The town to which they're headed is like a hundred other small Midwestern towns in the heartland of America: mom-and-pop shops, friendly residents, a handful of traffic signals.

It is home to two of Susanna's sister moms, Sandra and Paula, and their three children, twins Isabelle and Nicole, and their big sister, Bethany. As Susanna heads east on the highway, she looks forward to meeting these women and their children. And when she and her kids finally arrive, after a six-hour drive, she's not disappointed: the moms and their children are as welcoming as could be. They hug one another as though they've known each other for years.

The kids, who are aware they're half siblings, hit it off right from the start. The twins are Julianna's age, eight, and they are so alike, blond and tall for their age, "It's like having three Juliannas," says Susanna. They have similar personalities, too—curious and outgoing. The older sister, Bethany, a ten-year-old tomboy who is already into boys, attaches herself to Eric. Susanna recalls that moment with amusement: "We joked, 'should we tell her they can't get married?'"

As the children play, the adults talk about how similar their kids are. Like many others in the group, they are all tall, with blond hair and blue eyes. The half siblings in the group of 150 siblings live in four different countries, including Israel, England, and Canada. And many of the families get together often for playgroups, dinners, and some even go on vacations together to places such as Disney World.

"It's wild to see them all together," says one mother from the group. "They all look so much alike."

How does Susanna feel about her connection with the other families in the group of 150 kids? "We're more than just friends—we'll always be related," Susanna says. "The other mothers and I have this bond. You just have this incredible link with all these people."

It all started with Wendy Kramer's Donor Sibling Registry, created in 2000 with her son, Ryan, to help him find his own half siblings.

After they appeared on *Oprah* in 2002, donor families swarmed the site, actively searching for other families who had used the same sperm donor. Since then, thousands of children have found their half siblings through the site, and their stories, several shared in this book, are both life affirming and poignant. Like Susanna's group, many of the other donor-family groups that connected through DSR have become quite close.

When Susanna first learned about these other donor families in her children's group, she wondered how these new, complicated relationships would be structured. She's not alone. Donor-conceived families and their networks are incredibly complex and challenge the conventional concept of relationships. How do the children define their relations with each other? And what do the mothers call each other? In Susanna's group, they call each other sister moms to describe their close relationship to another woman whose child is a half sibling to their own son or daughter.

And while these donor-conceived family networks are connected by genes, they may share little else, such as religion, cultural background, or beliefs. Yet, the genetic ties between the children foster immediate, strong bonds. Many of the kids say they feel an instant connection with their siblings—as though they've known each other for years. They compare hands and feet and marvel at how much they look alike. The children are usually very tall for their age, which comes from choosing a sperm donor who is taller than average. Some become quite close and feel an uncanny sense that they've found the sister or brother they always wanted. That is the case for many of the children in Susanna's group.

Yet, its members have been secretive over the years, eschewing any contact with the media for fear that their kids would be looked on as freaks. That's why they contact each other mainly through their private Yahoo group, as do many other donor-sibling groups. The families in the group of 150 children are comprised of heterosexual couples, lesbians, and single mothers by choice, and they come from all different backgrounds. There are health nuts and fast-food junkies, families with twins, and a handful of children with autism. They come from red states and blue states, and are liberal and conservative, religious and secular.

As the creator and manager of the Yahoo group that connects all of the families born through Donor B155A, Cynthia Daily has a keen awareness of who the members in the group are, and how many children have been born. She knew from the beginning that the group was going to be large because it grew so quickly; within the first two years, there were almost fifty kids. The B155A group quickly outpaced other large donor sibling groups on the DSR.

Even with the large numbers, Cynthia wasn't worried that being a donor child would affect her son. And like Susanna, she didn't believe in keeping secrets about her child's origin from him, or from anyone else.

"I have no problem telling anyone how my son came to be," she says. "My son is a child of lesbians, and he goes to Catholic school. I don't think any more of a stigma could be attached to him."

When Cynthia and her partner used Donor B155A to conceive their child, they hoped that one day their son would get to know some of his half siblings. Now, their son, Mark, has more than twenty half siblings within a seventy-five-mile radius of their home, outside of Washington, D.C. They often meet with the other families for play dates and birthday parties. In their own way, they are a family.

"We started this group seven years ago with only seven families," says Cynthia. "Back then I thought, 'Oh my God, there are so many kids!' Now look at us!"

At the first meeting of donor families who lived nearby, they had fifteen kids together at a restaurant. The waitress asked if it was a family reunion because all the kids looked so much alike. And so many donor families live in the Washington, D.C., area that accidental meetings are not unusual. Sometimes, the families run into each other at local gay-pride rallies. "You see a lot of other kids that look like yours," says Cynthia.

Several years ago, Cynthia, her partner, and their son traveled to Disney World with thirty-five other parents and children from their donor group. While there, their son connected with another little girl from the group, and they eventually became best friends. "It was like they'd been together forever," she says. Now, whenever her son meets new half siblings, they become "new friends" and have an instant bond.

While the families in the group may be diverse, they're all linked by this strange commonality: they all have children who were fathered by the same, anonymous man. And with this remarkable connection to each other, they and others like them are helping to change the concept of family. Most social scientists agree that the definition of family has changed dramatically over the past few decades, and families related through sperm donors are one element of that transformation.

Susan McKinnon, an anthropology professor at the University of Virginia who studies families, says this new form of kinship presents new challenges in terms of how we define a family and how children conceptualize who is in their family and who is not. That's not an easy thing to establish when a child might have 150 half siblings. In fact, she says, this new world complicates the social, cultural, and economic meanings of family. But ultimately, she says, it can be a positive experience.

"There's something about the number 150 that puts it in a new category. In polygamous families, they might have 150 children. But for us, we have two or three kids. There's something extraordinary about it. But on the whole, I think it's positive. It makes all kinds of loving relations quite possible," she says.

Since my *New York Times* story about Susanna's group was first published in 2011, the number of children has actually grown, from 150 to around 200 kids. Many mothers in the group think the number could actually be much higher—possibly as high as 400 children. While this donor's sperm is no longer available through sperm banks, many of the mothers kept extra vials of the frozen sperm, so that their kids would have full siblings if they decided one day to have more children. Other women purchased the sperm on the gray market—that is, from other mothers in the group.

These super-extended donor-conceived families or clans, such as Susanna's, are stretching the meaning of family even more. They're also adding a new wrinkle, for while the children in these families do have a biological link, they also must *choose* to connect with one another and call each other family.

Much of this is happening now as donor-conceived children are starting to come of age. Sperm donation started gaining in popularity in the late 1990s, so there are more donor-conceived children in the their teens and early twenties now. Their stories are often quite moving and demonstrate a new openness that many donor-conceived children have about their origin.

Sarah Malley made a shocking discovery when she was nineteen years old. She had grown up in New Jersey with a mother and father, but her dad was much older than her mom and he died of prostate cancer when she was just eight.

One day, her twin sister called from college, asking for her social security number so that she could apply for a job. Sarah happened to be at home visiting, so she went to the bank with her mother to find the information in their safety deposit box. While they were digging around, looking for the card, Sarah happened upon a mysterious large, thick envelope, with hers and her sister's names written on the outside. Her mother said it was nothing, and not to worry about it. But when she opened the envelope, she found papers inside with a description of a man and the words, *California Cryobank*. She knew she'd found something important.

Finally, her mother told her the truth: she and her sister had been born through a sperm donor because their father's illness had made him infertile. She had been waiting until the right time to tell both of them. Sarah's mother expected her to be angry with her for keeping this secret, but in fact, her response was quite surprising.

"Standing there in Valley National Bank, I had this huge revelation about myself. I think my mom thought I'd be furious, but I actually thought it was hilarious. Once I got over the surprise, I think I released the longest string of profanities that she'd ever heard," she remembers.

After debating all day what and when to tell her sister, Sarah finally decided to call her at school in Boston and break the news. Her sister, Jenna, was in a noisy robotics meeting and at first couldn't hear what she was saying.

"I said, 'Jenna, I have life-changing news for you. You're never going to believe this, but we were born from a sperm donor.' She didn't believe it at first, and said, 'Very funny, what's the real news?' Then she started asking me all these questions," says Sarah. "I don't think she was angry, either."

Once the information sunk in, Sarah began thinking about her donor and wondering who he was. He'd been an anonymous donor, but she thought she might be able to find out some information about him. She went online and looked up: "how to find your sperm donor." The search engine led her to the Donor Sibling Registry. She read through the site, and when she figured out that she could use it to try and find her donor, Sarah used the emergency credit card that her mother had given her to pay the $75 membership fee. She quickly entered her donor's identifying number. As soon as she did, she was stunned when eleven results popped up—one was for her donor, and the other ten were for her half siblings. "The idea of half siblings hadn't even crossed my mind!" she says.

First, she emailed her sperm donor, whom she discovered was named Todd. She sent him an awkward email: "I was like, 'Hey, I'm pretty sure I'm your daughter. I don't want any money or anything. Cool. Talk to you soon? Bye.' I walked around the rest of the day, wondering if he'd write back."

By the next morning, she'd heard from him. His response was better than anything she could have imagined. He told her that he was very happy to be in contact with her, and he was glad that she existed. Then he told her a little about himself and his health, adding that he hoped he wasn't giving her too much information. Too much information! She couldn't believe that he even wanted to be in touch.

The emails were followed by a phone call, in which Sarah asked him about her ten half siblings. That was when Todd set her straight—he said no, you actually have *twenty-one* half siblings. Again, she took this development in her stride. Sarah is not someone who gets ruffled easily by unexpected news. She also learned that Todd lived in California and worked as an executive for Apple. He promised to stay in contact.

Sarah reached out to some of her half siblings, sending what she describes as more awkward emails. Again, the responses were better than she could have expected. Everyone seemed happy to welcome her into the clan. One mother of three of her half siblings mentioned that some of them were planning to meet in Cape Cod soon for a family reunion of sorts, and asked if Sarah and her sister would like to join them? Todd would be there, too—in fact, he had rented a house big enough for all of them to stay there together.

"I was still like, is this really happening to me? But we decided to go," says Sarah.

A couple of months before the trip, Sarah and Jenna celebrated their twentieth birthdays. They both woke up to an email from Todd, wishing them a happy birthday. At the end of the email, he asked, "By the way, do you want an iPhone 6 or an iPhone 6-plus for your birthday?"

"It was overwhelmingly nice of him! It still feels like, 'Is this real?'" she says.

Sarah's mother was supportive and happy that her daughters had been in contact with their donor and half siblings, but she was cautious, too—she didn't want them to get hurt. She came along with them to Cape Cod to make sure it all worked out. She needn't have worried.

When they got to the house, Sarah first met three of her half brothers, ages ten, thirteen, and seventeen. They looked a lot like her twin sister, Jenna, who has blond hair and blue eyes (Sarah has dark hair and greenish eyes). "I just ran out to them and said, 'Oh my god, we're related!' I thought, that's crazy, they look just like my sister. My mom could see how much we all looked alike."

She hit it off with the older boy, Keegan, and they started chatting right away about school and their interests. Then, the next group arrived, including her sister, some of the other families, and her sperm donor, Todd. Sarah says the first meeting is all a blur. "We were all running and hugging each other! My biggest fear was that we'd all just sit there awkwardly, not knowing what to say. But right off the bat, it wasn't like that."

She'd been most apprehensive about meeting Todd; she was afraid that he'd be quiet and buttoned up, and might not approve of her, since she was a young woman with purple hair and four tattoos. "I thought I'd have nothing in common with him. But Todd was the opposite of what I expected—he was very funny and down to earth," she says. "He's playful and fun. I think that's where I get it from. He's also incredibly smart and was valedictorian of his class. My mom is trying to use that now to inspire me to get good grades in college!"

Right away, she saw the resemblance between Todd, who is fair, and her sister, Jenna. Sarah also met two of her other half siblings, with whom she is now very close—her half sister, Carey, who was twenty-two, and her half brother, Gavin, who is a year younger than her. That's when the crazy coincidences started to happen. Sarah and her donor, Todd, kept making the same jokes at the same time. Then her sister, Jenna, realized that she and Carey had the same random birthmark on their legs. When they all plugged their cell phones in to charge, they kept getting them mixed up because they all had the same music on their phones. And none of them ever made it to the beach, because they were all afraid that their fair skin would burn.

"I never would have thought this was possible—it was bizarre," she says. "It was one of the most fun weekends of my life!"

For three days, the families played miniature golf, laser tag, and went boating. But mostly, they just sat around chatting, catching up on lost time. They'd stay up talking until four in the morning, without even realizing it was so late. Most of Sarah's half siblings are math and science people, which she believes they inherited from Todd. He and Sarah's sister, Jenna, who is a science major, often talk about chemistry and technology when they get together. Her mother was excited to get to know Todd, and when she finally met him for the first time, she said, "Thanks for helping me out here," and pointed to her daughters.

In many ways, Todd sounds like the perfect sperm donor dad. Last year, he invited his offspring to go on vacation with him to Turkey, and he has been talking about taking them all somewhere on holiday the following summer.

"Todd says he thinks of himself as an uncle. He's not trying to take over the parenting. He says if we need him, he's here for us," says Sarah. "He likes to come and visit and spend time with us when he can. I don't have enough nice things to say about him. I feel so lucky. All I was hoping for was for my donor to say, 'Have a great life.' This is so far beyond anything I could have asked for or expected."

Todd, who is forty-nine, started donating sperm while he was in graduate school at Stanford University. California Cryobank had daily advertisements in the college newspaper looking for donors, and he thought it might be a good idea to contribute and help other families to have the children they so badly wanted. He continued to donate two to three times a week for nearly four years. Occasionally, he thought about the offspring that he was helping to create, but he knew that they wouldn't be able to try and contact him until they were eighteen (according to the sperm bank), so he felt like that was a long way away. He was open to meeting his children, even if they wanted to reach out to him before they turned eighteen—but the cryobank was adamant that the children had to be adults before they could get in touch. So he made sure to update his contact information whenever he moved, in case there were any follow-up questions for him from the cryobank or any of the other families.

"I was definitely curious about the kids. I always thought I'd meet them someday. I wondered what their lives were like, and what they were doing, but I assumed that they had happy families who were taking good care of them," says Todd.

He is an unusual sperm donor in that he has always been open to meeting his donor offspring and to having them in his life. He has never felt uncomfortable with the idea, nor has he ever been ashamed of it.

Todd had been married twice before and had two children through a previous marriage, but they live in France and he doesn't get to see them very often. He sees his donor offspring more, but he doesn't regard them as his kids. "They're the children of the families that raised them. There's a biological connection there with me," he says, adding that he also considers himself more of an uncle to them. "I felt like I had an obligation to at least meet them, and if they were in any serious trouble, [I wanted them to know that] they could always contact me."

After the Cape Cod visit, Sarah went to visit a friend in Los Angeles, and Todd invited her to extend her trip and come stay with him in San Francisco, helping to pay her airfare. She did, and they had a great time. After that visit, Sarah became curious and went back to read his donor packet. She was particularly interested in the part where he was given three lines to describe himself.

"He said, 'I am generally very easygoing and funny, but sometimes if I get upset, it may take me a long time to calm down.' I thought, that's exactly how I would describe my personality! So this is where I get it from," says Sarah.

Instead of trying to find the perfect donor ("Though in my opinion, they did a pretty good job," says Sarah), her parents tried to find someone similar in appearance to her father. So they found a donor who had an Irish background, with blue eyes and fair coloring. Many heterosexual couples do this to avoid any embarrassing questions once their children are born. She found out that when Todd was asked why he wanted to donate, he said that if a family was willing to go through all the trouble of using a sperm donor to have a child, then they must really want a kid badly, and he thought that child would be really loved. (Sarah thought this was a great answer.)

Now, Sarah keeps in touch with Todd and her half siblings, Carey and Gavin, through a group chat that includes her sister. They message each other every couple of days—silly things about what they're doing, or they send pictures of themselves going out to dinner or to parties.

In some ways, she says that the hardest part about these new relationships has been figuring out the language she should use when referring to her donor and her half siblings. While many of their half siblings call Todd their "Dad," Sarah and Jenna don't call him that, because she says they already had a Dad. Her mother had worried that they would forget the father they had grown up with, but Sarah says that would never happen. Sometimes she and her sister call Todd their father, or their sperm-donor dad. The confusion around what to call each other is something that many donor-conceived children struggle with. It's all new—nobody has had to navigate these kinds of relationships before.

"We're slowly building our lexicon. It's sensitive with Jenna and me. We never wanted anyone to think that the man who raised us wasn't our dad. That was the most difficult part to come to terms with. I'm glad I have my twin sister, because she gets it," says Sarah.

She calls her half siblings her sisters and brothers. Most of them were born to single mothers by choice or lesbians and are only children. Through Todd, she discovered that she and her sister also had a young half sibling who lived in the next town over from them in New Jersey. She contacted the mother of the three-year-old boy and found that they'd actually attended the same town events without even knowing the other family existed. They keep in touch, but they don't spend a lot of time together since this brother is so young.

For Todd, having connections with all these children has, indeed, made his life fuller. "It's pretty awesome overall. I have fun interacting with the kids, and it's been great watching them grow up."

In fact, the morning that I spoke to Todd, he had just been to visit his six-year-old donor daughter who lives in Arizona. This was actually his second visit there. His first was a few months before, when she asked if he would attend a father-daughter dance with her at her school. He generously agreed and flew out there to join her.

And for the past two Christmas vacations, he's traveled to Europe with two of his offspring, both of whom are now in their twenties. He says that traveling with them, through England, Ireland, and Turkey, has been the most fun and rewarding part of being a sperm donor. They discovered while traveling together that they shared common interests, such as going to museums, seeing live theater and comedy, and even sleeping in late. "That's been an unanticipated bonus of the whole thing," says Todd.

His positive interactions with his kids have persuaded him to put out the message, by appearing on TV news and talk shows and in articles, about how rewarding the experience has been for him. "I've never been asked for money or for someone to come live with me," he says. "It's been great so far, and I expect it to continue. It's been a real upside to my life. Maybe other donors will consider meeting their kids as well."

Sarah has also found meeting Todd and her half siblings to be positive on many levels. Her friends and family—especially her mother—have been supportive of her through this journey and have never been critical. Now she feels like she has a whole new group of family and friends that she wants to spend time with.

"There's a comfort there. It's made my life richer—and it gives me a lot to talk about at parties!" she jokes. "There's so much more love in my life now. It's a really good feeling."

These days, Sarah's experience is not exactly unique. In 2013, Wendy Kramer helped produce a series for MTV called *Generation Cryo*, which followed a seventeen-year-old girl named Breeanna, who was conceived through an anonymous sperm donor, as she traveled through the country to meet some of her fifteen half siblings. She was trying to find out more about her family's history through her connections with these new family members. The meetings didn't always go so well.

These new relationships can be fraught and sometimes difficult to navigate, says Philip N. Cohen, a sociology professor at the University of Maryland who studies families. "You could have ambiguity and confusion. It's painful when you see someone as a member of your family, and they don't see you that way. If family becomes this thing where two people have to agree that they're related, it could be a point of disharmony. And for kids, it's important for their development phase to know who is in their circle of trust and who isn't. They need to know who they're close to," he says.

Still, even traditional families can have problems and disagreements. Cohen says these new groups illustrate how many different ways there are to create families.

Writer Andrew Solomon defines family as relationships that involve love and caretaking. "We love them because we take care of them. Let people use the word 'family' as they see fit. Even thirty years ago, the term family couldn't be nailed down." He sees families with multiple half siblings as something exciting, especially since meeting one's half brothers and half sisters could help children learn more about themselves. But he also agrees that it could bring with it some heartbreak, since some family members might be interested in connecting, while others might be alien and distant.

Solomon understands these nontraditional families well, since his own family is quite remarkable. As a gay man, he had always struggled with his desire to have a child, but didn't think he would have the chance. In 2003, he offered to have a child with a close, single female friend who had always wanted a baby. Their daughter now lives in Texas with his friend and her new husband, and Solomon visits them frequently. Solomon's husband, John Habich, also has two biological children; he acted as a sperm donor to lesbian friends in Minneapolis named Laura and Tammy.

When Solomon and Habich decided they wanted their own child together, one that would live with *them,* they searched for an egg donor and a surrogate, after they were told that having different women provide these services for them would mean that neither could fully claim to be the mother. While they were searching for a surrogate, they mentioned their plan to friends in Minneapolis. One of the women, Laura, kindly offered to be their surrogate as a way to thank them for Habich's generosity in being their sperm donor. It was an unbelievable offer. The men discussed it and accepted. They decided that Solomon would provide the sperm for their first child, while Habich would supply his sperm if they decided to have another child.

Their son, George, was born in 2009. By the time he arrived, Solomon and his partner had embraced the children that Habich had helped to father with his friends, and the kids were calling the men Daddy and Papa John. Solomon had gone from thinking he would never have his own children, to having four kids in his life, and he was amazed by his good fortune.

Yet, the families had to work out how they would all navigate these new, unusual relationships with six adults and four children in three different states. Somehow, they made it work. But without the ability to use a surrogate or an egg donor—as would be the case in other countries, where it is illegal—things would be very different for him. Solomon believes in "reproductive libertarianism."

"When people are given the most choices, love expands," he says.

The desire to meet other family members in donor-conceived groups is starting to spread. In Victoria, Australia, The Voluntary Register is starting to link member families, and in the UK, the Donor Conceived Register is doing the same thing, as is the state-run Human Fertilisation and Embryology Authority. In addition to the Donor Sibling Registry, some sperm banks in the U.S. are starting to connect donor-conceived families. In research conducted by the DSR, it was found that in a small sample of adolescents who were curious about their donor's identity, nearly 90 percent showed interest in other children who shared the same donor. Of the Donor Sibling Registry's 45,000 members, more than 13,000 have had a match with a donor or another donor-conceived person.

For several years, The Sperm Bank of California in Berkeley has been helping to connect families who use their services. Joanna Scheib, who has been the research director there since 2000, says that while their clients have long shown an interest in finding out more about their donors, now more people are looking to connect with other families as well.

"Their curiosity about these others is the number one motivator among donor-conceived adults to meet each other. They want to know, are they like me? Do they look like me? They share a donor, and they also share this incredibly unique experience of growing up donor conceived. There are not that many people out there who have a sperm donor, but it's getting more common," she says.

Around 25 percent of all families who use the sperm bank will join its family contact list, says Scheib. Many do so because they're curious about meeting the other families in their donor group and want to see what the other kids are like. For those who use anonymous donors, getting to know donor siblings can help kids find out more about themselves by seeing if they share traits or characteristics. Others want to avoid any chances of consanguinity among the half siblings. But some families—especially single mothers by choice and lesbians—are realizing that there's a potential to create an extended family for their children. Sometimes when they meet, there is an instant connection—especially when they see someone who looks a lot like themselves or their family.

That was the case for Erin Kelly and her partner, Michelle. Erin was twenty-four when she became pregnant with their first child, using a sperm donor from The Sperm Bank of California. They now have three children, ages fifteen, twelve, and five—all born through the same donor.

The couple has met three other families in their donor-sibling group through the sperm bank's family match program, and Erin says it's been an incredible experience for them all. Their eldest daughter, Olivia, was two when they met the first family: Cathy, a single mother by choice who lived in Chicago with her young son. Soon after, Erin and her family (by then their second child, a son, had been born) were visiting the city for a wedding, and she arranged for them to meet the other mother and her child.

"We immediately had a wonderful connection with her and her son. The kids had a great time together! And they all looked alike—they all have dark features, big eyes, and the same heart-shaped face," says Erin, a high school social studies teacher.

Since then, Erin's family has also connected with a lesbian couple in Vermont, who invited them to stay on their farm with them and their son, a half sibling to their children. Again, the families hit it off, instantly feeling close with one another. Her daughter was five years old at the time and was beginning to understand that she was somehow related to this other child. In the beginning, she would call her half siblings her "half brother" or "half sister," but now, more often than not, she uses "brother" and "sister." She gets to choose the language, says Erin.

Soon another lesbian couple, this time from Colorado, reached out to them. They had a daughter who was six months older than Olivia. A few summers later, Erin and Michelle invited all the families to stay with them at their home in Berkeley so that they could get to know each other, and the kids could bond.

All these connections made Olivia even more curious about any other half siblings that she might have out there, so whenever she met someone close in age to her who had two moms, or a single mom, she'd ask, "Do you know your donor number?" One day, it paid off. Olivia asked a girl in her hiking club this question. The girl didn't know her number and went home to ask one of her mothers. The following week, when Erin picked up her daughter, she said, "Mom, I want to introduce you to these people." Incredibly, she'd met her half sister while hiking. Her moms hadn't known about the sperm bank's family match program and hadn't thought that their daughter might have some half siblings. Now, their daughter—an only child—has a chaotic extended family of two brothers and a sister, says Erin, cheerfully. The families only live fifteen minutes apart, and the girls have become quite close.

Erin says it's been extraordinary getting to know these other children who are related to her kids. "They feel like my nieces and nephews. I really care about them as whole people. It's fascinating to watch them grow up. And the relationships with the other moms has been really easy. Some of these women have become good friends; I feel like they're lifelong friends. It's something I never expected. We have more people to care about, and [more people] who care about our children."

She hopes that having these connections with their half siblings will help her own children if they ever need someone to talk to, and she's grateful that her kids have that in their lives.

These remarkable relationships between donor-conceived families are sparking growing interest by researchers, who are fascinated by these new forms of kinship.

In a 2010 study, donor offspring were interviewed about their experiences in searching for and contacting their donor siblings. Most said they searched out of curiosity and to gain a better understanding of their genetic identity. Some of the offspring who already had children said they were seeking to provide a sense of their ancestral history for their kids.

The majority of the children who found their half siblings described the experience as positive and said they remained in regular contact with them. Those who found out about their conception when they were over the age of eighteen tended to search for medical reasons, while those who found out when they were younger, searched mainly out of inquisitiveness. Not surprisingly, the study also found that single mothers and lesbian couples were more open about their child's origin than heterosexual couples, who didn't have to explain why their son or daughter didn't have a father. It also noted that single moms and lesbians tended to be more accepting of a child's desire to find his or her donor siblings.

A sixteen-year-old male from a heterosexual couple family had this to say about meeting six of his half siblings: "It has become like a common occurrence, and I don't expect any of the meetings to go badly, because it is like we have known each other all our lives even though we did not grow up together."

The study also found that, like adopted individuals, donor offspring often began searching for their relatives after an important change in their lives, such as becoming a teenager, having a child, or getting married. Many said they were trying to gain a more complete sense of their own identity. The study, conducted by the Centre for Family Research at the University of Cambridge and the Donor Sibling Registry, was published in the journal *Reproductive BioMedicine* in 2010.

While connecting with donor-conceived family members, or even one's donor, can be exciting and fulfilling, it can also create a whole new set of questions. For instance, how should the law define these relationships?

Naomi Cahn, a law professor from George Washington University who specializes in fertility issues, believes that we need to accept and acknowledge that these new donor-conceived families are forming. "How should the law recognize these new relationships? It could facilitate them by creating a government-sponsored donor sibling registry that would help people find their siblings, as well as some information about their donors," says Cahn, who wrote the books, *Test Tube Families: Why the Fertility Market Needs Legal Regulation* and *The New Kinship: Constructing Donor-Conceived Families*.

She says that in addition to helping to foster these new forms of kinship, the government should clarify what the legal relationships are among donors, recipients, and offspring. The most important thing that needs to be clear is that the donor has no obligation of support for the child or children, but also has no rights to visitation. Even if an anonymous donor is found, he should not be able to go to court and say, "I have a legal right to see these children," says Cahn.

In an unusual twist on these issues, the state of Kansas has ordered a sperm donor to pay child support for a baby he helped to conceive. A lesbian couple advertised on Craigslist, looking for a sperm donor. When the couple split up, one of the women went on welfare to help support her child. The state decided that the donor must provide for the child since he is the girl's father—even though he signed documents waiving his parental rights. A judge in the case found that because the couple did not abide by Kansas law, which states that a licensed doctor must be part of the artificial insemination process (the women performed the procedure at home), he must pay. The donor vows to keep fighting. The case is being watched closely to see how it plays out in the courts.

There are many other astonishing cases involving sperm donation and embryos that are being heard in court—many of them involving celebrities. Actress Sofia Vergara has been fighting with her ex, businessman Nick Loeb, over several frozen embryos that they created together. Although they signed an agreement stating that both parties had to agree to bring the embryos to term, Loeb is now suggesting that Vergara's insistence on keeping the embryos frozen is "tantamount to killing them." It's an interesting case—does a man have a right to keep his half of an embryo alive, even if the woman doesn't agree?

A particularly vitriolic case involves the actor Jason Patric and his ex-girlfriend, to whom he once donated his sperm, apparently with the stipulation that she not expect child support nor tell anyone that he was the father. But when the couple got back together, Patric spent some time with the boy, named Gus, and he grew attached to him. Patric sued for custody, and in 2014, a judge ruled that he was the legal father of the child, and that the pair should come up with an agreement detailing custody, visitation, and support. The actor went so far as to create an organization called Stand Up for Gus, which he hopes will eventually help to change the laws for the rights of sperm donors in the U.S. His case even helped spawn new bills in California, such as the Modern Family Act, which would protect and define the rights of all nontraditional parents, including LGBTQ families and in cases where a sperm or egg donor seeks the role of a parent in a child's life. In the case of LGBTQ families, the new law would speed up the process by which one partner has to adopt the child at birth, while the other is the biological parent. Supporters say cases such as Patric's shows that laws have not kept up with technology and social change.

In yet another complex case that Cahn cites, two women who were in a relationship each used the same sperm donor to get pregnant, but they later split up, each taking one of the children. Now, the question is, do the half siblings have any right to see each other, once the women have separated? In some states, children have associational rights, meaning the right to associate with others and to join or form associations. But that's not the case everywhere. "The Supreme Court has never said that children have an associational right," says Cahn. "So do you treat donor children differently from other siblings?"

She says that, as more of these cases appear, it's important for the courts to weigh in on these issues.

With less than half of all kids today living in a "traditional family," what does the redefinition of family mean for society at large?

Lenna Nepomnyaschy, a sociology professor at Rutgers University who is also a single mother by choice, says that as more of these nontraditional families are being accepted by society, places that say only "families" are allowed, such as country clubs, will have to be open to allowing all kinds of family members. Of course, there will always be critics of these new families, such as the Catholic Church, which says that assisted reproduction undermines the traditional family. But no doubt these new donor-conceived families will eventually become part of the social fabric, in the same way that blended families have become commonly accepted.

Some children and parents, especially single mothers, may find these large, extended families to be reassuring, says Nepomnyaschy. "The thought of having other kids you can connect with seems like a beautiful situation. There's this family that's created just for you."

But while having all these new family members can seem very comforting on the surface, she cautions that, just like your own family, you may not like these people who are your new extended family, and you may not agree with the way they are raising their kids.

"Here's this weird amalgam of families, and you tell your kids stories about how they're connected so they understand that they have a place in the world," says Nepomnyaschy. "But if you don't feel comfortable around these people, it can get complicated."

In a way, that's what happened to Chase Kimball, the sperm donor from Salt Lake City, Utah. When a third donor-conceived child of his contacted him, he was thrilled to meet her. But it didn't exactly work out the way he planned.

Lori contacted him on Facebook and said that she believed she was his daughter. She told him she was writing to obtain some health information from him and mentioned that she had a full brother, who was Chase's son. But she maintained that she was not looking for a relationship with him—she merely wanted some questions answered.

He told her he was happy to help, and they talked on the phone for an hour. Then he asked if he could come visit her for a weekend so that they could get to know each other, and she agreed. Lori lived in Seattle, so he hopped on his motorcycle and rode out there. They had a nice time getting acquainted, and he was amazed to see how much they had in common.

"She's super geeky like me, and she loves games. She's also into costume play (dressing up like characters in a movie or comic book) and likes anime. She's everything I would expect from one of my daughters," he says. "It's cool to see myself in someone who has never met me before."

Chase also had a chance to meet Lori's fiancé, and he thought they all got along great. A few months later, he flew Lori out to Salt Lake City for a long weekend so that he could spend more time with her, and she could meet her half sisters. But since then, their communication has tapered off, and now they barely speak to each other. He was sorely disappointed about the way things turned out.

"I'm not surprised or hurt or anything. She told me from the beginning that she didn't want a relationship," he says. Still, he admits that he had hoped for more. And though he would have liked to have met her brother (his son), Lori insisted that he was not interested in getting to know Chase.

Something very different happened when two mothers who used the same sperm donor connected. One of the women, Valerie Interrante, who lives in Philadelphia, had been trying to buy more vials of sperm from her donor so that she and her partner could have another child. In 2009, she posted a message about it on the Donor Sibling Registry—as many mothers do in this situation. Another mother from the same donor-sibling group, Laurie Bertolacci from San Francisco, responded that, indeed, she had some leftover vials and was willing to part with them. She and her partner had had a daughter through this sperm donor, and she felt like they were done.

"I said, this is good stuff. Our donor is awesome, and our daughter is adorable," says Laurie. By the time she wrote back though, Valerie had already received some sperm from the sperm bank. She and her partner were able to conceive a second child, a girl. Still, since their children were related—they were half siblings after all—the two women kept in touch, connecting occasionally through Facebook, and exchanging pictures of their kids. They continued doing this for about four years.

The women had a lot in common: in addition to having children from the same sperm donor, they both came from Italian families, and they were both outgoing and gregarious. When Laurie read one day on Facebook that Valerie's father had passed away, she sent her a private message expressing her condolences. Laurie's mother had died a few years before, so she felt like she understood what Valerie was going through. The exchange brought them closer together, and they continued to email back and forth.

Over time, both Laurie's and Valerie's relationships with their partners unraveled, for different reasons. Soon after, in February 2014, Laurie learned that she had to travel to Philadelphia for work. She decided to contact Valerie, since she felt they had a certain bond with each other, as well as having kids who were half siblings to her daughter, and asked Valerie if she'd like to meet while she was in town. Valerie agreed, and even offered to pick Laurie up at the airport.

The next day, Valerie invited Laurie over to her house to meet her kids. Laurie was unsure, but when she mentioned the invitation to her work colleagues, they urged her to go. She was very glad that she did.

"When I went into her house, I felt this incredible familiarity. It was so comfortable; it was as if I was home," Laurie remembers. "I met the kids and it was surreal—they looked so much like my daughter. That's when I felt like there was something going on there. I felt like there was a deeper connection between us."

Valerie made the first move, telling Laurie that when she'd stepped out of the airport, she was taken aback by her feelings for her. For her, it was love at first sight.

Eventually, Laurie started to feel the same way about Valerie. "I thought she was great," she says. They soon started dating—long distance. And in time, they realized that their connection was real. "I remind her of her dad, and she reminds me of my mom," says Laurie. "People say, 'You could be sisters.'"

When they finally told their kids about each other, the children were thrilled and couldn't wait to meet. Eventually, the moms planned a meeting in New York City, where everyone got along well.

In January, after the women had dated for two years, they decided to move in together. Valerie and her kids made the big move out to San Francisco to live with Laurie and her daughter.

"Everyone is like, your story is incredible, it's so unique," says Laurie. "I love that Valerie is so real, and she helps me to be real. She has so much passion for life. She's so caring, and she has a very big heart.

She's helping to make me a better person, especially in the different ways that I can approach life."

Still, the families have had a lot of adjustments to make. They're not just blending a family, but they're combining a family that includes half siblings. It's a completely different dynamic, says Laurie, though she doesn't regret it for a minute.

Like Laurie and Valerie, the majority of those who are reaching out to other donor-conceived families are women. A 2016 study conducted by The Sperm Bank of California backs this up.[1] The study also noted that single mothers are the most likely to contact donor-linked families, since they are the sole decision makers when it comes to joining a registry or deciding whether reaching out to others in their donor groups would benefit their children. Heterosexual couples, on the other hand, may find it more complicated to form relationships with other families or with the donor—especially if the husband's infertility or choice to use a donor was kept a secret.

Stephen Lee, one of the study's authors, is also a parent. He and his wife used a sperm donor from The Sperm Bank of California to have a child, and they later reached out to other families in their donor-sibling group. Lee and his wife, Susan Czark, then decided to make a documentary observing the interactions of their group over an eleven-year period. In that film, *An Extended Family,* one can see how the relationships develop over time.[2]

First, the families start with exchanging emails and photos, and then they move on to phone calls, in which parents share their stories and medical information. Once the families start to meet in person, the parents watch the children interact.

The parents have observed that the children's interactions resemble simultaneously those among siblings, cousins, and friends. The children (seven boys and two girls, ages fifteen to eighteen) seemed almost magnetically drawn to each other. They roughhoused with one another, even the children who typically shied away from such activity. One of the mothers observed that all the children seemed drawn to touch their half siblings, "almost like they are trying to put engrams [a mental recording] of themselves on each other." Another mother commented that the children also appeared to be more engaged and more forgiving of each other than they were with their other peers.

One parent described an early meeting of the families as "we were like parents at our kids' play date, but with more at stake." Another parent described the relationship between the parents as "similar to in-laws, but without the negative connotations." The adults also lacked a term that accurately described the parents' relationships to each other, according to the study.

It also found that the children had an easier time describing their relationships, fluidly going from calling each other "half siblings" to "brother" and "sister" once they became closer. But did they consider each other family? The answer to that varied, but one teen put it aptly, noting, "I think family is more about the people you want to be with than who you're related to."

That's one of the things that Susanna is trying to teach her own children. Through their remarkable journey, she hopes that her kids will understand that having all these people connected to them around the country is a good thing, a wonderful thing.

She hopes the rest of their visits will go as well as the one with Cynthia and her son. She knows that her own son, Eric, and Cynthia's son, Mark, really bonded, and she hoped that they would keep in touch and cement their new relationship.

It's more than halfway through their trip when Susanna and her kids make it to the New Jersey suburbs to visit Angela and her young son, Liam. Despite all the jokes she's heard about New Jersey, Susanna finds this northern part of the state to be lush, green, and beautiful. Angela, a single mother by choice, in her early forties, is fun and vivacious, and thrilled to have a child—even if she is doing it all on her own. She's warm, friendly, and down to earth.

"I love her—she's wonderful. I like her spunk," says Susanna. "She's a single mom whose done it all herself—she doesn't need a guy. She has a very sweet son and her own house. I'm proud of her for all she's accomplished. She says, 'this is what I want,' and she makes it happen."

That night, the kids play outside Angela's suburban home, catching fireflies. Liam, who is five years old, has never caught them before, so Susanna's kids have fun introducing him to it. They bring out the butterfly nets and bug boxes that Susanna bought them on the trip, and spend the next few hours teaching their young half brother the magic of catching the bright flashing insects.

With his childish enthusiasm, Liam dives at them. At one point, he stumbles and skins his knee while capturing one and bursts into tears when he thinks he's killed it. But Susanna's kids, sympathetic, patiently explain to him that fireflies play dead to avoid getting caught.

Later that evening, Liam falls asleep under the warm glow of a box full of fireflies; Julianna and Eric do the same when they retire to the guest room. While the children sleep, Susanna and Angela take the boxes outside and release the insects, which flash away into the night.

It's a beautiful night, so the two moms sit in the backyard listening to the crickets chirp and talk about their kids. Angela says that she is delighted to have a son. He is the light of her life and the center of her world.

Like many of the other single moms in the group, Angela discovered that sperm donation meant that she didn't need to wait around for the right man to come into her life to start a family—she could do it all on her own. In a way, assisted reproductive technology helped Angela and others like her to become more independent. She wanted a family, so she made it happen.

When Susanna and her kids say goodbye to Angela and Liam the next day, it's with the warmth of kinship. Like their experience meeting Cynthia, and then Sandra and Paula, this visit is also a bonding success. Amid warm hugs and waves goodbye, the trio hit the road toward their next stop: Providence, Rhode Island, where Susanna and her kids will meet another single mother by choice and her three-year-old daughter, Emily.

Providence is situated at the head of Narragansett Bay and at more than 3,000 miles away from California, it's the furthest point on their trip. Roger Williams, a religious exile from the Massachusetts Bay Colony, founded the tiny city of Providence in 1636 as a refuge for religious minorities. And his legacy created a welcome environment for others who may not conform to mainstream society, making it an ideal place for Jessica, a single mother who is a social worker. Her daughter was born through an egg donor, using sperm from Donor B155A.

On this hot, sweaty day in July, Jessica, Susanna, and their children have dinner at a Friday's restaurant, then wander over to a nearby playground, where the moms have a chance to get to know each other while the kids play. With their matching shoulder-length blond hair set off by bangs, Jessica and Susanna can easily be mistaken for sisters.

Jessica tells Susanna how she kept her plans to have a baby on her own a secret from her colleagues and some of her friends, because she feared how they would react. She was surprised by how supportive they were when she announced she was pregnant with Emily. Jessica had longed for a baby for many years when she finally decided to have a child on her own. She'd gone to South Africa for the IVF treatments because the procedure was so much less expensive there.

But still, being a single mom was not easy. Jessica confessed that she struggled to stay afloat on her small salary and was thinking of moving elsewhere so that she could earn more money. She was devoted to making her young child happy and supporting her in the best way she could.

Susanna says she bonded with Jessica immediately.

"Frankly, I liked *all* of the mothers that we met. We all made the same choice—to have kids with this method, and with this same guy," she says. "We all have this independent mind-set. And I had this instant connection with Jessica—I guess because we knew that our kids were half siblings. I hope I get to see her again."

Her kids also enjoyed their time in Providence, and they thought that Emily was cute. But since they were only together for a few hours, Susanna's kids didn't bond with Emily as much as they did with some of their other half siblings.

Having made it to the eastern most edge of their trip, Susanna and her kids head back west and cross through the heart of the country into Milwaukee, where they plan to meet Susanna's sister mom, Joanne, and her daughter, Katie.

Before the trip, they learned that Katie, their half sibling who is eight years old, has autism. Susanna wonders if knowing that someone related to them is autistic will have an influence on how her children view disabilities. She once worked as a special education teacher and plans to go back to the field one day. It's important to her that her children have an understanding of disabilities and know that they should treat those who have them with respect.

They meet at the Milwaukee County Zoo. It's already hot out, but the kids are delighted to see all the animals, especially the newest addition to the park, the Humboldt Penguin flock. They watch a female chick named Liberty swim and dive in the exhibit pool. Katie is friendly and says whatever is on her mind. While Julianna had fun playing with Katie, Eric found the girl's sometimes-erratic behavior uncomfortable and didn't interact with her much.

After the zoo, the group stops for pizza, then heads to the park so the kids can run around for a bit. By this time, however, Katie is overwhelmed by all the day's activities and has a meltdown right there in the park. She is kicking and screaming and fighting her mother, Joanne, who practically has to carry the girl out of the park. Julianna and Eric are upset by her behavior, but Susanna reassures them that she's fine. A woman who happens to be in the park is also disturbed by the scene and asks if they need help. But once Susanna explains that Katie is autistic, the woman relaxes.

Everyone is exhausted by this time.

Joanne, who is a single mother by choice, invites Susanna and her kids to stay with them at their home in Madison. The evening goes better. Julianna and Katie play in the basement with stuffed animals, while Eric hangs out upstairs with the adults. The next morning, they all have blueberry pancakes for breakfast and decide to beat the heat by going swimming in a nearby lake.

As soon as they park, Katie jumps out of the car and runs straight into the water. Soon, Susanna's kids join in and they have fun playing in the warm water until the seaweed drifts over toward the area where they're swimming. Paddling in seaweed isn't much fun, they decide. Katie begins to cry, and although Julianna is uncomfortable by her reaction, she still feels bad because she is unable to console her. After the swim, Susanna rounds up her kids to say their goodbyes. They're finally heading home, and they're ready.

"When we left, we hugged each other goodbye," says Susanna. "I definitely felt close to her. Julianna really liked Katie, but Eric was ready to go by that point." She's secretly glad to be moving on—though she feels slightly guilty about it.

"It was eye opening spending time with a child with special needs," says Susanna. "The child is very bright, but she doesn't have social skills. Joanne just wanted to have a baby. She didn't know what she was in for."

There are a few other children in the group with autism, which could have a genetic link. Susanna wonders if Katie and the other kids could have inherited their autism from their donor. Unfortunately, there is currently no way to tell whether or not autism can be inherited, and no way to test whether a donor is genetically predisposed to it.

As they hit the road in their now very broken-in Prius, Susanna contemplates all the new and spectacular experiences that she and the kids had on their trip, and all the amazing people that they met, especially Cynthia, who is so open about everything, and her son, Mark. Susanna remembers that beautiful moment when Mark realized how he and her son, Eric, were connected.

"So kids, what did you think of our great adventure?"

"It was good," says Eric. "I'm glad we did it."

"Yeah, I liked meeting all the other kids," says Julianna. "They felt like friends, like cousins. Will we get to see them again?"

"Sure!" says Susanna. "They're family. We'll definitely see them again. Maybe we'll do this trip another time. Would you like that?"

"Yes, but let's do it with Dad next time," says Eric. "I miss him."

"I miss him, too," says Julianna. "And our pets."

Susanna nods her head. "We all miss Daddy—and the pets. We'll be home soon enough. But I hope you guys don't forget all the wonderful people we met on our trip."

"I'll never forget them!" says Julianna.

"Me either," says Eric.

Before they know it, the Prius crosses the boarder into California and they're home, richer for their collection of experiences and the profound awareness that they have of true family all over the United States. Susanna can't wait to step into her house and see her husband, Larry, and tell him about all the incredible experiences they had and the people they met. For her children, the cross-country trip expanded their vision of the world, both literally (in terms of the size of the United States), and figuratively (in terms of their family). "Now they know that the world is so much bigger than being right here at home," she says. "For them, seeing these connections they have with so many people all over the country helped them understand their place in the world."

Susanna's husband, Larry, also felt the trip had a profound impact on his wife and children.

"There's a comfort in knowing that you have family around that will hopefully care for you if you needed them to," he says. "Whether they are close or distant, you might feel like a complete stranger at first, but you know that you're family and they will probably treat you like one of their own. And that's a great feeling."

For his kids, especially, he says that knowing they have this family all over may lead them to one day want to rekindle their connection to the people they've met, and maybe they'll have their kids meet their half-sibling's kids, and in the process create a whole new part of their family.

Larry understands the deeper connection that can arise from getting to know new family members. He and his wife recently met a man through their local Rotary Club who happened to have the same last name as them—Wahl. Larry and this man even looked quite a bit alike, and mused that they must be related somehow. People asked if they were relatives. Now, they treat each other like brothers or cousins, even though they never took the genetic tests that would prove that they are. Larry says he felt an instant bond with this man, one that was significant and deep.

And that's what he believes happened to his children when they met their half siblings on their trip. "Meeting your family helps you define yourself—especially when you look alike, and many of these kids had the same facial features as Eric and Julianna, even some of the same mannerisms," he says. "It helps you figure out who you are in the world, in a very beautiful way."

Afterword

What Does the Future Hold?

The desire to have a baby is one of the most fundamental human biological urges. In fact, reproduction is the keystone of evolution, for in order for a species to persist, it must pass its genes to the next generation.

Yet, few could have predicted that this evolutionary urge could have led to the extraordinary result of one man fathering 150 children.

A perfect storm now exists in the fertility world, the result of advances in reproductive technology, minimal regulation, and corruption within some segments of the industry. Sperm is sold again and again, without any limits, and there are thousands of men, women, and children who are being negatively affected.

Likewise, assisted reproduction is growing so rapidly that regulators, lawmakers, and ethicists are struggling to keep up. For instance, as more couples turn to surrogates to have their babies, thorny legal issues arise between the rights of "intended parents" versus those of the surrogate, or birth mother, during and after pregnancy.

Additionally, as more women choose to have babies in their thirties and forties, when fertility naturally diminishes, the demand for technology such as in vitro fertilization intensifies. In fact, the use of IVF has doubled over the past decade. More than one million people in the United States alone were conceived via a donor.

So what does the future hold? What are the technological innovations that we can expect from the assisted reproduction industry? And should we be concerned?

One thing is certain, it's a "moment of market expansion," and companies are taking notice. A recent trade show in New York City titled "Fertility Planit" emphasized hopeful breakthroughs for couples trying to have a baby. The tradeshow slogan was "Everything You Need to Create Your Family," and it showcased the latest inventions in the world of reproductive medicine—from genetic testing and embryo thawing techniques to genome sequencing that could identify potential diseases or produce designer babies.

While such events can provide helpful information to hopeful parents-to-be, they can also prey on couples distressed over their unsuccessful efforts to have children. Exhibitors at Fertility Planit included those promoting expensive fertility treatments, diets that increase fertility, semen analysis, egg freezing and fertility preservation, and alternative healing, such as sessions of positive visualization with mind/body (or mind/belly) gurus.

Another telling indicator of the zeitgeist is the fact that some Fortune 500 companies are even including assisted reproduction into their health benefits packages for employees. In 2014, a number of large Silicon Valley businesses, including Google, Facebook, and Apple, said their new health plans would cover the cost of egg extraction for female employees who opted to freeze their eggs for later in vitro fertilization. That's generous, since each round of extraction can cost up to $10,000.

Freezing eggs is just the beginning when it comes to advanced reproductive technology. We're already confronting the extraordinary prospect of surrogacy battles, cloning, adopting embryos, artificial wombs, gender selection, and designer babies. And it's going to get even stranger.

Already, doctors have the ability to create babies that are born to three parents. This controversial procedure is used when a mother has faulty mitochondria, which could result in a baby born with devastating genetic diseases, such as muscular dystrophy, mental retardation, and problems with vital organs, including the heart. Doctors can replace a small amount of the mother's faulty DNA in her egg with healthy DNA from another woman. That means that a child would inherit genes from a father and two mothers. The procedure has already been approved in Britain. It is still not allowed in the United States, but the FDA is considering it.

Further advances include uterine transplants for women who were either born without a uterus or lost it due to illness or trauma—giving them a chance to become pregnant. The first uterus transplant in the U.S. was carried out in February 2016, but it failed after a few days due to an infection, and had to be removed. Sweden, however, documented its first successful birth from a uterus transplant in 2014. Since then, five healthy babies have been born from this method and nine women have received a transplant—many from their own mother. That means their own child will develop in the same womb that they were born from. It doesn't get much stranger than that.

But why even use a human uterus, when scientists may have come up with a way to create an artificial womb? Known as extracorporeal pregnancy, or extrauterine fetal incubation, researchers at Cornell University have been working on making artificial wombs out of engineered tissue. They have already grown a mouse fetus close to full term in a synthetic womb made of biodegradable "scaffolding." Scientists believe this innovation could be ready for human use in the next few decades.

One day soon, sperm donation might also become obsolete if researchers are successful in finding a way for women to have a child without a man. Researchers at the Institute for Reproductive Medicine and Genetics in Los Angeles have discovered that they can use a combination of chemicals to trick a human egg into forming an embryo without the need to be fertilized by a sperm. A baby born this way would be female and a genetic clone of her mother, prompting medical ethicists to warn of a world that could one day be dominated by females.

Another team of researchers, at the Gurdon Institute in Cambridge, say they have found a way to create primitive forms of artificial sperm and eggs out of skin tissue. That means that in the future, two men could reproduce via stem cells and an artificial womb, and women could have their own babies without men. Perhaps less controversially, it could also allow infertile men and women to regain their ability to reproduce.

Some bioethicists, such as Marcy Darnovsky, find many of these advances troubling. Darnovsky is the executive director of the Center for Genetics and Society, a nonprofit organization that she co-created to encourage responsible use of genetic and reproductive technologies.

"We haven't really developed the public understanding of these powerful new technologies and how they can shape our lives and society. And we don't consider that these technologies should be subject to democratic debate and governance," she says. "There are all sorts of indications that we need more regulation and oversight of the reproductive industry."

She says that scientists want to regulate themselves, but she doesn't believe this is practical. "Some of these scientists are getting carried away by their enthusiasm, and what they're doing is amazing. But they can't even understand what we're saying [about our concerns]—they just want to be left alone in their lab. The public doesn't realize the social consequences of this new technology."

Darnovsky is especially concerned about the work being done on genetic modification of embryos. She says that at a recent international summit on human gene editing at the National Academy in Washington, D.C., she was the only public interest advocate to speak among a bevy of scientists, and only a small minority of scientists actually questioned the technology.

Detractors of this technology, like Darnovsky, fear that allowing genetic modification of embryos could lead to designer babies. And the prospect of parents choosing their baby based on sex, hair and eye color, or certain characteristics, such as athletic ability or intelligence, *is* chilling. Designer babies can be created either through genetic screening or genetic modification.

Genetic screening involves testing embryos for medical reasons, before they are implanted through IVF. This technology can be profoundly beneficial: for example, providing an early warning that a child is at risk of inheriting serious diseases such as sickle cell anemia or cystic fibrosis. Couples that fear their child may face such a risk can use this type of embryo screening, also known as "preimplantation genetic diagnosis," to avoid having to make the difficult decision to terminate a pregnancy if the fetus later tests positive for one of these illnesses. But how far will parents go—or should they go—to screen their potential children?

Two British couples recently had their embryos tested for the BRCA mutations, the gene associated with an increased risk of breast cancer. Both came from families that had the disease and they wanted to remove the gene from their lineage. The embryos tested positive for the BRCA gene and were destroyed. While detractors say this crosses the line and will lead to the use of medical genetics in parents' quest for the perfect baby, Dartmouth College ethics professor Ronald M. Green argues that this isn't necessarily a bad thing. He believes that screening for things like obesity and dyslexia could lead to happier, healthier people.

But who is to say that having dyslexia makes a particular individual unhappy?

Charis Thompson, who holds dual appointments at UC Berkeley and the London School of Economics and Political Science, has written extensively about bioethical issues. As a fellow at UC Berkeley's Center for Science, Technology, and Medicine in Society, Thompson is concerned that genetic modification or screening could be used to single out people based on their disability. "What does it mean in terms of whose lives are valuable? When people start declaring who is and isn't of value to society, without speaking to people with that disability, it's a problem."

Genetic modification is far more invasive than genetic screening. It involves actually altering the DNA in an embryo to effectively repair its genes and remove genetic abnormalities such as Down syndrome. In theory, this technology could also be used to select a child's characteristics, making them taller, more athletic, better looking, or even smarter. Many equate this drive for a perfect—or at least "improved"—child with eugenics. Because the most advanced of these technologies will inevitably be expensive, there is a fear that it could lead to an "underclass" of humans who cannot afford to buy the best genes. This is partly why there has been such vehement opposition to the technology.

This kind of genetic editing is currently banned in the U.S., but in February 2016, the UK's Human Fertilisation and Embryology Authority made a landmark decision to allow resident scientists to genetically edit human embryos. Scientists will experiment on donated embryos, which will not be allowed to live beyond fourteen days and will not be implanted into a womb. The research involves finding ways to treat the main causes of infertility. Researchers believe if they can prove their work could help women achieve successful pregnancies through IVF treatment, these scientists might soon be allowed to bring genetically edited embryos to term.

"This whole question of genetically modifying human beings is a huge controversy right now," says Darnovsky. "Are we going to use biotechnology in a responsible way to alleviate disease and human suffering, or are we going to create a brave new world of genetically modified human beings?"

Lee Silver, a Princeton professor of molecular biology, has been known as a champion of "designer babies" since the publication of his groundbreaking 1996 book, *Remaking Eden: How Genetic Engineering and Cloning Will Transform the American Family*. Silver presciently coined the term "reprogenetics" to describe the fusion of reproductive technologies and genetics, and how the emerging technologies would enable prospective parents to choose which genes their children would receive.

At the time, Silver said that his explicit goal was to enable parents to select the genetic characteristics of their offspring, which he predicted would trigger major social changes. On the one hand, it would significantly reduce genetic diseases. But it could also permit the breeding of superior humans. Silver speculated on a dystopian future, with the divergence of genetically enhanced "GenRich" and unenhanced "naturals" into separate species. He predicted a world where class differences between the rich and poor became genetic differences.

Said one critic, "Silver's argument will not persuade many who are religious and will be offended by the spectacle of parents playing God . . . but a lot of parents, religious and otherwise, will confront the choice between average kids and great kids, and go for the great kids. It is hard to believe they can be stopped."[1]

Silver was harshly criticized by many within the scientific community for *Remaking Eden*'s positive view on human cloning and designer babies.[2]

In fact, Darnovsky says she decided to start her center on bioethics after reading Silver's book because she was surprised that no one was speaking out against his theories.

"The idea of designing future human beings is a terrible one," she says. "At the core of it, you're setting off an arms race for parents trying to upgrade their offspring, and the most well-off people will produce children who will have these genetic enhancements. It sets in motion some troubling social, economic, and political dynamics. It could put us in that science fiction world."

Since his book came out, Silver says he has reversed his position on designer babies.

In 2012, he established a company, GenePeeks, which tests the DNA of sperm donors and women to help prevent babies being born with serious genetic illnesses. It does this by predicting which diseases these children might have. But there is concern that, in the future, the company's technology could also allow parents to select specific traits and create designer babies.

Silver and his business partner say they have no intention of doing this, but the implications of the new technology are dramatic.

Renowned Harvard geneticist George Church says, "You could imagine that the closer we get to try to perfect offspring, the more it changes the usual contact we have with our child, that unconditional love, but this starts ticking the balance. Parents might say, 'we did everything we could to make sure you're biologically great, so you better be great.'"

What does this mean for the future? Many say it's time for regulatory intervention, at the very least, of the fertility industry. There are calls for limits on how many offspring a sperm donor may help to create, on how many times a man may donate his sperm, more and better testing of sperm donors, and an end to anonymous sperm donation. After my *New York Times* story about the prolific sperm donor was published, New York Assemblywoman Deborah Glick introduced legislation that would regulate sperm donations. Glick, a Manhattan Democrat who was the first openly gay member of the state legislature when she took office in 1990, wanted to establish a registry that would limit the number of children conceived from one sperm donor.

"While the best possible solution would be federal controls that prevent circumventing state-by-state laws, we cannot wait to address the obvious problem that has developed. For some years we have heard of young people seeking out their half siblings and a growing number of web-based registries and search groups. There needs to be a standard of behavior for all sperm banks," Glick said in September 2011.

Despite the bill having a senate sponsor, it never made it to the floor for a vote. An aide to Glick said, "No one knew how to deal with it."

That same year, Washington State passed a law requiring sperm and egg donors to provide identifying information to fertility clinics, along with a medical history. It also allowed donor-conceived children to request their donor's identifying and medical information once they turned eighteen.

However, one of the issues with making any laws dealing with reproduction is the fear that the legislation could cross over into the abortion debate.

This is the dawn of a challenging moment in time for assisted reproduction. With technology evolving rapidly, it's time for legislators and policymakers to start acknowledging these changes and examine the consequences of an unregulated industry. Hopefully, this book will help to bring to light the stories of individuals whose lives have been affected by this brave new world.

Acknowledgments

I'd like to thank all the many, many people who let me share their stories in this book, especially Susanna and Larry Wahl and their charming family, as well as all the families in their donor-sibling group. Susanna and Larry warmly welcomed me to spend time with their family. Cynthia Daily was also particularly helpful and supportive.

Chase Kimball and his family were giving with their time, and always willing to talk, whenever I contacted them. They were delightful hosts when I visited them in Utah.

Wendy Kramer was invaluable. Her contacts, insights, and advice made researching this book possible. Her son, Ryan, was also incredibly helpful and perceptive, and he was generous in sharing his story.

There were many others that I interviewed who were important to this book, but I'd like to thank, in particular, Sharine Kretchmar and her family, for sharing their son's inspiring and moving story. I must thank Susan Frankel for her help and insight, and her lovely daughter, Zoe, and her sperm donor, Randy, for talking to me so openly. Michael Rubino, for telling me about his amazing life and his children. Marcy Darnovsky was a font of wisdom on bioethical matters and talked to me about where reproductive technology is heading. Jane Mattes helpfully connected me with other single mothers by choice and kindly shared her own story. Alana Newman's fierce determination was an inspiration.

This book would not exist without my amazing agents, Jane Dystel and Miriam Goderich, who believed in me and in the importance of this subject.

Krista Lyons, Laura Mazer, and Merrik Bush-Pirkle were incredibly insightful, smart, and talented, and made the whole process of writing this book a joy.

I'd also like to thank the following:

Andrew Solomon, for his gentle guidance and encouragement.

Naomi Cahn, for skillfully explaining the legal aspects of reproductive technology.

Deborah Davis, for her sage advice, and for being so positive and encouraging throughout this process.

Stacy McCarthy, for generously letting me stay with her in San Francisco while I did my research.

My writing group, Candy Cooper and Elinor Meeks, who were so supportive and were especially helpful in the early stages of writing this book.

My *New York Times* editors, David Corcoran and Mike Mason, for skillfully editing, and for publishing, the original story that I wrote about a sperm donor with 150 kids.

The Montclair Public Library, for their help in tracking down research that I needed. The library is also where I worked on much of my book.

My children, Lucas, Will, and Owen, always cheered me on and made me feel like I was doing something worthwhile and important.

My sister, Michelle, for her inspiration in writing this book. She tirelessly and enthusiastically read my chapters and gave me feedback and always rooted for me. I'd also like to thank my mother, Rosa, for her support.

And finally, I want to thank my husband, Simon, for putting up with it all and for encouraging me to write this book from the start.

Notes

Chapter 4

1. www.britannica.com/topic/Lupercalia
2. oasis.lib.harvard.edu/oasis/deliver/~med00073
3. www.amjmed.com/article/S0002-9343(12)00080-0/abstract
4. http://www.bl.uk/collection-items/john-hunter-residence
5. http://www.sciencemuseum.org.uk/broughttolife/people /johnhunter.aspx
6. http://www.theguardian.com/lifeandstyle/2011/jan/11/irish -giant-genetic-mutation-growth-disorder
7. https://thechirurgeonsapprentice.com/2012/07/29/the-hunter -hunted-searching-for-the-body-of-an-anatomist/
8. http://www.amjmed.com/article/S0002-9343(12)00080-0/abstract
9. http://www.ncbi.nlm.nih.gov/pmc/articles/PMC4498171/
10. Ibid.
11. http://www.reproductivefacts.org/George_Washingtons_infertility _Why_was_the_father_of_our_country_never_a_father/
12. http://www.ncbi.nlm.nih.gov/pubmed/21229203
13. http://www.history-of-the-microscope.org/anton-van -leeuwenhoek-microscope-history.php
14. Ibid.
15. http://www.britannica.com/biography/Lazzaro-Spallanzani
16. https://embryo.asu.edu/pages/lazzaro-spallanzani-1729-1799
17. https://embryo.asu.edu/pages/karl-ernst-von-baer-1792-1876
18. http://www.ncbi.nlm.nih.gov/pmc/articles/PMC2563360/
19. https://www.mja.com.au/system/files/issues/178_12_160603 /dec10116_fm.pdf
20. https://embryo.asu.edu/pages/james-marion-simss-treatment -vesico-vaginal-fistula
21. http://www.ncbi.nlm.nih.gov/pmc/articles/PMC2563360/

22. http://www.theatlantic.com/health/archive/2016/01/first-artificial
-insemination/423198/
23. http://www.ncbi.nlm.nih.gov/pmc/articles/PMC2563360/
24. https://www.uvm.edu/~lkaelber/eugenics/MS/MS.html
25. http://www.ferris.edu/isar/archives/eliminating-inferior.htm
26. https://www.uvm.edu/~lkaelber/eugenics/
27. http://www.eugenicsarchive.org/html/eugenics/essay8text.html
28. Ibid.
29. http://www.revolvy.com/main/index.php?s=Carrie%20Buck
30. http://rockcenter.nbcnews.com/_news/2011/11/07/8640744
-victims-speak-out-about-north-carolina-sterilization-program-which
-targeted-women-young-girls-and-blacks
31. http://www.journals.uchicago.edu/doi/abs/10.1086/674007?
mobileUi=0&journalCode=ajs
32. Ibid.
33. Ibid.
34. Ibid.
35. http://scholarship.law.stjohns.edu/cgi/viewcontent.cgi?article=1046
&context=tcl
36. http://www.huffingtonpost.com/wendy-kramer/a-brief-history-of
-donor-conception_b_9814184.html
37. http://digitalcommons.law.villanova.edu/cgi/viewcontent.cgi?
article=1595&context=vlr
38. Ibid.
39. http://www.pbs.org/wgbh/americanexperience/features/general
-article/babies-americas-first/

Chapter 5

1. http://ir.uiowa.edu/cgi/viewcontent.cgi?article=1645&context
=annals-of-iowa
2. https://books.google.com/books?id=3hihAwAAQBAJ&printsec
=frontcover&dq=banking+on+the+body&hl=en&sa=X&ved=0ahUKEwi
EhceYttzNAhWMcD4KHfKSAAYQ6AEIHTAA#v=onepage&q=banking
%20on%20the%20body&f=false
3. https://books.google.com/books?id=JfTh62uefU4C&printsec=
frontcover&dq=exposing+men+the+science&hl=en&sa=X&ved=0ah
UKEwiJ_NzQttzNAhXCdj4KHRPvA9oQ6AEIHTAA#v=onepage&q
=exposing%20men%20the%20science&f=false

4. https://books.google.com/books?id=XaiF6MeXFmQC&printsec
=frontcover&dq=geneticist+and+Nobel+Prize+winner+Hermann
+Muller+advocated+for+planned+human+breeding+so+that
+only+the+best+men+could+be+used+to+reproduce+future
+generations&hl=en&sa=X&ved=0ahUKEwif1OSEt9zNAhWCP
z4KHd6qAssQ6AEIJTAB#v=onepage&q=herman%20muller&f=false

5. http://www.nature.com/nature/journal/v172/n4382/abs/172767
b0.html

6. http://ir.uiowa.edu/cgi/viewcontent.cgi?article=1645&context
=annals-of-iowa

7. https://www.princeton.edu/~ota/disk2/1988/8804/8804.PDF

8. https://books.google.com/books?id=YXvEmBHnOD8C&pg
=PA48&lpg=PA48&dq=survey+doctors+using+sperm+from+other
+men+published+by+the+University+of+Wisconsin+in+the+1970s
&source=bl&ots=2tSfX_WVLw&sig=UnZtS88u_K7v5kLPnKvSKH0
FXI8&hl=en&sa=X&ved=0ahUKEwiQ0rmnutzNAhVSID4KHdPiAo0Q
6AEIITAB#v=onepage&q=survey%20doctors%20using%20sperm%20
from%20other%20men%20published%20by%20the%20University%20
of%20Wisconsin%20in%20the%201970s&f=false

9. https://books.google.com/books?id=VjLRCwAAQBAJ&pg=PA
90&dq=There+were+reports+that+six+women+in+the+U.S.+had+been
+infected+with+HIV+through+donor+insemination.&hl=en&sa=X
&ved=0ahUKEwiCmfO-utzNAhWHQD4KHd4HA5YQ6AEIHTAA
#v=onepage&q=There%20were%20reports%20that%20six%20women%20
in%20the%20U.S.%20had%20been%20infected%20with%20HIV%20
through%20donor%20insemination.&f=false

10. http://www.npr.org/2015/07/27/426842589/donors-sue-fertility
-industry-for-caps-on-egg-prices

11. http://www.nytimes.com/2005/07/01/arts/the-genius-factory-the
-curious-history-of-the-nobel-prize-sperm-bank.html

12. http://www.dailymail.co.uk/femail/article-2667262/Why-British
-women-giving-birth-Viking-babies-conceived-Danish-donors.html

Chapter 7

1. http://www.ncbi.nlm.nih.gov/pmc/articles/PMC3987373/

2. http://www.fertstert.org/article/S0015-0282(16)30004-8/abstract
?cc=y=

3. https://www.britannica.com/topic/kin-selection

Chapter 8

1. https://www.donorsiblingregistry.com/sites/default/files/files
/Rolling%20the%20genetic%20dice%20with%20a%20sperm%20donor%20
-%20AmericaNowNews_com.pdf

Chapter 9

1. http://www.pewsocialtrends.org/2010/05/06/the-new-demography
-of-american-motherhood/

2. http://www.pewsocialtrends.org/2014/09/24/record-share-of
-americans-have-never-married/

3. http://www.nytimes.com/1983/05/02/style/single-mothers-by
-choice-perils-and-joys.html

4. http://humrep.oxfordjournals.org/content/18/5/1115.full

Chapter 10

1. http://scheib.faculty.ucdavis.edu/wp-content/uploads/sites
/89/2014/07/Scheib_Ruby_Lee2016.pdf

2. http://www.firstpictures.org/an-extended-family/

Afterword

1. http://www.forbes.com/forbes/1998/0706/6201110a.html

2. http://www.geneticsandsociety.org/article.php?id=3540

About the Author

JACQUELINE MROZ is a veteran journalist specializing in reproductive and family issues. She writes for national magazines and newspapers, and she is a former radio journalist for the BBC World News Service. Her 2012 article for the *New York Times* on a sperm donor who fathered 150 children garnered national attention. She has taught journalism at Montclair State University and Rutgers University and attended the University of Massachusetts, Amherst. She lives in Montclair, New Jersey, with her husband and three children.